GARETH MOORE

WORD FALL

350 PUZZLES INSPIRED BY YOUR FAVORITE ONLINE WORD GAME

HARVEST

An Imprint of WILLIAM MORROW

HarperCollins books may be purchased for educational,
business, or sales promotional use. For information, please email
the Special Markets Department at SPsales@harpercollins.com.

Originally published as *Word Fall 1* in Great Britain in 2022
by Yellow Kite, an Imprint of Hodder & Stoughton.

FIRST HARVEST PAPERBACK EDITION 2022

Puzzles designed by Dr. Gareth Moore
Cover and internal design by Goldust Design

Library of Congress Cataloging-in-Publication Data
has been applied for.

ISBN 978-0-06-328071-7

22 23 24 25 26   LSC   10 9 8 7 6 5 4 3 2 1

CONTENTS

INTRODUCTION

Not since Sudoku took the world by storm has a puzzle entered the popular imagination in the way that *Wordle* has. But even *Wordle* itself is a wonderful version of a decades-old two-player game where you try to guess a secret word, relying on a second person (instead of *Wordle*) to tell you which letters are correct.

But what if, I wondered, we could create a pencil-and-paper version of the game, which could be played at any time and without a second person? Now you would be able to play even if your device was out of battery or you were having screen-free time, and you could invent your own house rules if you wished.

Enter *Word Fall*. In this re-imagining of the game, you can now play offline and solo – it's just you and your intellect pitted against the printed boxes on the page. It remains just as fiendish to solve as any online version, but with the added drama of a letter-by-letter reveal as you check each guess. Not only that, but the secret words have been carefully chosen to be as fair as possible, with no obscurities or UK-/US-only terms.

Good luck on your *Word Fall* adventure!

Gareth Moore

HOW TO USE THIS BOOK

The aim of Word Fall is to find a secret word by making a series of up to six guesses, each of which should be an English word. After each guess, you check each letter to find out whether it appears in the secret word or not. If the letter does appear, you're also told if it is in the correct position within that word or not.

So far, so *Wordle*. But now we enter the realm of paper solving:

☐ **Each page has two puzzles on it**. One on the left, and one on the right. Pick the one you're going to use. The puzzle consists of the six rows of squares, plus the three or four rows of numbers listed immediately beneath it.

☐ **Each page has an A-Z letter table**, at the bottom, which is **shared by both puzzles**.

☐ For each letter you've placed, **find that letter in the table**, then find the column that corresponds with the position you've placed the letter in. This gives you a number.

☐ **If that number appears in the list** for that puzzle, the letter is correct. If it's also underlined, it's in the correct position.

And that's it! That's all you need to know to play *Word Fall*! For a quick-start video, visit www.drgarethmoore.com/wordfall

8

It's also worth knowing that:

☐ **There are no repeated letters** within a word. So, for example, you would not find 'TITLE' as one of the secret words in this book because it has two 'T's. I designed the puzzles like this because I find it fairer. Note that you can still guess a word with repeated letters if you want, but bear in mind that – if the repeated letter is correct – it will only appear once in the secret word, even though each occurrence will be marked as correct by the puzzle.

☐ **To keep track of letters you have used**, you can cross them out down the left-hand side of the letter table (for the left-hand puzzle) or the right-hand side of the letter table (for the right-hand puzzle) if you wish. Because letters can't repeat, you can confidently cross out all used letters in the same way – you won't need to consider that some may be used again.

☐ **There are no separate printed solutions**. This is to avoid the near certainty of accidentally seeing another answer, which would ruin that puzzle. Instead, if you need a solution – or a hint – then just pick a number from the list beneath the puzzle and find it in the table. This will tell you that the letter appears in the word. Or pick an underlined number and you will also find out the column that the letter appears in. By looking up all five underlined numbers in the puzzle, you'll find the full solution.

☐ **There's no such thing as cheating!** It's up to you what rules you use. I suggest playing only words found in a dictionary, but it's your call. You can even make the game harder, if you want, by allowing only guesses which use all your correct letters, and requiring those in known positions to stay in place.

Word Fall

By way of example, let's solve the left-hand puzzle on the opposite page. I've drawn in the letters and results described below.

☐ Write in your first guess at the top. There are competing opinions, but you might want to choose a word with several common letters (A, E, I, N, R, S, T are the most common); or some people prefer a word with lots of vowels, such as ADIEU. I chose TEARS.

☐ Now we check the letters, column-by-column. Check the first column in row 'T' in the table below. You'll see that the value is 63. Now we look in the list of numbers beneath the puzzle, and discover that there *is* a 63. So we know that there is a 'T' in the answer. It isn't underlined, however, so circle your letter 'T' to remember that it is correct, but in the wrong position. (This is equivalent to being yellow in *Wordle*)

☐ Next we check the second letter, 'E', so look in the second column in the 'E' row, where we find a 10. This isn't in the number list beneath the puzzle, so we cross out the 'E' to show it's wrong. (Grey in *Wordle*)

☐ Now we check 'A'. In column 3 of the 'A' row we find 34. This isn't in the number list beneath the puzzle, so it's also wrong. Cross it out.

☐ Check 'R'. In column 4 of the 'R' row we find 83. This appears in the list beneath the puzzle *and* is underlined, so we know it is both correct *and* in the right position. (Green in *Wordle*). Draw an arrow pointing down, to show that the letter 'falls' down. Or you might prefer to underline it, draw a square, or copy it into the relevant boxes below.

☐ Check the 'S' in the table and find 44. Correct letter, wrong position.

☐ Now we know we have T, R and S, of which only the R is in the correct position, and there is no E or A in the secret word.

☐ We now guess again. I tried SHORT, and the results are shown.

☐ Finally I guessed STORY, and found I was correct. Puzzle solved!

Now you can try the right-hand puzzle. I've already put in a first guess, STORE, and marked the resulting correct letters. Can you complete it?

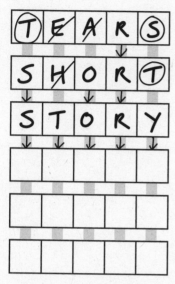

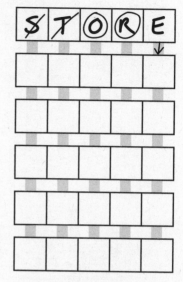

12 14 21 27 30 33 39 41 44
46 51 54 58 63 65 68 71 74
78 81 83 85 91 93 96

10 13 17 20 23 25 27 30 32
36 39 41 46 50 53 56 58 68
72 74 78 83 87 95 99

A	98	43	34	19	66	A
B	82	70	40	31	75	B
C	17	32	99	23	56	C
D	37	90	64	29	24	D
E	72	10	25	95	53	E
F	87	13	50	36	20	F
G	76	60	84	42	15	G
H	45	97	28	89	80	H
I	38	16	48	62	55	I
J	69	59	77	35	18	J
K	92	26	57	11	52	K
L	22	73	86	47	80	L
M	97	84	49	89	59	M

N	64	88	92	37	73	N
O	39	41	78	58	27	O
P	98	19	11	62	38	P
Q	15	75	90	29	42	Q
R	30	46	68	83	74	R
S	12	85	96	51	44	S
T	63	33	21	14	91	T
U	18	40	66	26	76	U
V	28	57	43	67	34	V
W	86	70	55	48	82	W
X	79	24	16	52	45	X
Y	54	81	71	65	93	Y
Z	22	35	94	47	77	Z

5-LETTER PUZZLES

Word Fall

1

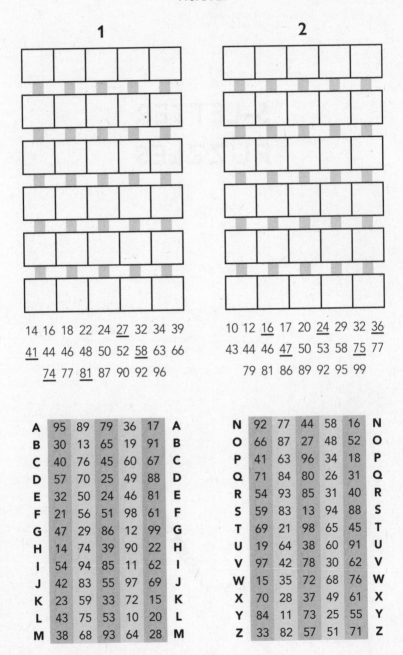

14 16 18 22 24 <u>27</u> 32 34 39
<u>41</u> 44 46 48 50 52 <u>58</u> 63 66
<u>74</u> 77 <u>81</u> 87 90 92 96

2

10 12 <u>16</u> 17 20 <u>24</u> 29 32 <u>36</u>
43 44 46 <u>47</u> 50 53 58 <u>75</u> 77
79 81 86 89 92 95 99

A	95	89	79	36	17	A
B	30	13	65	19	91	B
C	40	76	45	60	67	C
D	57	70	25	49	88	D
E	32	50	24	46	81	E
F	21	56	51	98	61	F
G	47	29	86	12	99	G
H	14	74	39	90	22	H
I	54	94	85	11	62	I
J	42	83	55	97	69	J
K	23	59	33	72	15	K
L	43	75	53	10	20	L
M	38	68	93	64	28	M

N	92	77	44	58	16	N
O	66	87	27	48	52	O
P	41	63	96	34	18	P
Q	71	84	80	26	31	Q
R	54	93	85	31	40	R
S	59	83	13	94	88	S
T	69	21	98	65	45	T
U	19	64	38	60	91	U
V	97	42	78	30	62	V
W	15	35	72	68	76	W
X	70	28	37	49	61	X
Y	84	11	73	25	55	Y
Z	33	82	57	51	71	Z

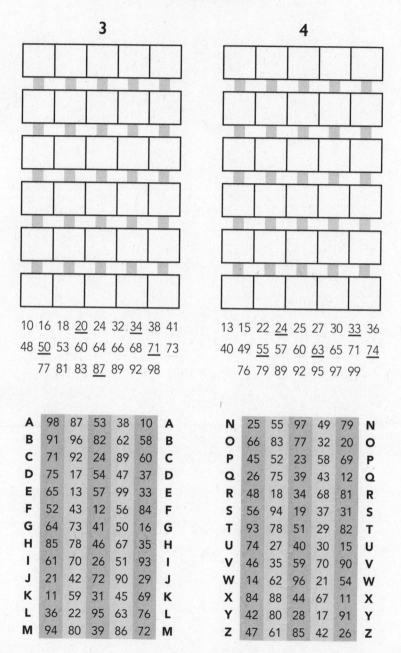

3

10 16 18 <u>20</u> 24 32 <u>34</u> 38 41
48 <u>50</u> 53 60 64 66 68 <u>71</u> 73
77 81 83 <u>87</u> 89 92 98

4

13 15 22 <u>24</u> 25 27 30 <u>33</u> 36
40 49 <u>55</u> 57 60 <u>63</u> 65 71 <u>74</u>
76 79 89 92 95 97 99

A	98	87	53	38	10	A
B	91	96	82	62	58	B
C	71	92	24	89	60	C
D	75	17	54	47	37	D
E	65	13	57	99	33	E
F	52	43	12	56	84	F
G	64	73	41	50	16	G
H	85	78	46	67	35	H
I	61	70	26	51	93	I
J	21	42	72	90	29	J
K	11	59	31	45	69	K
L	36	22	95	63	76	L
M	94	80	39	86	72	M

N	25	55	97	49	79	N
O	66	83	77	32	20	O
P	45	52	23	58	69	P
Q	26	75	39	43	12	Q
R	48	18	34	68	81	R
S	56	94	19	37	31	S
T	93	78	51	29	82	T
U	74	27	40	30	15	U
V	46	35	59	70	90	V
W	14	62	96	21	54	W
X	84	88	44	67	11	X
Y	42	80	28	17	91	Y
Z	47	61	85	42	26	Z

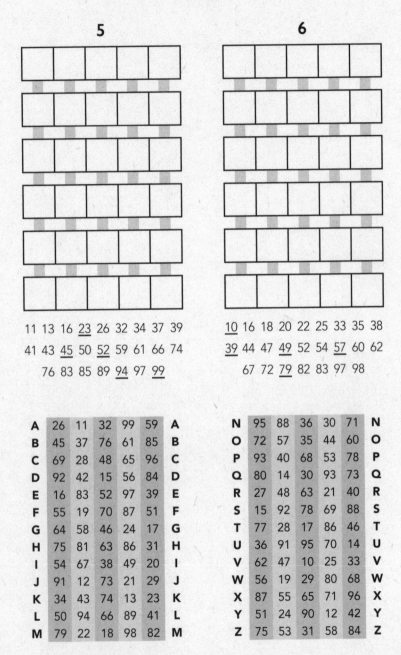

Word Fall

5

11 13 16 <u>23</u> 26 32 34 37 39
41 43 <u>45</u> 50 <u>52</u> 59 61 66 74
76 83 85 89 <u>94</u> 97 <u>99</u>

6

<u>10</u> 16 18 20 22 25 33 35 38
<u>39</u> 44 47 <u>49</u> 52 54 <u>57</u> 60 62
67 72 <u>79</u> 82 83 97 98

A	26	11	32	99	59	**A**
B	45	37	76	61	85	**B**
C	69	28	48	65	96	**C**
D	92	42	15	56	84	**D**
E	16	83	52	97	39	**E**
F	55	19	70	87	51	**F**
G	64	58	46	24	17	**G**
H	75	81	63	86	31	**H**
I	54	67	38	49	20	**I**
J	91	12	73	21	29	**J**
K	34	43	74	13	23	**K**
L	50	94	66	89	41	**L**
M	79	22	18	98	82	**M**

N	95	88	36	30	71	**N**
O	72	57	35	44	60	**O**
P	93	40	68	53	78	**P**
Q	80	14	30	93	73	**Q**
R	27	48	63	21	40	**R**
S	15	92	78	69	88	**S**
T	77	28	17	86	46	**T**
U	36	91	95	70	14	**U**
V	62	47	10	25	33	**V**
W	56	19	29	80	68	**W**
X	87	55	65	71	96	**X**
Y	51	24	90	12	42	**Y**
Z	75	53	31	58	84	**Z**

7

8

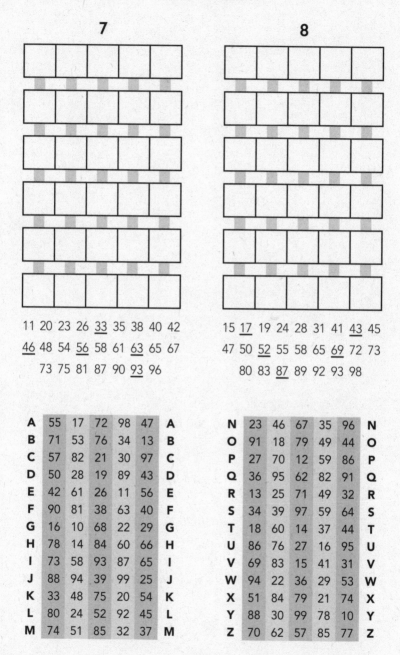

11 20 23 26 <u>33</u> 35 38 40 42
<u>46</u> 48 54 <u>56</u> 58 61 <u>63</u> 65 67
73 75 81 87 90 <u>93</u> 96

15 <u>17</u> 19 24 28 31 41 <u>43</u> 45
47 50 <u>52</u> 55 58 65 <u>69</u> 72 73
80 83 <u>87</u> 89 92 93 98

A	55	17	72	98	47	A
B	71	53	76	34	13	B
C	57	82	21	30	97	C
D	50	28	19	89	43	D
E	42	61	26	11	56	E
F	90	81	38	63	40	F
G	16	10	68	22	29	G
H	78	14	84	60	66	H
I	73	58	93	87	65	I
J	88	94	39	99	25	J
K	33	48	75	20	54	K
L	80	24	52	92	45	L
M	74	51	85	32	37	M

N	23	46	67	35	96	N
O	91	18	79	49	44	O
P	27	70	12	59	86	P
Q	36	95	62	82	91	Q
R	13	25	71	49	32	R
S	34	39	97	59	64	S
T	18	60	14	37	44	T
U	86	76	27	16	95	U
V	69	83	15	41	31	V
W	94	22	36	29	53	W
X	51	84	79	21	74	X
Y	88	30	99	78	10	Y
Z	70	62	57	85	77	Z

Word Fall

9

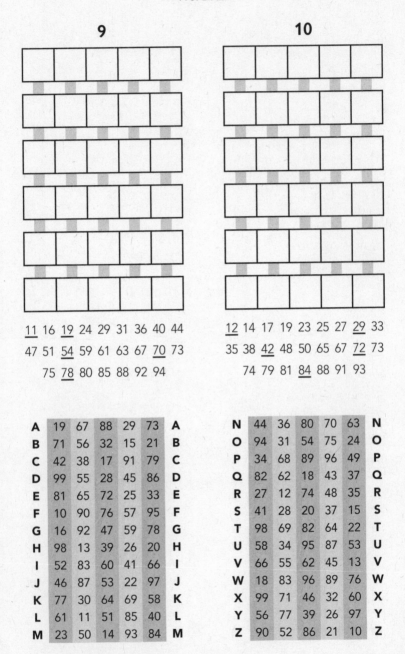

11 16 19 24 29 31 36 40 44
47 51 54 59 61 63 67 70 73
75 78 80 85 88 92 94

10

12 14 17 19 23 25 27 29 33
35 38 42 48 50 65 67 72 73
74 79 81 84 88 91 93

A	19	67	88	29	73	A
B	71	56	32	15	21	B
C	42	38	17	91	79	C
D	99	55	28	45	86	D
E	81	65	72	25	33	E
F	10	90	76	57	95	F
G	16	92	47	59	78	G
H	98	13	39	26	20	H
I	52	83	60	41	66	I
J	46	87	53	22	97	J
K	77	30	64	69	58	K
L	61	11	51	85	40	L
M	23	50	14	93	84	M

N	44	36	80	70	63	N
O	94	31	54	75	24	O
P	34	68	89	96	49	P
Q	82	62	18	43	37	Q
R	27	12	74	48	35	R
S	41	28	20	37	15	S
T	98	69	82	64	22	T
U	58	34	95	87	53	U
V	66	55	62	45	13	V
W	18	83	96	89	76	W
X	99	71	46	32	60	X
Y	56	77	39	26	97	Y
Z	90	52	86	21	10	Z

11

12

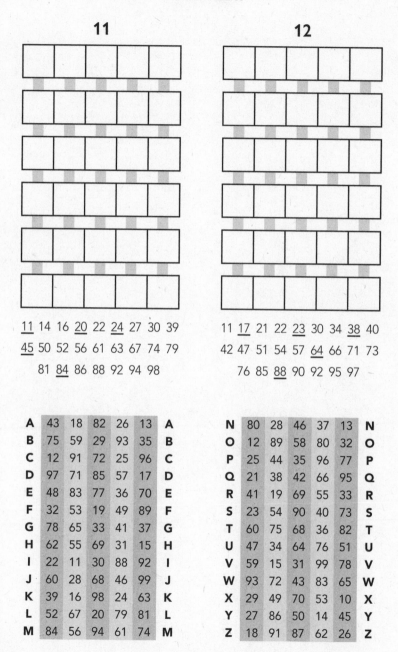

11 14 16 20 22 24 27 30 39
45 50 52 56 61 63 67 74 79
81 84 86 88 92 94 98

11 17 21 22 23 30 34 38 40
42 47 51 54 57 64 66 71 73
76 85 88 90 92 95 97

A	43	18	82	26	13
B	75	59	29	93	35
C	12	91	72	25	96
D	97	71	85	57	17
E	48	83	77	36	70
F	32	53	19	49	89
G	78	65	33	41	37
H	62	55	69	31	15
I	22	11	30	88	92
J	60	28	68	46	99
K	39	16	98	24	63
L	52	67	20	79	81
M	84	56	94	61	74

N	80	28	46	37	13
O	12	89	58	80	32
P	25	44	35	96	77
Q	21	38	42	66	95
R	41	19	69	55	33
S	23	54	90	40	73
T	60	75	68	36	82
U	47	34	64	76	51
V	59	15	31	99	78
W	93	72	43	83	65
X	29	49	70	53	10
Y	27	86	50	14	45
Z	18	91	87	62	26

13

14

13 19 <u>21</u> 26 <u>28</u> 30 <u>35</u> 38 41

44 49 54 <u>59</u> 63 67 69 71 75

78 80 <u>83</u> 86 90 92 95

15 18 19 21 24 28 30 <u>34</u> 37

41 <u>42</u> 45 54 55 58 63 <u>64</u> 68

70 71 73 <u>80</u> 88 <u>90</u> 98

A	75	83	95	44	38	A
B	56	46	79	39	66	B
C	17	74	87	91	62	C
D	54	71	21	63	80	D
E	24	98	34	73	55	E
F	42	68	58	88	18	F
G	94	85	72	47	53	G
H	57	50	33	40	82	H
I	19	90	41	28	30	I
J	12	51	77	65	97	J
K	29	25	60	93	43	K
L	52	36	76	20	14	L
M	22	84	48	27	89	M

N	70	45	37	64	15	N
O	13	92	78	67	59	O
P	99	11	31	16	66	P
Q	87	97	72	47	52	Q
R	35	49	86	69	26	R
S	14	85	48	53	43	S
T	20	79	61	11	96	T
U	82	33	65	39	23	U
V	16	27	91	60	40	V
W	25	50	46	10	74	W
X	57	17	36	81	12	X
Y	89	31	76	22	62	Y
Z	77	93	32	11	99	Z

15

16

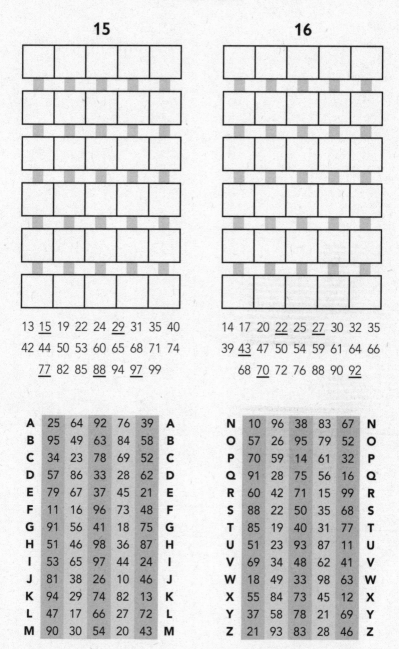

13 <u>15</u> 19 22 24 <u>29</u> 31 35 40
42 44 50 53 60 65 68 71 74
<u>77</u> 82 85 <u>88</u> 94 <u>97</u> 99

14 17 20 <u>22</u> 25 <u>27</u> 30 32 35
39 <u>43</u> 47 50 54 59 61 64 66
68 <u>70</u> 72 76 88 90 <u>92</u>

A	25	64	92	76	39	A
B	95	49	63	84	58	B
C	34	23	78	69	52	C
D	57	86	33	28	62	D
E	79	67	37	45	21	E
F	11	16	96	73	48	F
G	91	56	41	18	75	G
H	51	46	98	36	87	H
I	53	65	97	44	24	I
J	81	38	26	10	46	J
K	94	29	74	82	13	K
L	47	17	66	27	72	L
M	90	30	54	20	43	M

N	10	96	38	83	67	N
O	57	26	95	79	52	O
P	70	59	14	61	32	P
Q	91	28	75	56	16	Q
R	60	42	71	15	99	R
S	88	22	50	35	68	S
T	85	19	40	31	77	T
U	51	23	93	87	11	U
V	69	34	48	62	41	V
W	18	49	33	98	63	W
X	55	84	73	45	12	X
Y	37	58	78	21	69	Y
Z	21	93	83	28	46	Z

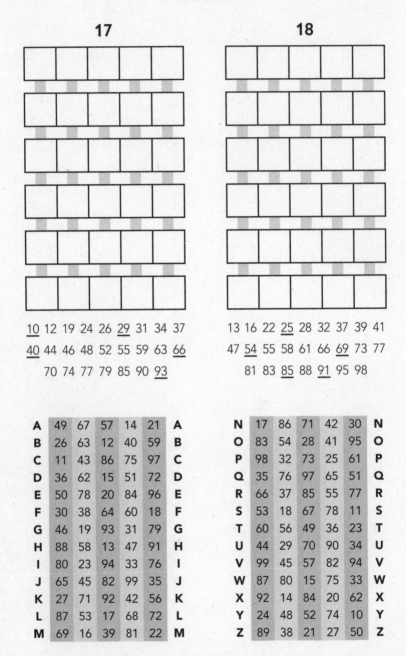

17

<u>10</u> 12 19 24 26 <u>29</u> 31 34 37
<u>40</u> 44 46 48 52 55 59 63 <u>66</u>
70 74 77 79 85 90 <u>93</u>

18

13 16 22 <u>25</u> 28 32 37 39 41
47 <u>54</u> 55 58 61 66 <u>69</u> 73 77
81 83 <u>85</u> 88 <u>91</u> 95 98

A	49	67	57	14	21	A
B	26	63	12	40	59	B
C	11	43	86	75	97	C
D	36	62	15	51	72	D
E	50	78	20	84	96	E
F	30	38	64	60	18	F
G	46	19	93	31	79	G
H	88	58	13	47	91	H
I	80	23	94	33	76	I
J	65	45	82	99	35	J
K	27	71	92	42	56	K
L	87	53	17	68	72	L
M	69	16	39	81	22	M

N	17	86	71	42	30	N
O	83	54	28	41	95	O
P	98	32	73	25	61	P
Q	35	76	97	65	51	Q
R	66	37	85	55	77	R
S	53	18	67	78	11	S
T	60	56	49	36	23	T
U	44	29	70	90	34	U
V	99	45	57	82	94	V
W	87	80	15	75	33	W
X	92	14	84	20	62	X
Y	24	48	52	74	10	Y
Z	89	38	21	27	50	Z

19

20

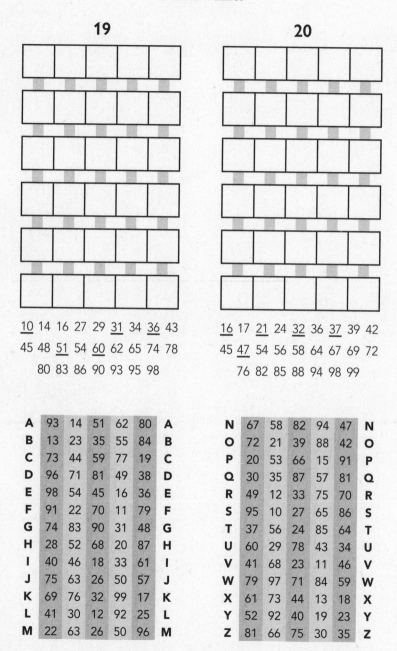

10 14 16 27 29 31 34 36 43
45 48 51 54 60 62 65 74 78
80 83 86 90 93 95 98

16 17 21 24 32 36 37 39 42
45 47 54 56 58 64 67 69 72
76 82 85 88 94 98 99

A	93	14	51	62	80	A
B	13	23	35	55	84	B
C	73	44	59	77	19	C
D	96	71	81	49	38	D
E	98	54	45	16	36	E
F	91	22	70	11	79	F
G	74	83	90	31	48	G
H	28	52	68	20	87	H
I	40	46	18	33	61	I
J	75	63	26	50	57	J
K	69	76	32	99	17	K
L	41	30	12	92	25	L
M	22	63	26	50	96	M

N	67	58	82	94	47	N
O	72	21	39	88	42	O
P	20	53	66	15	91	P
Q	30	35	87	57	81	Q
R	49	12	33	75	70	R
S	95	10	27	65	86	S
T	37	56	24	85	64	T
U	60	29	78	43	34	U
V	41	68	23	11	46	V
W	79	97	71	84	59	W
X	61	73	44	13	18	X
Y	52	92	40	19	23	Y
Z	81	66	75	30	35	Z

21

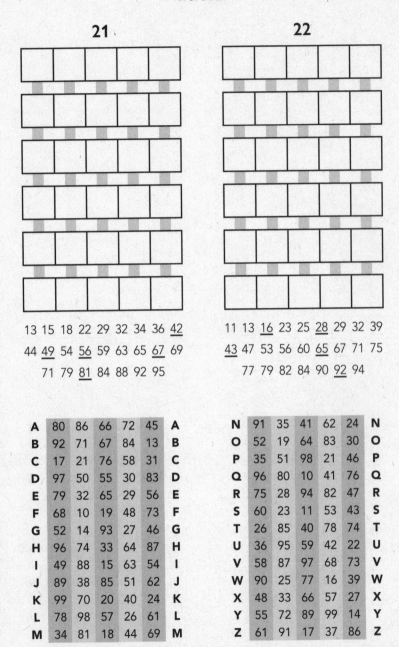

13 15 18 22 29 32 34 36 <u>42</u>
44 <u>49</u> 54 <u>56</u> 59 63 65 <u>67</u> 69
71 79 <u>81</u> 84 88 92 95

22

11 13 <u>16</u> 23 25 <u>28</u> 29 32 39
<u>43</u> 47 53 56 60 <u>65</u> 67 71 75
77 79 82 84 90 <u>92</u> 94

A	80	86	66	72	45	A
B	92	71	67	84	13	B
C	17	21	76	58	31	C
D	97	50	55	30	83	D
E	79	32	65	29	56	E
F	68	10	19	48	73	F
G	52	14	93	27	46	G
H	96	74	33	64	87	H
I	49	88	15	63	54	I
J	89	38	85	51	62	J
K	99	70	20	40	24	K
L	78	98	57	26	61	L
M	34	81	18	44	69	M

N	91	35	41	62	24	N
O	52	19	64	83	30	O
P	35	51	98	21	46	P
Q	96	80	10	41	76	Q
R	75	28	94	82	47	R
S	60	23	11	53	43	S
T	26	85	40	78	74	T
U	36	95	59	42	22	U
V	58	87	97	68	73	V
W	90	25	77	16	39	W
X	48	33	66	57	27	X
Y	55	72	89	99	14	Y
Z	61	91	17	37	86	Z

23

24

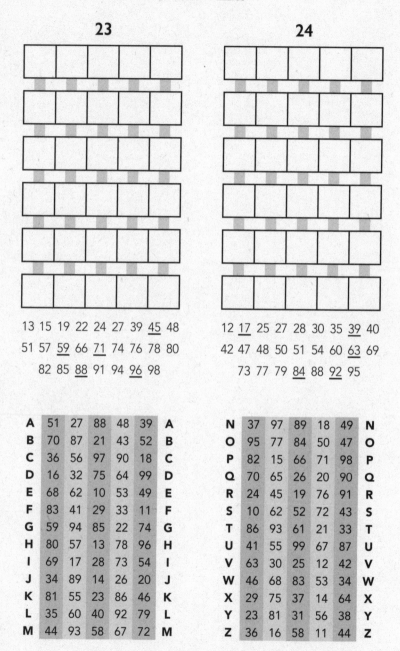

13 15 19 22 24 27 39 <u>45</u> 48
51 57 <u>59</u> 66 <u>71</u> 74 76 78 80
82 85 <u>88</u> 91 94 <u>96</u> 98

12 <u>17</u> 25 27 28 30 35 <u>39</u> 40
42 47 48 50 51 54 60 <u>63</u> 69
73 77 79 <u>84</u> 88 <u>92</u> 95

A	51	27	88	48	39	A
B	70	87	21	43	52	B
C	36	56	97	90	18	C
D	16	32	75	64	99	D
E	68	62	10	53	49	E
F	83	41	29	33	11	F
G	59	94	85	22	74	G
H	80	57	13	78	96	H
I	69	17	28	73	54	I
J	34	89	14	26	20	J
K	81	55	23	86	46	K
L	35	60	40	92	79	L
M	44	93	58	67	72	M

N	37	97	89	18	49	N
O	95	77	84	50	47	O
P	82	15	66	71	98	P
Q	70	65	26	20	90	Q
R	24	45	19	76	91	R
S	10	62	52	72	43	S
T	86	93	61	21	33	T
U	41	55	99	67	87	U
V	63	30	25	12	42	V
W	46	68	83	53	34	W
X	29	75	37	14	64	X
Y	23	81	31	56	38	Y
Z	36	16	58	11	44	Z

25

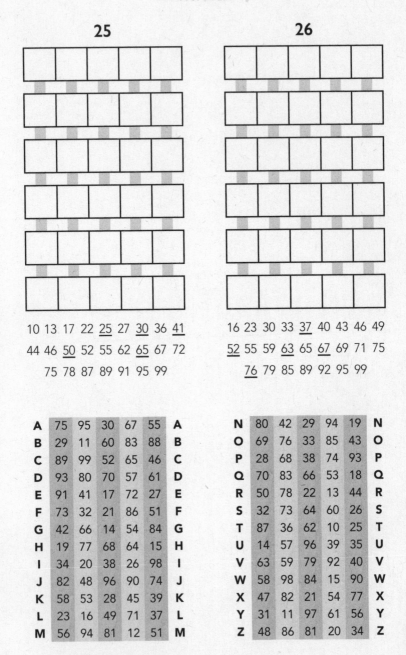

10 13 17 22 <u>25</u> 27 <u>30</u> 36 <u>41</u>
44 46 <u>50</u> 52 55 62 <u>65</u> 67 72
75 78 87 89 91 95 99

26

16 23 30 33 <u>37</u> 40 43 46 49
<u>52</u> 55 59 <u>63</u> 65 <u>67</u> 69 71 75
<u>76</u> 79 85 89 92 95 99

A	75	95	30	67	55	A
B	29	11	60	83	88	B
C	89	99	52	65	46	C
D	93	80	70	57	61	D
E	91	41	17	72	27	E
F	73	32	21	86	51	F
G	42	66	14	54	84	G
H	19	77	68	64	15	H
I	34	20	38	26	98	I
J	82	48	96	90	74	J
K	58	53	28	45	39	K
L	23	16	49	71	37	L
M	56	94	81	12	51	M

N	80	42	29	94	19	N
O	69	76	33	85	43	O
P	28	68	38	74	93	P
Q	70	83	66	53	18	Q
R	50	78	22	13	44	R
S	32	73	64	60	26	S
T	87	36	62	10	25	T
U	14	57	96	39	35	U
V	63	59	79	92	40	V
W	58	98	84	15	90	W
X	47	82	21	54	77	X
Y	31	11	97	61	56	Y
Z	48	86	81	20	34	Z

27

28

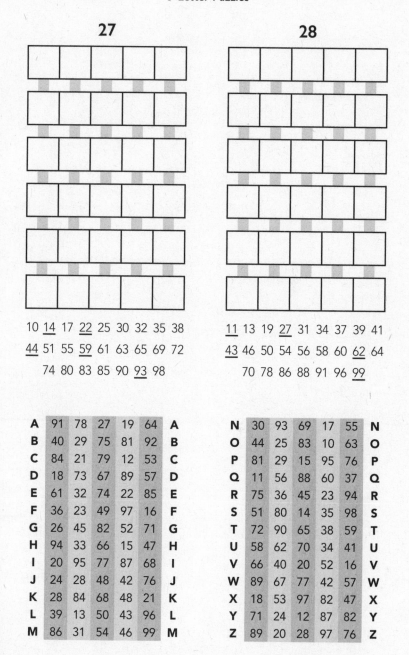

10 <u>14</u> 17 <u>22</u> 25 30 32 35 38
<u>44</u> 51 55 <u>59</u> 61 63 65 69 72
74 80 83 85 90 <u>93</u> 98

<u>11</u> 13 19 <u>27</u> 31 34 37 39 41
<u>43</u> 46 50 54 56 58 60 <u>62</u> 64
70 78 86 88 91 96 <u>99</u>

A	91	78	27	19	64	**A**
B	40	29	75	81	92	**B**
C	84	21	79	12	53	**C**
D	18	73	67	89	57	**D**
E	61	32	74	22	85	**E**
F	36	23	49	97	16	**F**
G	26	45	82	52	71	**G**
H	94	33	66	15	47	**H**
I	20	95	77	87	68	**I**
J	24	28	48	42	76	**J**
K	28	84	68	48	21	**K**
L	39	13	50	43	96	**L**
M	86	31	54	46	99	**M**

N	30	93	69	17	55	**N**
O	44	25	83	10	63	**O**
P	81	29	15	95	76	**P**
Q	11	56	88	60	37	**Q**
R	75	36	45	23	94	**R**
S	51	80	14	35	98	**S**
T	72	90	65	38	59	**T**
U	58	62	70	34	41	**U**
V	66	40	20	52	16	**V**
W	89	67	77	42	57	**W**
X	18	53	97	82	47	**X**
Y	71	24	12	87	82	**Y**
Z	89	20	28	97	76	**Z**

Word Fall

29

30

13 16 <u>23</u> 27 29 32 <u>36</u> 40 <u>42</u>
47 51 55 62 <u>64</u> 67 70 <u>72</u> 76
79 81 83 87 89 95 98

16 <u>18</u> 21 27 <u>31</u> 35 42 <u>44</u> 47
50 56 59 <u>62</u> 65 67 69 72 79
<u>81</u> 84 86 90 93 95 99

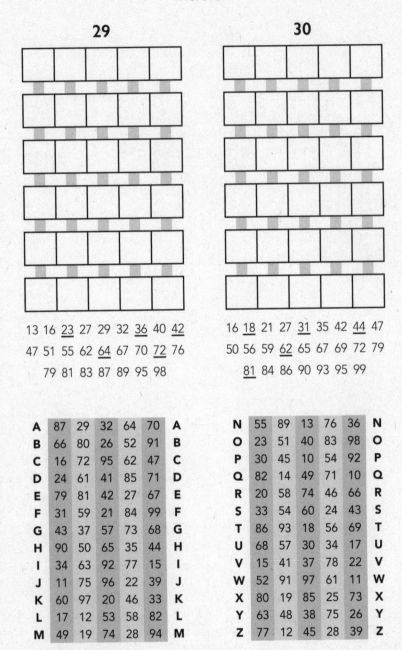

A	87	29	32	64	70
B	66	80	26	52	91
C	16	72	95	62	47
D	24	61	41	85	71
E	79	81	42	27	67
F	31	59	21	84	99
G	43	37	57	73	68
H	90	50	65	35	44
I	34	63	92	77	15
J	11	75	96	22	39
K	60	97	20	46	33
L	17	12	53	58	82
M	49	19	74	28	94

N	55	89	13	76	36
O	23	51	40	83	98
P	30	45	10	54	92
Q	82	14	49	71	10
R	20	58	74	46	66
S	33	54	60	24	43
T	86	93	18	56	69
U	68	57	30	34	17
V	15	41	37	78	22
W	52	91	97	61	11
X	80	19	85	25	73
Y	63	48	38	75	26
Z	77	12	45	28	39

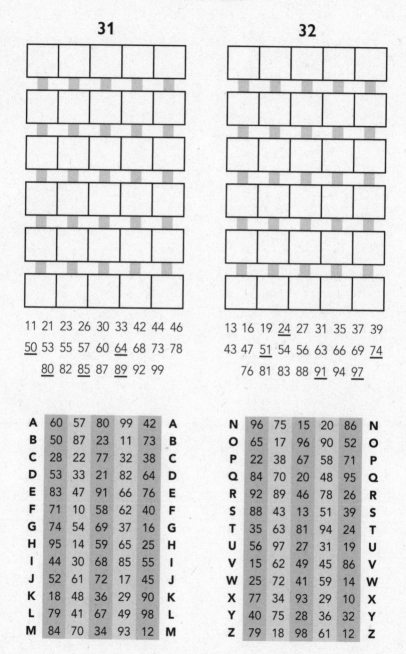

31

11 21 23 26 30 33 42 44 46
<u>50</u> 53 55 57 60 <u>64</u> 68 73 78
80 82 <u>85</u> 87 <u>89</u> 92 99

A	60	57	80	99	42	A
B	50	87	23	11	73	B
C	28	22	77	32	38	C
D	53	33	21	82	64	D
E	83	47	91	66	76	E
F	71	10	58	62	40	F
G	74	54	69	37	16	G
H	95	14	59	65	25	H
I	44	30	68	85	55	I
J	52	61	72	17	45	J
K	18	48	36	29	90	K
L	79	41	67	49	98	L
M	84	70	34	93	12	M

32

13 16 19 <u>24</u> 27 31 35 37 39
43 47 <u>51</u> 54 56 63 66 69 <u>74</u>
76 81 83 88 <u>91</u> 94 <u>97</u>

N	96	75	15	20	86	N
O	65	17	96	90	52	O
P	22	38	67	58	71	P
Q	84	70	20	48	95	Q
R	92	89	46	78	26	R
S	88	43	13	51	39	S
T	35	63	81	94	24	T
U	56	97	27	31	19	U
V	15	62	49	45	86	V
W	25	72	41	59	14	W
X	77	34	93	29	10	X
Y	40	75	28	36	32	Y
Z	79	18	98	61	12	Z

Word Fall

33

10 15 <u>19</u> 23 25 27 29 32 <u>40</u>
48 52 56 59 62 64 67 <u>71</u> 76
78 83 85 <u>87</u> 91 <u>94</u> 97

34

12 15 <u>16</u> 21 25 27 30 38 40
43 <u>47</u> 52 54 57 <u>59</u> 61 64 <u>67</u>
71 77 80 <u>84</u> 85 90 99

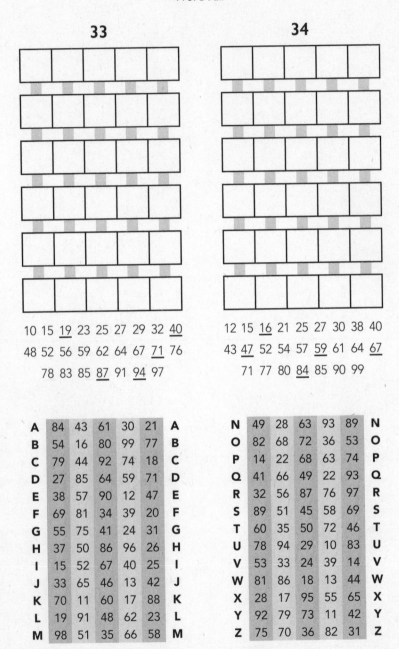

A	84	43	61	30	21	A
B	54	16	80	99	77	B
C	79	44	92	74	18	C
D	27	85	64	59	71	D
E	38	57	90	12	47	E
F	69	81	34	39	20	F
G	55	75	41	24	31	G
H	37	50	86	96	26	H
I	15	52	67	40	25	I
J	33	65	46	13	42	J
K	70	11	60	17	88	K
L	19	91	48	62	23	L
M	98	51	35	66	58	M

N	49	28	63	93	89	N
O	82	68	72	36	53	O
P	14	22	68	63	74	P
Q	41	66	49	22	93	Q
R	32	56	87	76	97	R
S	89	51	45	58	69	S
T	60	35	50	72	46	T
U	78	94	29	10	83	U
V	53	33	24	39	14	V
W	81	86	18	13	44	W
X	28	17	95	55	65	X
Y	92	79	73	11	42	Y
Z	75	70	36	82	31	Z

35

36

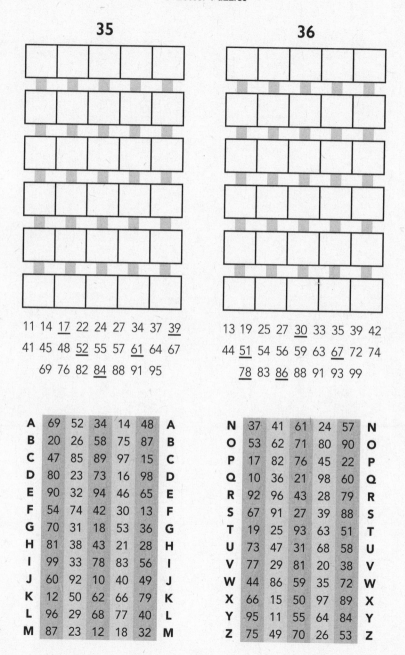

11 14 <u>17</u> 22 24 27 34 37 <u>39</u>
41 45 48 <u>52</u> 55 57 <u>61</u> 64 67
69 76 82 <u>84</u> 88 91 95

13 19 25 27 <u>30</u> 33 35 39 42
44 <u>51</u> 54 56 59 63 <u>67</u> 72 74
<u>78</u> 83 <u>86</u> 88 91 93 99

A	69	52	34	14	48	A
B	20	26	58	75	87	B
C	47	85	89	97	15	C
D	80	23	73	16	98	D
E	90	32	94	46	65	E
F	54	74	42	30	13	F
G	70	31	18	53	36	G
H	81	38	43	21	28	H
I	99	33	78	83	56	I
J	60	92	10	40	49	J
K	12	50	62	66	79	K
L	96	29	68	77	40	L
M	87	23	12	18	32	M

N	37	41	61	24	57	N
O	53	62	71	80	90	O
P	17	82	76	45	22	P
Q	10	36	21	98	60	Q
R	92	96	43	28	79	R
S	67	91	27	39	88	S
T	19	25	93	63	51	T
U	73	47	31	68	58	U
V	77	29	81	20	38	V
W	44	86	59	35	72	W
X	66	15	50	97	89	X
Y	95	11	55	64	84	Y
Z	75	49	70	26	53	Z

Word Fall

37

38

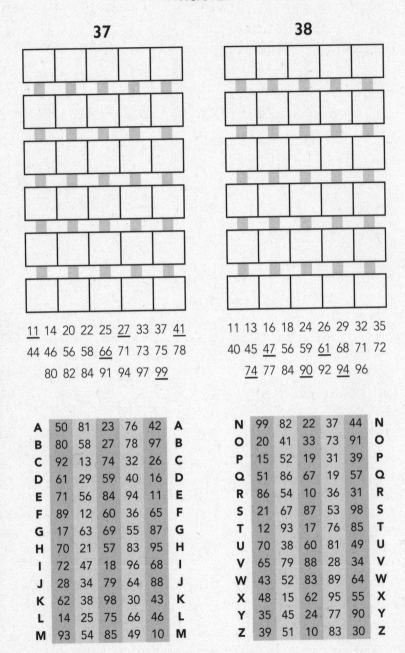

37

<u>11</u> 14 20 22 25 <u>27</u> 33 37 <u>41</u>
44 46 56 58 <u>66</u> 71 73 75 78
80 82 84 91 94 97 <u>99</u>

38

11 13 16 18 24 26 29 32 35
40 45 <u>47</u> 56 59 <u>61</u> 68 71 72
<u>74</u> 77 84 <u>90</u> 92 <u>94</u> 96

A	50	81	23	76	42	A
B	80	58	27	78	97	B
C	92	13	74	32	26	C
D	61	29	59	40	16	D
E	71	56	84	94	11	E
F	89	12	60	36	65	F
G	17	63	69	55	87	G
H	70	21	57	83	95	H
I	72	47	18	96	68	I
J	28	34	79	64	88	J
K	62	38	98	30	43	K
L	14	25	75	66	46	L
M	93	54	85	49	10	M

N	99	82	22	37	44	N
O	20	41	33	73	91	O
P	15	52	19	31	39	P
Q	51	86	67	19	57	Q
R	86	54	10	36	31	R
S	21	67	87	53	98	S
T	12	93	17	76	85	T
U	70	38	60	81	49	U
V	65	79	88	28	34	V
W	43	52	83	89	64	W
X	48	15	62	95	55	X
Y	35	45	24	77	90	Y
Z	39	51	10	83	30	Z

39

40

11 <u>13</u> 17 21 26 29 32 <u>35</u> 39
41 44 <u>46</u> 49 51 54 60 67 69
71 73 <u>78</u> 80 <u>89</u> 91 98

12 15 19 22 24 30 33 37 43
<u>47</u> 52 57 61 63 66 <u>68</u> 72 74
<u>77</u> 81 83 <u>93</u> 95 97 <u>99</u>

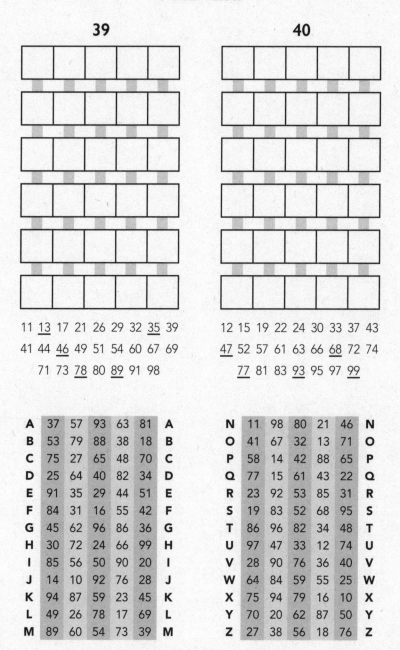

A	37	57	93	63	81	A
B	53	79	88	38	18	B
C	75	27	65	48	70	C
D	25	64	40	82	34	D
E	91	35	29	44	51	E
F	84	31	16	55	42	F
G	45	62	96	86	36	G
H	30	72	24	66	99	H
I	85	56	50	90	20	I
J	14	10	92	76	28	J
K	94	87	59	23	45	K
L	49	26	78	17	69	L
M	89	60	54	73	39	M

N	11	98	80	21	46	N
O	41	67	32	13	71	O
P	58	14	42	88	65	P
Q	77	15	61	43	22	Q
R	23	92	53	85	31	R
S	19	83	52	68	95	S
T	86	96	82	34	48	T
U	97	47	33	12	74	U
V	28	90	76	36	40	V
W	64	84	59	55	25	W
X	75	94	79	16	10	X
Y	70	20	62	87	50	Y
Z	27	38	56	18	76	Z

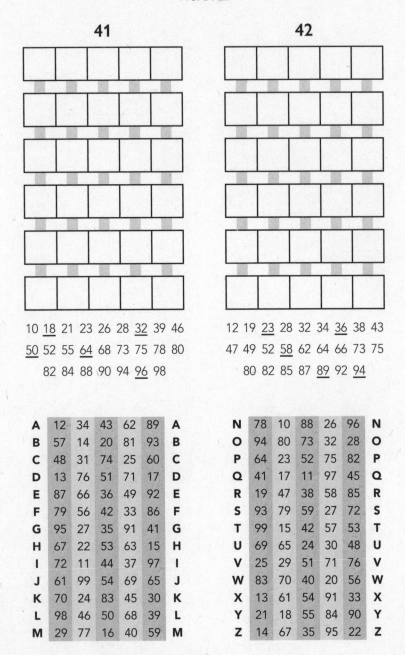

Word Fall

41

10 <u>18</u> 21 23 26 28 <u>32</u> 39 46
<u>50</u> 52 55 <u>64</u> 68 73 75 78 80
82 84 88 90 94 <u>96</u> 98

42

12 19 <u>23</u> 28 32 34 <u>36</u> 38 43
47 49 52 <u>58</u> 62 64 66 73 75
80 82 85 87 <u>89</u> 92 <u>94</u>

A	12	34	43	62	89	**A**
B	57	14	20	81	93	**B**
C	48	31	74	25	60	**C**
D	13	76	51	71	17	**D**
E	87	66	36	49	92	**E**
F	79	56	42	33	86	**F**
G	95	27	35	91	41	**G**
H	67	22	53	63	15	**H**
I	72	11	44	37	97	**I**
J	61	99	54	69	65	**J**
K	70	24	83	45	30	**K**
L	98	46	50	68	39	**L**
M	29	77	16	40	59	**M**

N	78	10	88	26	96	**N**
O	94	80	73	32	28	**O**
P	64	23	52	75	82	**P**
Q	41	17	11	97	45	**Q**
R	19	47	38	58	85	**R**
S	93	79	59	27	72	**S**
T	99	15	42	57	53	**T**
U	69	65	24	30	48	**U**
V	25	29	51	71	76	**V**
W	83	70	40	20	56	**W**
X	13	61	54	91	33	**X**
Y	21	18	55	84	90	**Y**
Z	14	67	35	95	22	**Z**

43

44

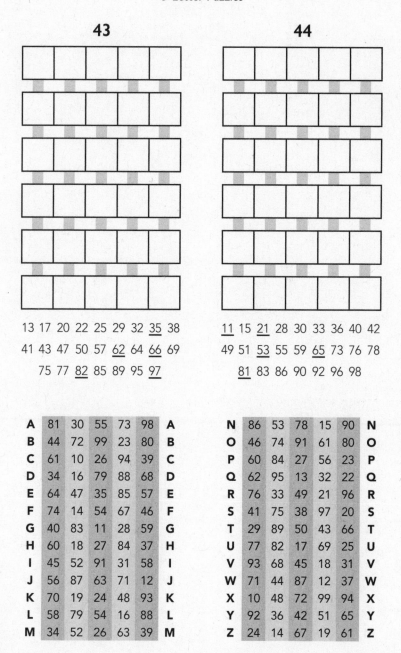

13 17 20 22 25 29 32 <u>35</u> 38
41 43 47 50 57 <u>62</u> 64 <u>66</u> 69
75 77 <u>82</u> 85 89 95 <u>97</u>

<u>11</u> 15 <u>21</u> 28 30 33 36 40 42
49 51 <u>53</u> 55 59 <u>65</u> 73 76 78
<u>81</u> 83 86 90 92 96 98

A	81	30	55	73	98	A
B	44	72	99	23	80	B
C	61	10	26	94	39	C
D	34	16	79	88	68	D
E	64	47	35	85	57	E
F	74	14	54	67	46	F
G	40	83	11	28	59	G
H	60	18	27	84	37	H
I	45	52	91	31	58	I
J	56	87	63	71	12	J
K	70	19	24	48	93	K
L	58	79	54	16	88	L
M	34	52	26	63	39	M

N	86	53	78	15	90	N
O	46	74	91	61	80	O
P	60	84	27	56	23	P
Q	62	95	13	32	22	Q
R	76	33	49	21	96	R
S	41	75	38	97	20	S
T	29	89	50	43	66	T
U	77	82	17	69	25	U
V	93	68	45	18	31	V
W	71	44	87	12	37	W
X	10	48	72	99	94	X
Y	92	36	42	51	65	Y
Z	24	14	67	19	61	Z

45

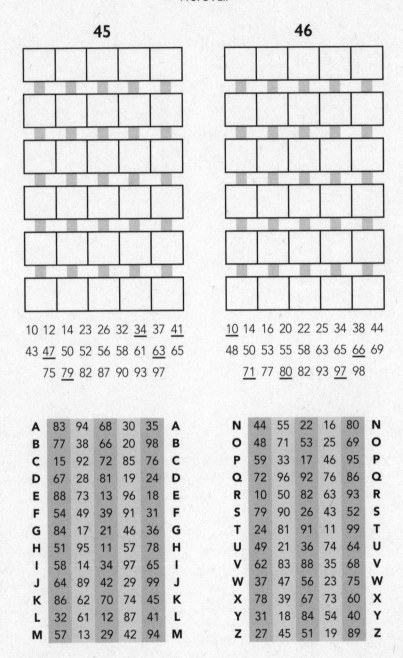

10 12 14 23 26 32 <u>34</u> 37 <u>41</u>
43 <u>47</u> 50 52 56 58 61 <u>63</u> 65
75 <u>79</u> 82 87 90 93 97

A	83	94	68	30	35
B	77	38	66	20	98
C	15	92	72	85	76
D	67	28	81	19	24
E	88	73	13	96	18
F	54	49	39	91	31
G	84	17	21	46	36
H	51	95	11	57	78
I	58	14	34	97	65
J	64	89	42	29	99
K	86	62	70	74	45
L	32	61	12	87	41
M	57	13	29	42	94

46

10 14 16 20 22 25 34 38 44
48 50 53 55 58 63 65 <u>66</u> 69
<u>71</u> 77 <u>80</u> 82 93 <u>97</u> 98

N	44	55	22	16	80
O	48	71	53	25	69
P	59	33	17	46	95
Q	72	96	92	76	86
R	10	50	82	63	93
S	79	90	26	43	52
T	24	81	91	11	99
U	49	21	36	74	64
V	62	83	88	35	68
W	37	47	56	23	75
X	78	39	67	73	60
Y	31	18	84	54	40
Z	27	45	51	19	89

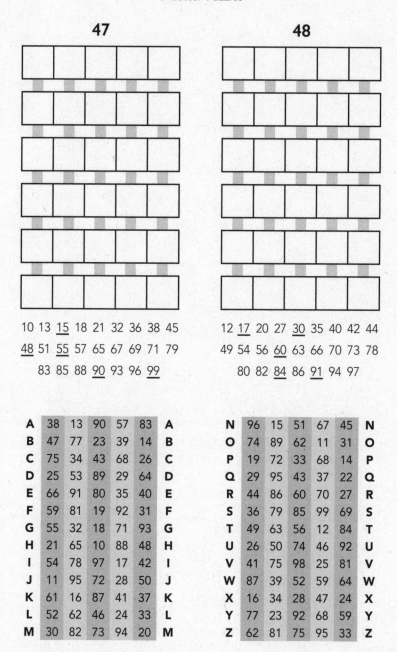

47

10 13 <u>15</u> 18 21 32 36 38 45
<u>48</u> 51 <u>55</u> 57 65 67 69 71 79
83 85 88 <u>90</u> 93 96 <u>99</u>

48

12 <u>17</u> 20 27 <u>30</u> 35 40 42 44
49 54 56 <u>60</u> 63 66 70 73 78
80 82 <u>84</u> 86 <u>91</u> 94 97

A	38	13	90	57	83	A
B	47	77	23	39	14	B
C	75	34	43	68	26	C
D	25	53	89	29	64	D
E	66	91	80	35	40	E
F	59	81	19	92	31	F
G	55	32	18	71	93	G
H	21	65	10	88	48	H
I	54	78	97	17	42	I
J	11	95	72	28	50	J
K	61	16	87	41	37	K
L	52	62	46	24	33	L
M	30	82	73	94	20	M

N	96	15	51	67	45	N
O	74	89	62	11	31	O
P	19	72	33	68	14	P
Q	29	95	43	37	22	Q
R	44	86	60	70	27	R
S	36	79	85	99	69	S
T	49	63	56	12	84	T
U	26	50	74	46	92	U
V	41	75	98	25	81	V
W	87	39	52	59	64	W
X	16	34	28	47	24	X
Y	77	23	92	68	59	Y
Z	62	81	75	95	33	Z

49

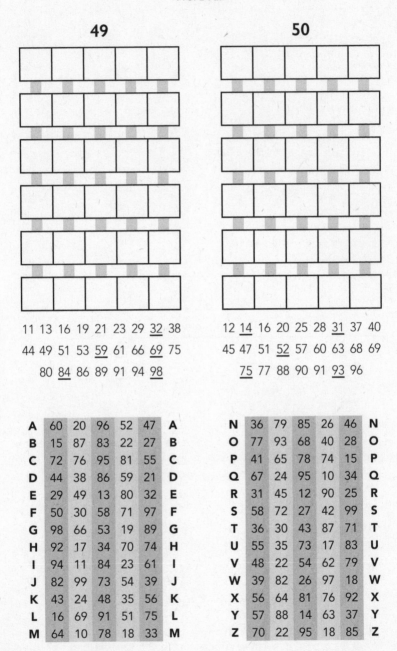

11 13 16 19 21 23 29 <u>32</u> 38
44 49 51 53 <u>59</u> 61 66 <u>69</u> 75
80 <u>84</u> 86 89 91 94 <u>98</u>

50

12 <u>14</u> 16 20 25 28 <u>31</u> 37 40
45 47 51 <u>52</u> 57 60 63 68 69
<u>75</u> 77 88 90 91 <u>93</u> 96

A	60	20	96	52	47	A
B	15	87	83	22	27	B
C	72	76	95	81	55	C
D	44	38	86	59	21	D
E	29	49	13	80	32	E
F	50	30	58	71	97	F
G	98	66	53	19	89	G
H	92	17	34	70	74	H
I	94	11	84	23	61	I
J	82	99	73	54	39	J
K	43	24	48	35	56	K
L	16	69	91	51	75	L
M	64	10	78	18	33	M

N	36	79	85	26	46	N
O	77	93	68	40	28	O
P	41	65	78	74	15	P
Q	67	24	95	10	34	Q
R	31	45	12	90	25	R
S	58	72	27	42	99	S
T	36	30	43	87	71	T
U	55	35	73	17	83	U
V	48	22	54	62	79	V
W	39	82	26	97	18	W
X	56	64	81	76	92	X
Y	57	88	14	63	37	Y
Z	70	22	95	18	85	Z

51

52

11 13 15 24 28 <u>30</u> 32 34 43
45 49 53 <u>56</u> 59 63 65 67 70
74 <u>82</u> 84 89 <u>91</u> 95 <u>99</u>

<u>16</u> 18 <u>22</u> 25 27 31 <u>35</u> 39 41
45 48 <u>50</u> 52 54 61 67 <u>70</u> 72
76 79 82 87 90 95 97

A	89	53	91	15	34	A
B	85	98	42	20	93	B
C	47	62	57	75	10	C
D	32	84	28	74	56	D
E	76	25	18	50	39	E
F	83	88	38	46	73	F
G	82	70	67	95	45	G
H	71	17	77	58	94	H
I	96	60	26	81	21	I
J	36	29	64	14	80	J
K	68	23	12	51	44	K
L	49	99	13	24	63	L
M	92	55	78	86	37	M

N	11	59	65	30	43	N
O	22	41	87	54	61	O
P	40	69	19	33	10	P
Q	92	80	23	47	55	Q
R	72	97	16	48	31	R
S	52	79	27	90	35	S
T	33	60	21	69	12	T
U	58	14	64	78	26	U
V	81	19	57	42	86	V
W	94	44	17	38	71	W
X	68	51	96	83	88	X
Y	37	85	77	73	62	Y
Z	75	29	36	20	93	Z

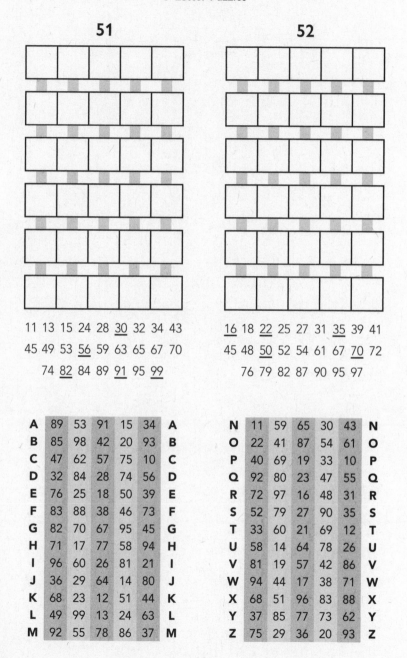

Word Fall

53

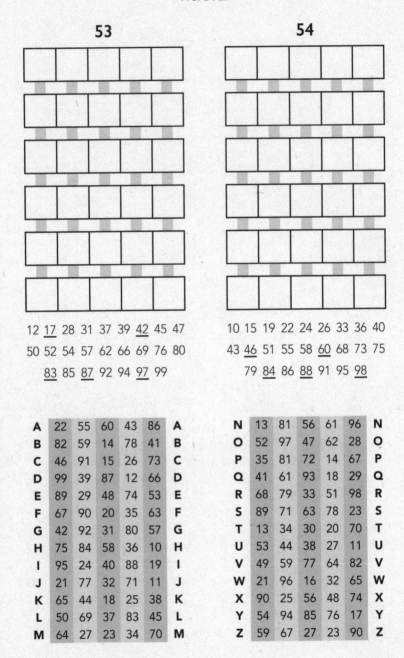

12 <u>17</u> 28 31 37 39 <u>42</u> 45 47
50 52 54 57 62 66 69 76 80
<u>83</u> 85 <u>87</u> 92 94 <u>97</u> 99

54

10 15 19 22 24 26 33 36 40
43 <u>46</u> 51 55 58 <u>60</u> 68 73 75
79 <u>84</u> 86 <u>88</u> 91 95 <u>98</u>

A	22	55	60	43	86	A
B	82	59	14	78	41	B
C	46	91	15	26	73	C
D	99	39	87	12	66	D
E	89	29	48	74	53	E
F	67	90	20	35	63	F
G	42	92	31	80	57	G
H	75	84	58	36	10	H
I	95	24	40	88	19	I
J	21	77	32	71	11	J
K	65	44	18	25	38	K
L	50	69	37	83	45	L
M	64	27	23	34	70	M

N	13	81	56	61	96	N
O	52	97	47	62	28	O
P	35	81	72	14	67	P
Q	41	61	93	18	29	Q
R	68	79	33	51	98	R
S	89	71	63	78	23	S
T	13	34	30	20	70	T
U	53	44	38	27	11	U
V	49	59	77	64	82	V
W	21	96	16	32	65	W
X	90	25	56	48	74	X
Y	54	94	85	76	17	Y
Z	59	67	27	23	90	Z

5-Letter Puzzles

55

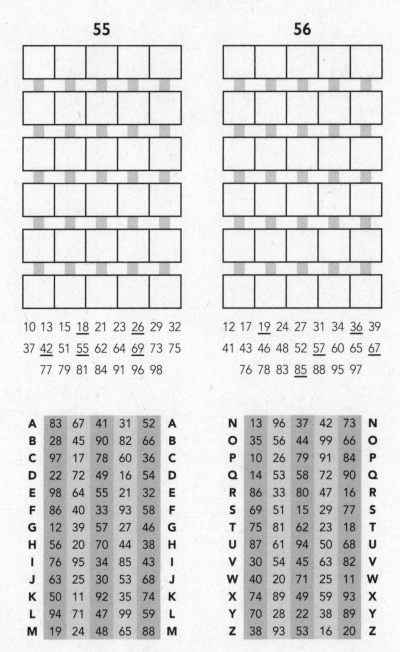

10 13 15 <u>18</u> 21 23 <u>26</u> 29 32
37 <u>42</u> 51 <u>55</u> 62 64 <u>69</u> 73 75
77 79 81 84 91 96 98

56

12 17 <u>19</u> 24 27 31 34 <u>36</u> 39
41 43 46 48 52 <u>57</u> 60 65 <u>67</u>
76 78 83 <u>85</u> 88 95 97

A	83	67	41	31	52	A
B	28	45	90	82	66	B
C	97	17	78	60	36	C
D	22	72	49	16	54	D
E	98	64	55	21	32	E
F	86	40	33	93	58	F
G	12	39	57	27	46	G
H	56	20	70	44	38	H
I	76	95	34	85	43	I
J	63	25	30	53	68	J
K	50	11	92	35	74	K
L	94	71	47	99	59	L
M	19	24	48	65	88	M

N	13	96	37	42	73	N
O	35	56	44	99	66	O
P	10	26	79	91	84	P
Q	14	53	58	72	90	Q
R	86	33	80	47	16	R
S	69	51	15	29	77	S
T	75	81	62	23	18	T
U	87	61	94	50	68	U
V	30	54	45	63	82	V
W	40	20	71	25	11	W
X	74	89	49	59	93	X
Y	70	28	22	38	89	Y
Z	38	93	53	16	20	Z

57

12 <u>15</u> 18 21 23 <u>26</u> 30 32 35
<u>40</u> 44 47 51 53 57 62 65 71
76 81 84 <u>89</u> 93 95 <u>99</u>

58

10 12 <u>19</u> 26 28 30 32 38 41
43 <u>44</u> 53 56 61 63 70 <u>74</u> 76
81 <u>83</u> 85 91 <u>93</u> 96 99

A	15	21	57	35	95	A
B	73	31	94	39	17	B
C	64	24	16	88	69	C
D	86	46	66	11	37	D
E	30	44	53	12	99	E
F	72	60	22	49	14	F
G	84	51	40	65	71	G
H	25	80	55	97	36	H
I	29	90	67	54	78	I
J	42	68	77	92	82	J
K	48	52	27	79	34	K
L	18	47	23	89	62	L
M	41	91	70	61	83	M

N	76	26	93	81	32	N
O	56	96	63	19	38	O
P	33	13	87	58	98	P
Q	59	75	45	50	20	Q
R	14	25	80	66	55	R
S	69	45	98	58	39	S
T	46	59	20	27	97	T
U	54	87	64	11	29	U
V	74	43	10	85	28	V
W	94	86	73	60	36	W
X	68	82	37	48	75	X
Y	24	34	77	88	17	Y
Z	50	22	31	92	79	Z

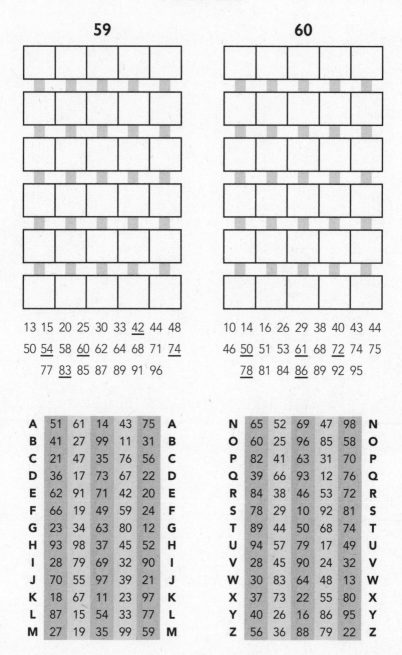

59

13 15 20 25 30 33 <u>42</u> 44 48
50 <u>54</u> 58 <u>60</u> 62 64 68 71 <u>74</u>
77 <u>83</u> 85 87 89 91 96

60

10 14 16 26 29 38 40 43 44
46 <u>50</u> 51 53 <u>61</u> 68 <u>72</u> 74 75
<u>78</u> 81 84 <u>86</u> 89 92 95

A	51	61	14	43	75	A
B	41	27	99	11	31	B
C	21	47	35	76	56	C
D	36	17	73	67	22	D
E	62	91	71	42	20	E
F	66	19	49	59	24	F
G	23	34	63	80	12	G
H	93	98	37	45	52	H
I	28	79	69	32	90	I
J	70	55	97	39	21	J
K	18	67	11	23	97	K
L	87	15	54	33	77	L
M	27	19	35	99	59	M

N	65	52	69	47	98	N
O	60	25	96	85	58	O
P	82	41	63	31	70	P
Q	39	66	93	12	76	Q
R	84	38	46	53	72	R
S	78	29	10	92	81	S
T	89	44	50	68	74	T
U	94	57	79	17	49	U
V	28	45	90	24	32	V
W	30	83	64	48	13	W
X	37	73	22	55	80	X
Y	40	26	16	86	95	Y
Z	56	36	88	79	22	Z

Word Fall

61

13 <u>15</u> 17 22 24 26 28 <u>31</u> 35
<u>37</u> 39 45 47 49 53 57 59 64
75 <u>80</u> 83 <u>86</u> 89 91 95

62

11 16 18 <u>20</u> 30 33 36 <u>38</u> 40
42 48 <u>50</u> 52 <u>55</u> 60 63 65 72
<u>76</u> 79 81 84 88 93 99

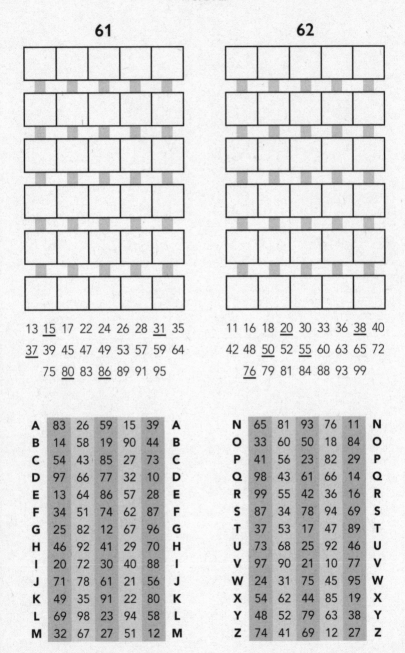

A	83	26	59	15	39	A
B	14	58	19	90	44	B
C	54	43	85	27	73	C
D	97	66	77	32	10	D
E	13	64	86	57	28	E
F	34	51	74	62	87	F
G	25	82	12	67	96	G
H	46	92	41	29	70	H
I	20	72	30	40	88	I
J	71	78	61	21	56	J
K	49	35	91	22	80	K
L	69	98	23	94	58	L
M	32	67	27	51	12	M

N	65	81	93	76	11	N
O	33	60	50	18	84	O
P	41	56	23	82	29	P
Q	98	43	61	66	14	Q
R	99	55	42	36	16	R
S	87	34	78	94	69	S
T	37	53	17	47	89	T
U	73	68	25	92	46	U
V	97	90	21	10	77	V
W	24	31	75	45	95	W
X	54	62	44	85	19	X
Y	48	52	79	63	38	Y
Z	74	41	69	12	27	Z

63

64

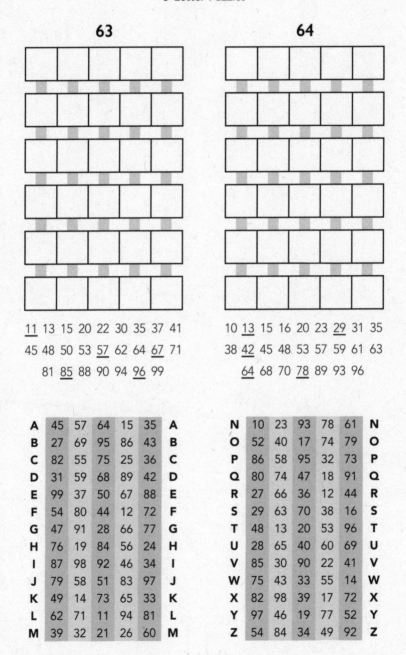

<u>11</u> 13 15 20 22 30 35 37 41
45 48 50 53 <u>57</u> 62 64 <u>67</u> 71
81 <u>85</u> 88 90 94 <u>96</u> 99

10 <u>13</u> 15 16 20 23 <u>29</u> 31 35
38 <u>42</u> 45 48 53 57 59 61 63
<u>64</u> 68 70 <u>78</u> 89 93 96

A	45	57	64	15	35	A
B	27	69	95	86	43	B
C	82	55	75	25	36	C
D	31	59	68	89	42	D
E	99	37	50	67	88	E
F	54	80	44	12	72	F
G	47	91	28	66	77	G
H	76	19	84	56	24	H
I	87	98	92	46	34	I
J	79	58	51	83	97	J
K	49	14	73	65	33	K
L	62	71	11	94	81	L
M	39	32	21	26	60	M

N	10	23	93	78	61	N
O	52	40	17	74	79	O
P	86	58	95	32	73	P
Q	80	74	47	18	91	Q
R	27	66	36	12	44	R
S	29	63	70	38	16	S
T	48	13	20	53	96	T
U	28	65	40	60	69	U
V	85	30	90	22	41	V
W	75	43	33	55	14	W
X	82	98	39	17	72	X
Y	97	46	19	77	52	Y
Z	54	84	34	49	92	Z

Word Fall

65

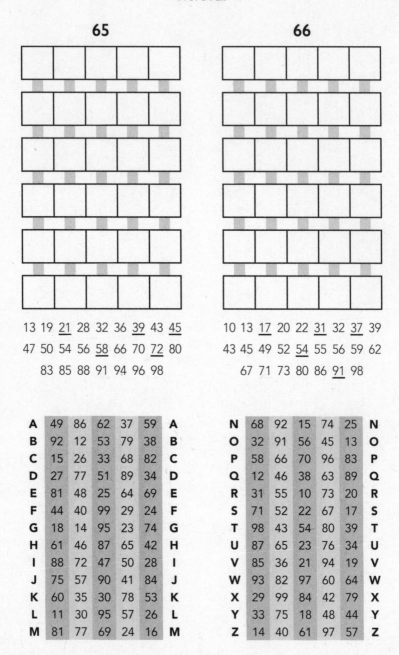

13 19 <u>21</u> 28 32 36 <u>39</u> 43 <u>45</u>
47 50 54 56 <u>58</u> 66 70 <u>72</u> 80
83 85 88 91 94 96 98

66

10 13 <u>17</u> 20 22 <u>31</u> 32 <u>37</u> 39
43 45 49 52 <u>54</u> 55 56 59 62
67 71 73 80 86 <u>91</u> 98

A	49	86	62	37	59	A
B	92	12	53	79	38	B
C	15	26	33	68	82	C
D	27	77	51	89	34	D
E	81	48	25	64	69	E
F	44	40	99	29	24	F
G	18	14	95	23	74	G
H	61	46	87	65	42	H
I	88	72	47	50	28	I
J	75	57	90	41	84	J
K	60	35	30	78	53	K
L	11	30	95	57	26	L
M	81	77	69	24	16	M

N	68	92	15	74	25	N
O	32	91	56	45	13	O
P	58	66	70	96	83	P
Q	12	46	38	63	89	Q
R	31	55	10	73	20	R
S	71	52	22	67	17	S
T	98	43	54	80	39	T
U	87	65	23	76	34	U
V	85	36	21	94	19	V
W	93	82	97	60	64	W
X	29	99	84	42	79	X
Y	33	75	18	48	44	Y
Z	14	40	61	97	57	Z

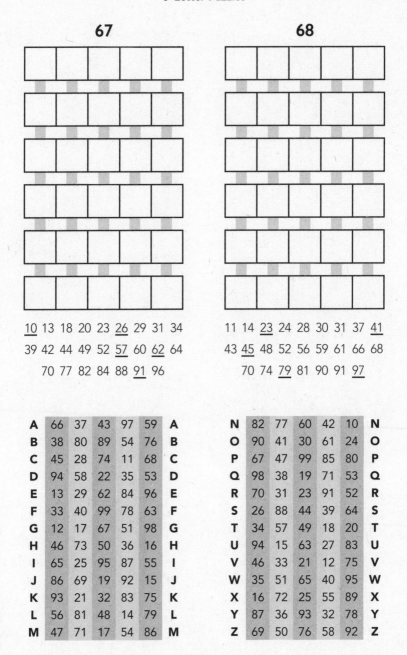

67

10 13 18 20 23 26 29 31 34
39 42 44 49 52 57 60 62 64
70 77 82 84 88 91 96

68

11 14 23 24 28 30 31 37 41
43 45 48 52 56 59 61 66 68
70 74 79 81 90 91 97

A	66	37	43	97	59	A
B	38	80	89	54	76	B
C	45	28	74	11	68	C
D	94	58	22	35	53	D
E	13	29	62	84	96	E
F	33	40	99	78	63	F
G	12	17	67	51	98	G
H	46	73	50	36	16	H
I	65	25	95	87	55	I
J	86	69	19	92	15	J
K	93	21	32	83	75	K
L	56	81	48	14	79	L
M	47	71	17	54	86	M

N	82	77	60	42	10	N
O	90	41	30	61	24	O
P	67	47	99	85	80	P
Q	98	38	19	71	53	Q
R	70	31	23	91	52	R
S	26	88	44	39	64	S
T	34	57	49	18	20	T
U	94	15	63	27	83	U
V	46	33	21	12	75	V
W	35	51	65	40	95	W
X	16	72	25	55	89	X
Y	87	36	93	32	78	Y
Z	69	50	76	58	92	Z

Word Fall

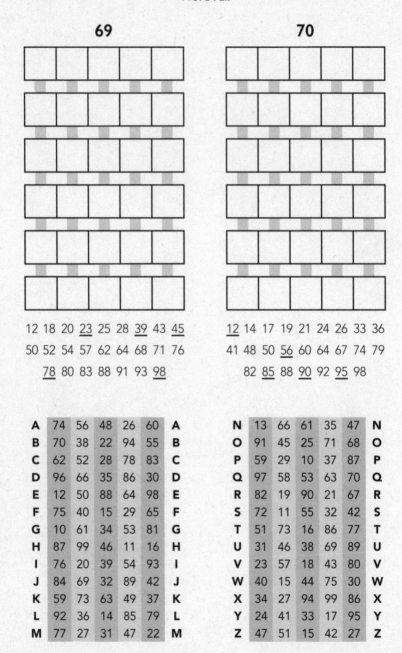

69

12 18 20 <u>23</u> 25 28 <u>39</u> 43 <u>45</u>
50 52 54 57 62 64 68 71 76
<u>78</u> 80 83 88 91 93 <u>98</u>

70

<u>12</u> 14 17 19 21 24 26 33 36
41 48 50 <u>56</u> 60 64 67 74 79
82 <u>85</u> 88 <u>90</u> 92 <u>95</u> 98

A	74	56	48	26	60	A
B	70	38	22	94	55	B
C	62	52	28	78	83	C
D	96	66	35	86	30	D
E	12	50	88	64	98	E
F	75	40	15	29	65	F
G	10	61	34	53	81	G
H	87	99	46	11	16	H
I	76	20	39	54	93	I
J	84	69	32	89	42	J
K	59	73	63	49	37	K
L	92	36	14	85	79	L
M	77	27	31	47	22	M

N	13	66	61	35	47	N
O	91	45	25	71	68	O
P	59	29	10	37	87	P
Q	97	58	53	63	70	Q
R	82	19	90	21	67	R
S	72	11	55	32	42	S
T	51	73	16	86	77	T
U	31	46	38	69	89	U
V	23	57	18	43	80	V
W	40	15	44	75	30	W
X	34	27	94	99	86	X
Y	24	41	33	17	95	Y
Z	47	51	15	42	27	Z

71

72

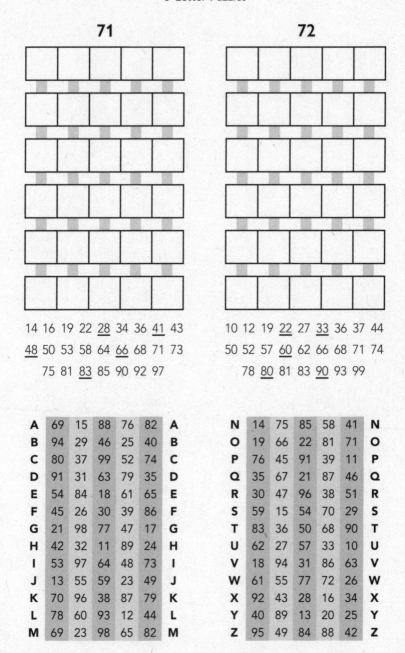

14 16 19 22 <u>28</u> 34 36 <u>41</u> 43
<u>48</u> 50 53 58 64 <u>66</u> 68 71 73
75 81 <u>83</u> 85 90 92 97

10 12 19 <u>22</u> 27 <u>33</u> 36 37 44
50 52 57 <u>60</u> 62 66 68 71 74
78 <u>80</u> 81 83 <u>90</u> 93 99

A	69	15	88	76	82	**A**
B	94	29	46	25	40	**B**
C	80	37	99	52	74	**C**
D	91	31	63	79	35	**D**
E	54	84	18	61	65	**E**
F	45	26	30	39	86	**F**
G	21	98	77	47	17	**G**
H	42	32	11	89	24	**H**
I	53	97	64	48	73	**I**
J	13	55	59	23	49	**J**
K	70	96	38	87	79	**K**
L	78	60	93	12	44	**L**
M	69	23	98	65	82	**M**

N	14	75	85	58	41	**N**
O	19	66	22	81	71	**O**
P	76	45	91	39	11	**P**
Q	35	67	21	87	46	**Q**
R	30	47	96	38	51	**R**
S	59	15	54	70	29	**S**
T	83	36	50	68	90	**T**
U	62	27	57	33	10	**U**
V	18	94	31	86	63	**V**
W	61	55	77	72	26	**W**
X	92	43	28	16	34	**X**
Y	40	89	13	20	25	**Y**
Z	95	49	84	88	42	**Z**

73

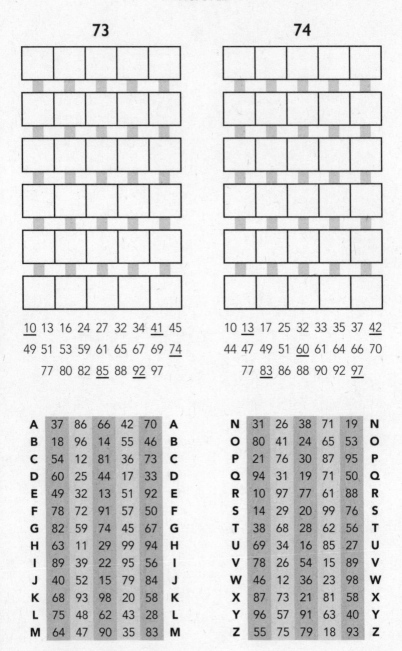

10 13 16 24 27 32 34 41 45
49 51 53 59 61 65 67 69 74
77 80 82 85 88 92 97

74

10 13 17 25 32 33 35 37 42
44 47 49 51 60 61 64 66 70
77 83 86 88 90 92 97

A	37	86	66	42	70	A
B	18	96	14	55	46	B
C	54	12	81	36	73	C
D	60	25	44	17	33	D
E	49	32	13	51	92	E
F	78	72	91	57	50	F
G	82	59	74	45	67	G
H	63	11	29	99	94	H
I	89	39	22	95	56	I
J	40	52	15	79	84	J
K	68	93	98	20	58	K
L	75	48	62	43	28	L
M	64	47	90	35	83	M

N	31	26	38	71	19	N
O	80	41	24	65	53	O
P	21	76	30	87	95	P
Q	94	31	19	71	50	Q
R	10	97	77	61	88	R
S	14	29	20	99	76	S
T	38	68	28	62	56	T
U	69	34	16	85	27	U
V	78	26	54	15	89	V
W	46	12	36	23	98	W
X	87	73	21	81	58	X
Y	96	57	91	63	40	Y
Z	55	75	79	18	93	Z

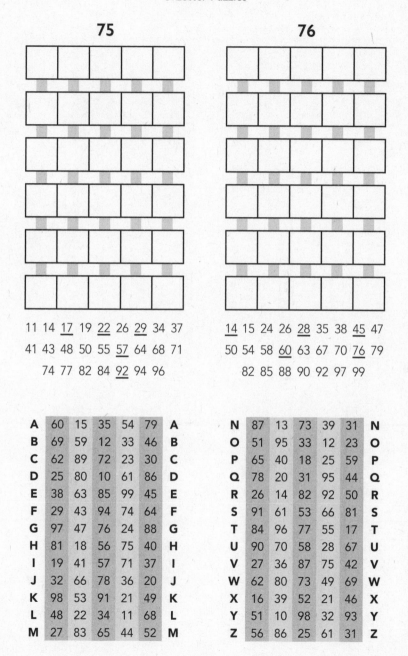

75

11 14 <u>17</u> 19 <u>22</u> 26 <u>29</u> 34 37
41 43 48 50 55 <u>57</u> 64 68 71
74 77 82 84 <u>92</u> 94 96

76

<u>14</u> 15 24 26 <u>28</u> 35 38 <u>45</u> 47
50 54 58 <u>60</u> 63 67 70 <u>76</u> 79
82 85 88 90 92 97 99

A	60	15	35	54	79	A
B	69	59	12	33	46	B
C	62	89	72	23	30	C
D	25	80	10	61	86	D
E	38	63	85	99	45	E
F	29	43	94	74	64	F
G	97	47	76	24	88	G
H	81	18	56	75	40	H
I	19	41	57	71	37	I
J	32	66	78	36	20	J
K	98	53	91	21	49	K
L	48	22	34	11	68	L
M	27	83	65	44	52	M

N	87	13	73	39	31	N
O	51	95	33	12	23	O
P	65	40	18	25	59	P
Q	78	20	31	95	44	Q
R	26	14	82	92	50	R
S	91	61	53	66	81	S
T	84	96	77	55	17	T
U	90	70	58	28	67	U
V	27	36	87	75	42	V
W	62	80	73	49	69	W
X	16	39	52	21	46	X
Y	51	10	98	32	93	Y
Z	56	86	25	61	31	Z

Word Fall

77

10 13 15 17 22 24 <u>26</u> 31 34
<u>40</u> 42 44 46 <u>51</u> 53 56 62 66
<u>70</u> 74 80 82 <u>84</u> 87 92

78

10 12 14 16 <u>25</u> 28 30 35 42
45 48 50 <u>54</u> 56 <u>58</u> 65 68 70
<u>75</u> 78 <u>82</u> 85 89 93 95

A	71	38	33	81	59	A
B	49	83	55	73	90	B
C	16	30	75	85	65	C
D	88	57	63	41	29	D
E	89	12	93	35	54	E
F	47	61	52	72	94	F
G	76	86	64	18	36	G
H	10	70	56	82	42	H
I	68	58	45	28	14	I
J	11	77	21	39	32	J
K	60	20	97	67	27	K
L	37	91	43	79	23	L
M	99	19	67	91	29	M

N	25	48	50	95	78	N
O	15	74	26	80	44	O
P	76	81	55	33	49	P
Q	52	61	77	86	37	Q
R	21	11	39	90	27	R
S	84	17	24	31	66	S
T	79	38	32	83	72	T
U	47	71	99	88	63	U
V	20	64	43	96	57	V
W	22	46	62	51	34	W
X	59	36	18	23	73	X
Y	13	53	87	92	40	Y
Z	69	98	19	81	76	Z

79

80

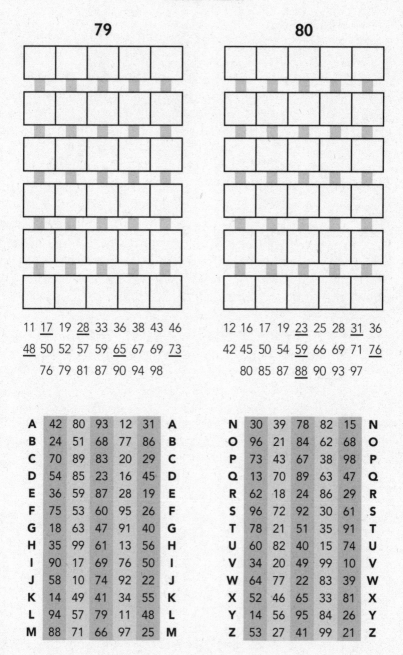

11 <u>17</u> 19 <u>28</u> 33 36 38 43 46
<u>48</u> 50 52 57 59 <u>65</u> 67 69 <u>73</u>
76 79 81 87 90 94 98

12 16 17 19 <u>23</u> 25 28 <u>31</u> 36
42 45 50 54 <u>59</u> 66 69 71 <u>76</u>
80 85 87 <u>88</u> 90 93 97

A	42	80	93	12	31	A	N	30	39	78	82	15	N
B	24	51	68	77	86	B	O	96	21	84	62	68	O
C	70	89	83	20	29	C	P	73	43	67	38	98	P
D	54	85	23	16	45	D	Q	13	70	89	63	47	Q
E	36	59	87	28	19	E	R	62	18	24	86	29	R
F	75	53	60	95	26	F	S	96	72	92	30	61	S
G	18	63	47	91	40	G	T	78	21	51	35	91	T
H	35	99	61	13	56	H	U	60	82	40	15	74	U
I	90	17	69	76	50	I	V	34	20	49	99	10	V
J	58	10	74	92	22	J	W	64	77	22	83	39	W
K	14	49	41	34	55	K	X	52	46	65	33	81	X
L	94	57	79	11	48	L	Y	14	56	95	84	26	Y
M	88	71	66	97	25	M	Z	53	27	41	99	21	Z

Word Fall

81

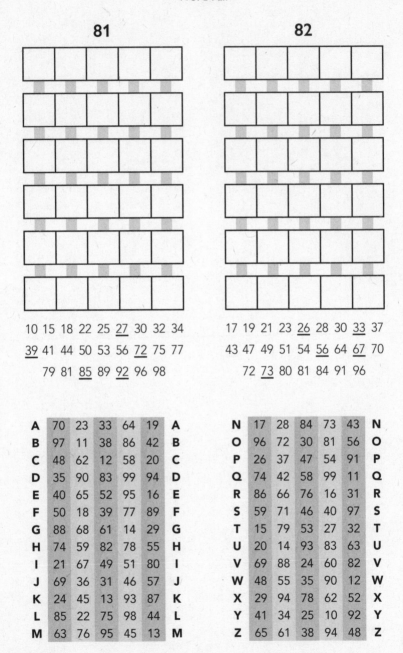

10 15 18 22 25 <u>27</u> 30 32 34
<u>39</u> 41 44 50 53 56 <u>72</u> 75 77
79 81 <u>85</u> 89 <u>92</u> 96 98

82

17 19 21 23 <u>26</u> 28 30 <u>33</u> 37
43 47 49 51 54 <u>56</u> 64 <u>67</u> 70
72 <u>73</u> 80 81 84 91 96

A	70	23	33	64	19	A
B	97	11	38	86	42	B
C	48	62	12	58	20	C
D	35	90	83	99	94	D
E	40	65	52	95	16	E
F	50	18	39	77	89	F
G	88	68	61	14	29	G
H	74	59	82	78	55	H
I	21	67	49	51	80	I
J	69	36	31	46	57	J
K	24	45	13	93	87	K
L	85	22	75	98	44	L
M	63	76	95	45	13	M

N	17	28	84	73	43	N
O	96	72	30	81	56	O
P	26	37	47	54	91	P
Q	74	42	58	99	11	Q
R	86	66	76	16	31	R
S	59	71	46	40	97	S
T	15	79	53	27	32	T
U	20	14	93	83	63	U
V	69	88	24	60	82	V
W	48	55	35	90	12	W
X	29	94	78	62	52	X
Y	41	34	25	10	92	Y
Z	65	61	38	94	48	Z

83

84

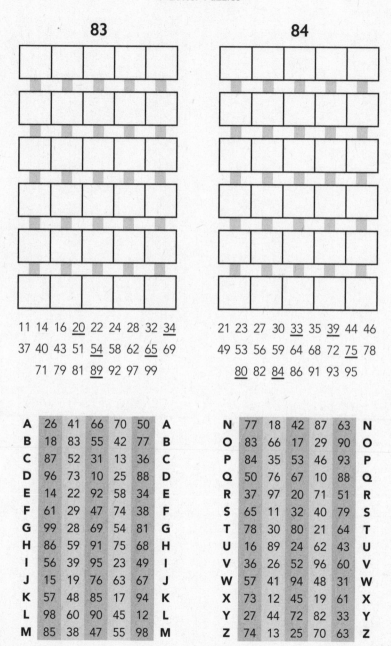

11 14 16 <u>20</u> 22 24 28 32 <u>34</u>
37 40 43 51 <u>54</u> 58 62 <u>65</u> 69
71 79 81 <u>89</u> 92 97 99

21 23 27 30 <u>33</u> 35 <u>39</u> 44 46
49 53 56 59 64 68 72 <u>75</u> 78
<u>80</u> 82 <u>84</u> 86 91 93 95

A	26	41	66	70	50	**A**
B	18	83	55	42	77	**B**
C	87	52	31	13	36	**C**
D	96	73	10	25	88	**D**
E	14	22	92	58	34	**E**
F	61	29	47	74	38	**F**
G	99	28	69	54	81	**G**
H	86	59	91	75	68	**H**
I	56	39	95	23	49	**I**
J	15	19	76	63	67	**J**
K	57	48	85	17	94	**K**
L	98	60	90	45	12	**L**
M	85	38	47	55	98	**M**

N	77	18	42	87	63	**N**
O	83	66	17	29	90	**O**
P	84	35	53	46	93	**P**
Q	50	76	67	10	88	**Q**
R	37	97	20	71	51	**R**
S	65	11	32	40	79	**S**
T	78	30	80	21	64	**T**
U	16	89	24	62	43	**U**
V	36	26	52	96	60	**V**
W	57	41	94	48	31	**W**
X	73	12	45	19	61	**X**
Y	27	44	72	82	33	**Y**
Z	74	13	25	70	63	**Z**

85

86

12 14 <u>17</u> 24 28 33 <u>37</u> 39 42
44 46 <u>49</u> 51 <u>53</u> 59 63 65 68
<u>72</u> 76 81 83 89 96 98

<u>11</u> 15 17 <u>22</u> 25 28 30 <u>36</u> 41
<u>44</u> 47 50 55 62 71 73 75 77
80 83 86 91 94 96 <u>99</u>

A	58	52	48	84	31	**A**
B	50	62	30	75	99	**B**
C	82	93	66	43	87	**C**
D	40	78	88	10	97	**D**
E	76	81	42	53	12	**E**
F	57	21	29	85	74	**F**
G	23	16	61	70	92	**G**
H	41	11	25	86	77	**H**
I	37	98	59	46	65	**I**
J	27	32	54	79	19	**J**
K	13	64	95	20	69	**K**
L	51	63	72	24	39	**L**
M	18	38	90	56	26	**M**

N	45	34	67	84	38	**N**
O	16	64	31	97	52	**O**
P	58	95	19	74	67	**P**
Q	48	27	78	18	35	**Q**
R	91	47	22	71	15	**R**
S	44	17	96	83	28	**S**
T	14	33	89	68	49	**T**
U	73	55	80	36	94	**U**
V	13	45	87	60	26	**V**
W	79	70	43	66	57	**W**
X	92	34	82	21	88	**X**
Y	32	10	93	54	40	**Y**
Z	69	20	85	31	97	**Z**

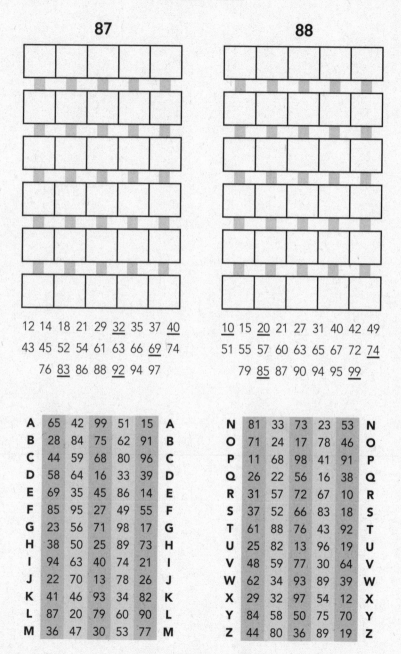

87

12 14 18 21 29 <u>32</u> 35 37 <u>40</u>
43 45 52 54 61 63 66 <u>69</u> 74
76 <u>83</u> 86 88 <u>92</u> 94 97

88

<u>10</u> 15 <u>20</u> 21 27 31 40 42 49
51 55 57 60 63 65 67 72 <u>74</u>
79 <u>85</u> 87 90 94 95 <u>99</u>

A	65	42	99	51	15	A
B	28	84	75	62	91	B
C	44	59	68	80	96	C
D	58	64	16	33	39	D
E	69	35	45	86	14	E
F	85	95	27	49	55	F
G	23	56	71	98	17	G
H	38	50	25	89	73	H
I	94	63	40	74	21	I
J	22	70	13	78	26	J
K	41	46	93	34	82	K
L	87	20	79	60	90	L
M	36	47	30	53	77	M

N	81	33	73	23	53	N
O	71	24	17	78	46	O
P	11	68	98	41	91	P
Q	26	22	56	16	38	Q
R	31	57	72	67	10	R
S	37	52	66	83	18	S
T	61	88	76	43	92	T
U	25	82	13	96	19	U
V	48	59	77	30	64	V
W	62	34	93	89	39	W
X	29	32	97	54	12	X
Y	84	58	50	75	70	Y
Z	44	80	36	89	19	Z

Word Fall

89

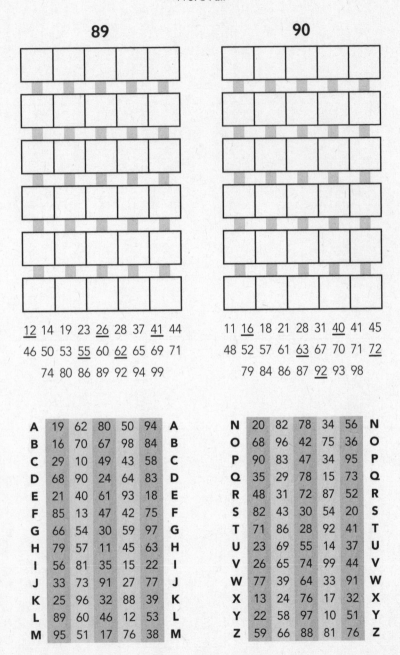

12 14 19 23 26 28 37 41 44
46 50 53 55 60 62 65 69 71
74 80 86 89 92 94 99

90

11 16 18 21 28 31 40 41 45
48 52 57 61 63 67 70 71 72
79 84 86 87 92 93 98

A	19	62	80	50	94	A
B	16	70	67	98	84	B
C	29	10	49	43	58	C
D	68	90	24	64	83	D
E	21	40	61	93	18	E
F	85	13	47	42	75	F
G	66	54	30	59	97	G
H	79	57	11	45	63	H
I	56	81	35	15	22	I
J	33	73	91	27	77	J
K	25	96	32	88	39	K
L	89	60	46	12	53	L
M	95	51	17	76	38	M

N	20	82	78	34	56	N
O	68	96	42	75	36	O
P	90	83	47	34	95	P
Q	35	29	78	15	73	Q
R	48	31	72	87	52	R
S	82	43	30	54	20	S
T	71	86	28	92	41	T
U	23	69	55	14	37	U
V	26	65	74	99	44	V
W	77	39	64	33	91	W
X	13	24	76	17	32	X
Y	22	58	97	10	51	Y
Z	59	66	88	81	76	Z

91

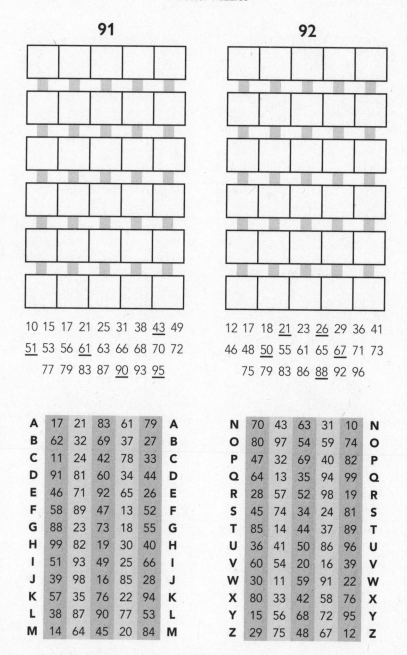

10 15 17 21 25 31 38 <u>43</u> 49
<u>51</u> 53 56 <u>61</u> 63 66 68 70 72
77 79 83 87 <u>90</u> 93 <u>95</u>

92

12 17 18 <u>21</u> 23 <u>26</u> 29 36 41
46 48 <u>50</u> 55 61 65 <u>67</u> 71 73
75 79 83 86 <u>88</u> 92 96

A	17	21	83	61	79	A
B	62	32	69	37	27	B
C	11	24	42	78	33	C
D	91	81	60	34	44	D
E	46	71	92	65	26	E
F	58	89	47	13	52	F
G	88	23	73	18	55	G
H	99	82	19	30	40	H
I	51	93	49	25	66	I
J	39	98	16	85	28	J
K	57	35	76	22	94	K
L	38	87	90	77	53	L
M	14	64	45	20	84	M

N	70	43	63	31	10	N
O	80	97	54	59	74	O
P	47	32	69	40	82	P
Q	64	13	35	94	99	Q
R	28	57	52	98	19	R
S	45	74	34	24	81	S
T	85	14	44	37	89	T
U	36	41	50	86	96	U
V	60	54	20	16	39	V
W	30	11	59	91	22	W
X	80	33	42	58	76	X
Y	15	56	68	72	95	Y
Z	29	75	48	67	12	Z

93

11 13 16 20 23 <u>26</u> 28 <u>30</u> 32
34 39 44 48 <u>53</u> 59 <u>61</u> 63 69
72 <u>74</u> 76 84 89 93 96

94

14 <u>19</u> 21 25 27 29 33 35 <u>37</u>
41 43 <u>49</u> 51 56 58 60 68 71
77 <u>80</u> 82 <u>87</u> 91 94 98

A	23	89	61	34	76	A
B	18	73	55	67	81	B
C	51	19	60	33	21	C
D	15	75	45	86	79	D
E	98	41	56	80	27	E
F	26	16	72	96	48	F
G	65	36	40	10	92	G
H	22	47	97	83	42	H
I	99	85	57	52	78	I
J	90	12	95	38	62	J
K	28	32	59	74	11	K
L	69	53	84	39	44	L
M	88	70	31	17	54	M

N	92	75	88	42	97	N
O	36	99	12	24	47	O
P	90	40	18	67	10	P
Q	79	17	52	57	62	Q
R	94	14	37	71	68	R
S	87	91	29	43	35	S
T	38	65	73	83	95	T
U	46	70	15	55	22	U
V	50	31	85	78	12	V
W	77	82	25	58	49	W
X	54	64	40	75	18	X
Y	20	93	63	13	30	Y
Z	81	73	22	88	10	Z

95

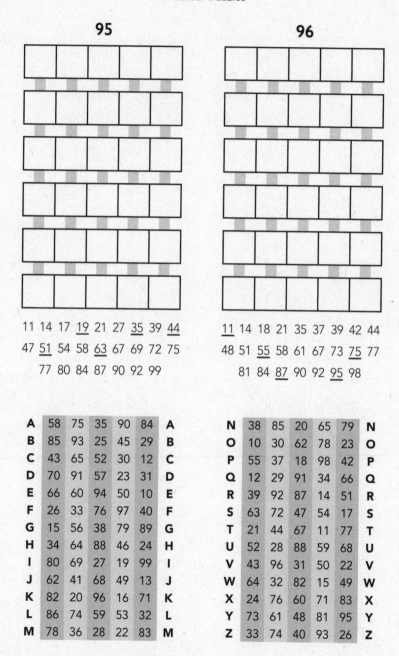

11 14 17 <u>19</u> 21 27 <u>35</u> 39 <u>44</u>
47 <u>51</u> 54 58 <u>63</u> 67 69 72 75
77 80 84 87 90 92 99

96

<u>11</u> 14 18 21 35 37 39 42 44
48 51 <u>55</u> 58 61 67 73 <u>75</u> 77
81 84 <u>87</u> 90 92 <u>95</u> 98

A	58	75	35	90	84	A
B	85	93	25	45	29	B
C	43	65	52	30	12	C
D	70	91	57	23	31	D
E	66	60	94	50	10	E
F	26	33	76	97	40	F
G	15	56	38	79	89	G
H	34	64	88	46	24	H
I	80	69	27	19	99	I
J	62	41	68	49	13	J
K	82	20	96	16	71	K
L	86	74	59	53	32	L
M	78	36	28	22	83	M

N	38	85	20	65	79	N
O	10	30	62	78	23	O
P	55	37	18	98	42	P
Q	12	29	91	34	66	Q
R	39	92	87	14	51	R
S	63	72	47	54	17	S
T	21	44	67	11	77	T
U	52	28	88	59	68	U
V	43	96	31	50	22	V
W	64	32	82	15	49	W
X	24	76	60	71	83	X
Y	73	61	48	81	95	Y
Z	33	74	40	93	26	Z

97

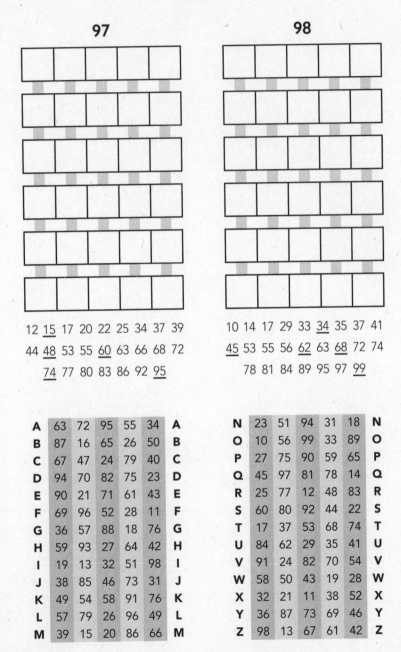

12 <u>15</u> 17 20 22 25 34 37 39
44 <u>48</u> 53 55 <u>60</u> 63 66 68 72
<u>74</u> 77 80 83 86 92 <u>95</u>

98

10 14 17 29 33 <u>34</u> 35 37 41
<u>45</u> 53 55 56 <u>62</u> 63 <u>68</u> 72 74
78 81 84 89 95 97 <u>99</u>

A	63	72	95	55	34	A
B	87	16	65	26	50	B
C	67	47	24	79	40	C
D	94	70	82	75	23	D
E	90	21	71	61	43	E
F	69	96	52	28	11	F
G	36	57	88	18	76	G
H	59	93	27	64	42	H
I	19	13	32	51	98	I
J	38	85	46	73	31	J
K	49	54	58	91	76	K
L	57	79	26	96	49	L
M	39	15	20	86	66	M

N	23	51	94	31	18	N
O	10	56	99	33	89	O
P	27	75	90	59	65	P
Q	45	97	81	78	14	Q
R	25	77	12	48	83	R
S	60	80	92	44	22	S
T	17	37	53	68	74	T
U	84	62	29	35	41	U
V	91	24	82	70	54	V
W	58	50	43	19	28	W
X	32	21	11	38	52	X
Y	36	87	73	69	46	Y
Z	98	13	67	61	42	Z

99

100

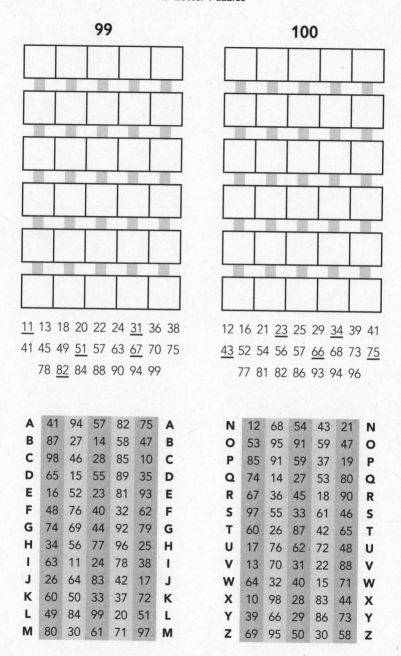

99

<u>11</u> 13 18 20 22 24 <u>31</u> 36 38
41 45 49 <u>51</u> 57 63 <u>67</u> 70 75
78 <u>82</u> 84 88 90 94 99

100

12 16 21 <u>23</u> 25 29 <u>34</u> 39 41
<u>43</u> 52 54 56 57 <u>66</u> 68 73 <u>75</u>
77 81 82 86 93 94 96

A	41	94	57	82	75	A
B	87	27	14	58	47	B
C	98	46	28	85	10	C
D	65	15	55	89	35	D
E	16	52	23	81	93	E
F	48	76	40	32	62	F
G	74	69	44	92	79	G
H	34	56	77	96	25	H
I	63	11	24	78	38	I
J	26	64	83	42	17	J
K	60	50	33	37	72	K
L	49	84	99	20	51	L
M	80	30	61	71	97	M

N	12	68	54	43	21	N
O	53	95	91	59	47	O
P	85	91	59	37	19	P
Q	74	14	27	53	80	Q
R	67	36	45	18	90	R
S	97	55	33	61	46	S
T	60	26	87	42	65	T
U	17	76	62	72	48	U
V	13	70	31	22	88	V
W	64	32	40	15	71	W
X	10	98	28	83	44	X
Y	39	66	29	86	73	Y
Z	69	95	50	30	58	Z

101

102

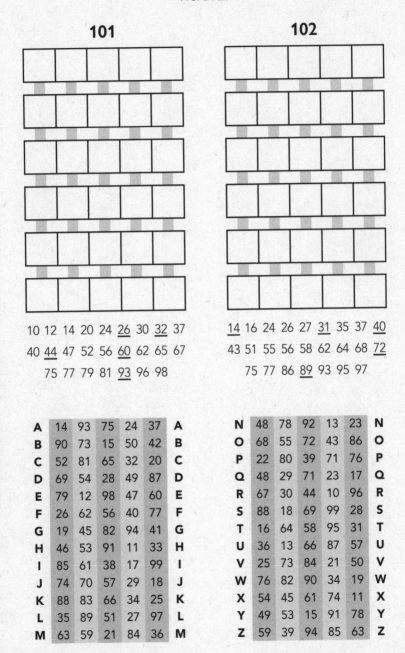

10 12 14 20 24 <u>26</u> 30 <u>32</u> 37
40 <u>44</u> 47 52 56 <u>60</u> 62 65 67
75 77 79 81 <u>93</u> 96 98

<u>14</u> 16 24 26 27 <u>31</u> 35 37 <u>40</u>
43 51 55 56 58 62 64 68 <u>72</u>
75 77 86 <u>89</u> 93 95 97

A	14	93	75	24	37	A
B	90	73	15	50	42	B
C	52	81	65	32	20	C
D	69	54	28	49	87	D
E	79	12	98	47	60	E
F	26	62	56	40	77	F
G	19	45	82	94	41	G
H	46	53	91	11	33	H
I	85	61	38	17	99	I
J	74	70	57	29	18	J
K	88	83	66	34	25	K
L	35	89	51	27	97	L
M	63	59	21	84	36	M

N	48	78	92	13	23	N
O	68	55	72	43	86	O
P	22	80	39	71	76	P
Q	48	29	71	23	17	Q
R	67	30	44	10	96	R
S	88	18	69	99	28	S
T	16	64	58	95	31	T
U	36	13	66	87	57	U
V	25	73	84	21	50	V
W	76	82	90	34	19	W
X	54	45	61	74	11	X
Y	49	53	15	91	78	Y
Z	59	39	94	85	63	Z

103

104

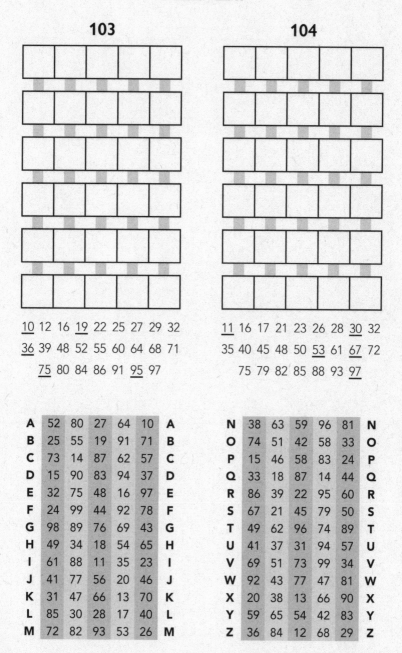

10 12 16 19 22 25 27 29 32

36 39 48 52 55 60 64 68 71

75 80 84 86 91 95 97

11 16 17 21 23 26 28 30 32

35 40 45 48 50 53 61 67 72

75 79 82 85 88 93 97

A	52	80	27	64	10	A
B	25	55	19	91	71	B
C	73	14	87	62	57	C
D	15	90	83	94	37	D
E	32	75	48	16	97	E
F	24	99	44	92	78	F
G	98	89	76	69	43	G
H	49	34	18	54	65	H
I	61	88	11	35	23	I
J	41	77	56	20	46	J
K	31	47	66	13	70	K
L	85	30	28	17	40	L
M	72	82	93	53	26	M

N	38	63	59	96	81	N
O	74	51	42	58	33	O
P	15	46	58	83	24	P
Q	33	18	87	14	44	Q
R	86	39	22	95	60	R
S	67	21	45	79	50	S
T	49	62	96	74	89	T
U	41	37	31	94	57	U
V	69	51	73	99	34	V
W	92	43	77	47	81	W
X	20	38	13	66	90	X
Y	59	65	54	42	83	Y
Z	36	84	12	68	29	Z

105

106

12 14 17 <u>20</u> 22 24 26 28 36
43 <u>46</u> 52 54 57 61 <u>63</u> 66 74
76 85 <u>87</u> 89 92 <u>94</u> 99

<u>16</u> 19 <u>22</u> 27 29 31 <u>37</u> 40 43
45 49 51 53 59 62 65 67 <u>71</u>
76 78 <u>81</u> 87 93 95 99

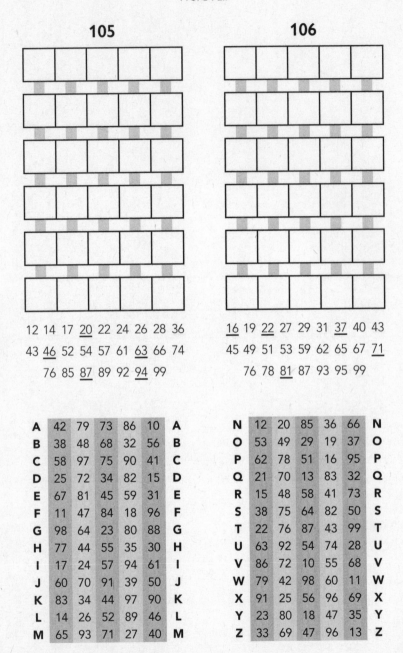

A	42	79	73	86	10	A
B	38	48	68	32	56	B
C	58	97	75	90	41	C
D	25	72	34	82	15	D
E	67	81	45	59	31	E
F	11	47	84	18	96	F
G	98	64	23	80	88	G
H	77	44	55	35	30	H
I	17	24	57	94	61	I
J	60	70	91	39	50	J
K	83	34	44	97	90	K
L	14	26	52	89	46	L
M	65	93	71	27	40	M

N	12	20	85	36	66	N
O	53	49	29	19	37	O
P	62	78	51	16	95	P
Q	21	70	13	83	32	Q
R	15	48	58	41	73	R
S	38	75	64	82	50	S
T	22	76	87	43	99	T
U	63	92	54	74	28	U
V	86	72	10	55	68	V
W	79	42	98	60	11	W
X	91	25	56	96	69	X
Y	23	80	18	47	35	Y
Z	33	69	47	96	13	Z

107

108

13 15 19 21 23 25 31 <u>33</u> 43
46 <u>49</u> 53 55 58 <u>61</u> 64 66 68
72 79 <u>81</u> 83 91 <u>93</u> 98

10 14 16 18 20 <u>27</u> 32 <u>36</u> 38
<u>44</u> 48 54 57 59 <u>65</u> 67 70 74
76 <u>78</u> 80 86 89 97 99

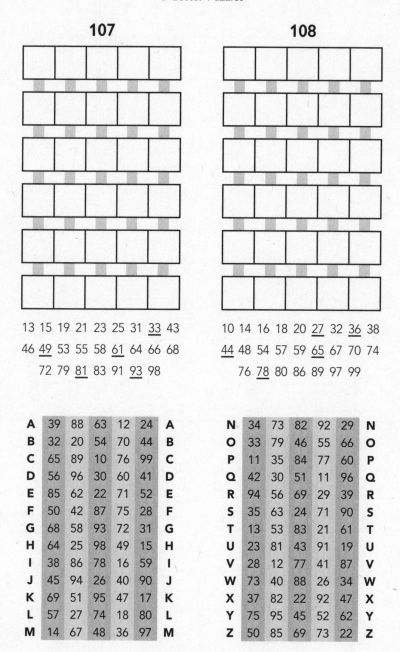

A	39	88	63	12	24	A
B	32	20	54	70	44	B
C	65	89	10	76	99	C
D	56	96	30	60	41	D
E	85	62	22	71	52	E
F	50	42	87	75	28	F
G	68	58	93	72	31	G
H	64	25	98	49	15	H
I	38	86	78	16	59	I
J	45	94	26	40	90	J
K	69	51	95	47	17	K
L	57	27	74	18	80	L
M	14	67	48	36	97	M

N	34	73	82	92	29	N
O	33	79	46	55	66	O
P	11	35	84	77	60	P
Q	42	30	51	11	96	Q
R	94	56	69	29	39	R
S	35	63	24	71	90	S
T	13	53	83	21	61	T
U	23	81	43	91	19	U
V	28	12	77	41	87	V
W	73	40	88	26	34	W
X	37	82	22	92	47	X
Y	75	95	45	52	62	Y
Z	50	85	69	73	22	Z

109

110

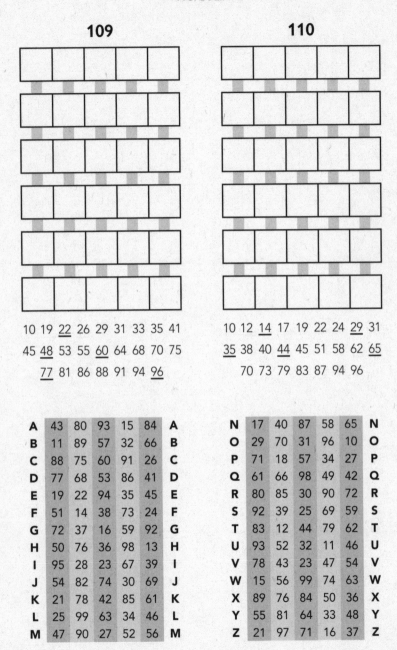

10 19 <u>22</u> 26 29 31 33 35 41
45 <u>48</u> 53 55 <u>60</u> 64 68 70 75
<u>77</u> 81 86 88 91 94 <u>96</u>

10 12 <u>14</u> 17 19 22 24 <u>29</u> 31
<u>35</u> 38 40 <u>44</u> 45 51 58 62 <u>65</u>
70 73 79 83 87 94 96

A	43	80	93	15	84	A
B	11	89	57	32	66	B
C	88	75	60	91	26	C
D	77	68	53	86	41	D
E	19	22	94	35	45	E
F	51	14	38	73	24	F
G	72	37	16	59	92	G
H	50	76	36	98	13	H
I	95	28	23	67	39	I
J	54	82	74	30	69	J
K	21	78	42	85	61	K
L	25	99	63	34	46	L
M	47	90	27	52	56	M

N	17	40	87	58	65	N
O	29	70	31	96	10	O
P	71	18	57	34	27	P
Q	61	66	98	49	42	Q
R	80	85	30	90	72	R
S	92	39	25	69	59	S
T	83	12	44	79	62	T
U	93	52	32	11	46	U
V	78	43	23	47	54	V
W	15	56	99	74	63	W
X	89	76	84	50	36	X
Y	55	81	64	33	48	Y
Z	21	97	71	16	37	Z

111

112

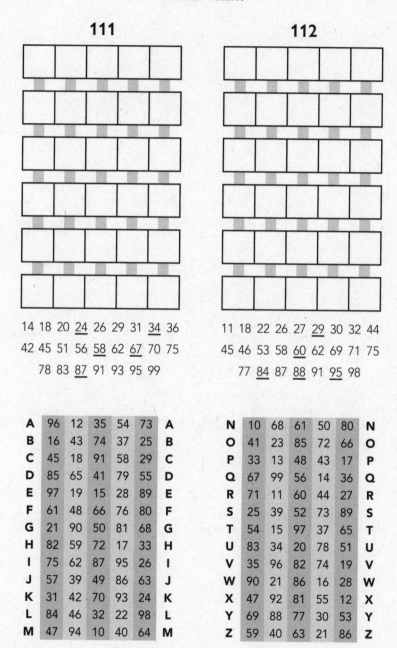

14 18 20 <u>24</u> 26 29 31 <u>34</u> 36
42 45 51 56 <u>58</u> 62 <u>67</u> 70 75
78 83 <u>87</u> 91 93 95 99

11 18 22 26 27 <u>29</u> 30 32 44
45 46 53 58 <u>60</u> 62 69 71 75
77 <u>84</u> 87 <u>88</u> 91 <u>95</u> 98

A	96	12	35	54	73	A
B	16	43	74	37	25	B
C	45	18	91	58	29	C
D	85	65	41	79	55	D
E	97	19	15	28	89	E
F	61	48	66	76	80	F
G	21	90	50	81	68	G
H	82	59	72	17	33	H
I	75	62	87	95	26	I
J	57	39	49	86	63	J
K	31	42	70	93	24	K
L	84	46	32	22	98	L
M	47	94	10	40	64	M

N	10	68	61	50	80	N
O	41	23	85	72	66	O
P	33	13	48	43	17	P
Q	67	99	56	14	36	Q
R	71	11	60	44	27	R
S	25	39	52	73	89	S
T	54	15	97	37	65	T
U	83	34	20	78	51	U
V	35	96	82	74	19	V
W	90	21	86	16	28	W
X	47	92	81	55	12	X
Y	69	88	77	30	53	Y
Z	59	40	63	21	86	Z

113

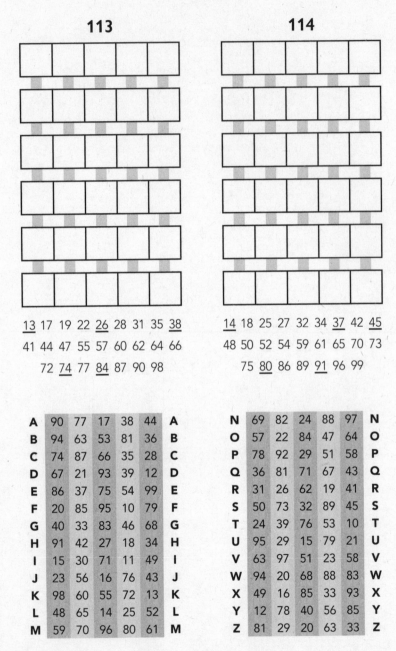

<u>13</u> 17 19 22 <u>26</u> 28 31 35 <u>38</u>
41 44 47 55 57 60 62 64 66
72 <u>74</u> 77 <u>84</u> 87 90 98

114

<u>14</u> 18 25 27 32 34 <u>37</u> 42 <u>45</u>
48 50 52 54 59 61 65 70 73
75 <u>80</u> 86 89 <u>91</u> 96 99

A	90	77	17	38	44	A
B	94	63	53	81	36	B
C	74	87	66	35	28	C
D	67	21	93	39	12	D
E	86	37	75	54	99	E
F	20	85	95	10	79	F
G	40	33	83	46	68	G
H	91	42	27	18	34	H
I	15	30	71	11	49	I
J	23	56	16	76	43	J
K	98	60	55	72	13	K
L	48	65	14	25	52	L
M	59	70	96	80	61	M

N	69	82	24	88	97	N
O	57	22	84	47	64	O
P	78	92	29	51	58	P
Q	36	81	71	67	43	Q
R	31	26	62	19	41	R
S	50	73	32	89	45	S
T	24	39	76	53	10	T
U	95	29	15	79	21	U
V	63	97	51	23	58	V
W	94	20	68	88	83	W
X	49	16	85	33	93	X
Y	12	78	40	56	85	Y
Z	81	29	20	63	33	Z

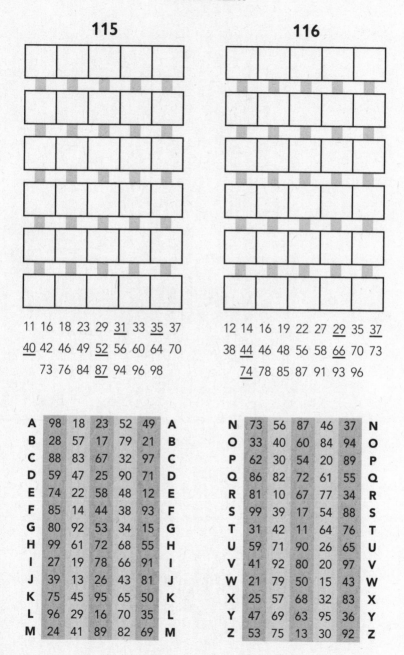

115

11 16 18 23 29 <u>31</u> 33 <u>35</u> 37
<u>40</u> 42 46 49 <u>52</u> 56 60 64 70
73 76 84 <u>87</u> 94 96 98

116

12 14 16 19 22 27 <u>29</u> 35 <u>37</u>
38 <u>44</u> 46 48 56 58 <u>66</u> 70 73
<u>74</u> 78 85 87 91 93 96

A	98	18	23	52	49	A
B	28	57	17	79	21	B
C	88	83	67	32	97	C
D	59	47	25	90	71	D
E	74	22	58	48	12	E
F	85	14	44	38	93	F
G	80	92	53	34	15	G
H	99	61	72	68	55	H
I	27	19	78	66	91	I
J	39	13	26	43	81	J
K	75	45	95	65	50	K
L	96	29	16	70	35	L
M	24	41	89	82	69	M

N	73	56	87	46	37	N
O	33	40	60	84	94	O
P	62	30	54	20	89	P
Q	86	82	72	61	55	Q
R	81	10	67	77	34	R
S	99	39	17	54	88	S
T	31	42	11	64	76	T
U	59	71	90	26	65	U
V	41	92	80	20	97	V
W	21	79	50	15	43	W
X	25	57	68	32	83	X
Y	47	69	63	95	36	Y
Z	53	75	13	30	92	Z

Word Fall

117

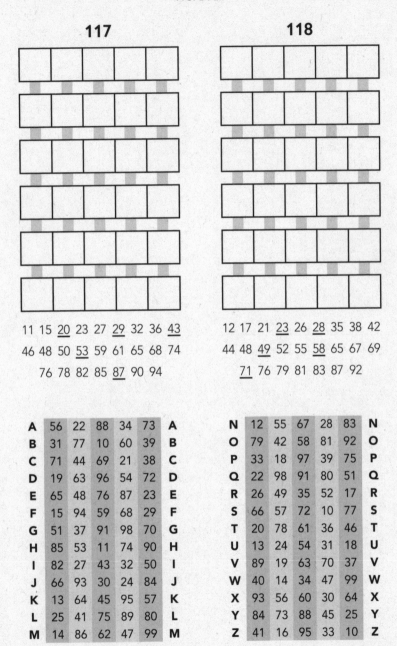

11 15 <u>20</u> 23 27 <u>29</u> 32 36 <u>43</u>
46 48 50 <u>53</u> 59 61 65 68 74
76 78 82 85 <u>87</u> 90 94

118

12 17 21 <u>23</u> 26 <u>28</u> 35 38 42
44 48 <u>49</u> 52 55 <u>58</u> 65 67 69
<u>71</u> 76 79 81 83 87 92

A	56	22	88	34	73	A
B	31	77	10	60	39	B
C	71	44	69	21	38	C
D	19	63	96	54	72	D
E	65	48	76	87	23	E
F	15	94	59	68	29	F
G	51	37	91	98	70	G
H	85	53	11	74	90	H
I	82	27	43	32	50	I
J	66	93	30	24	84	J
K	13	64	45	95	57	K
L	25	41	75	89	80	L
M	14	86	62	47	99	M

N	12	55	67	28	83	N
O	79	42	58	81	92	O
P	33	18	97	39	75	P
Q	22	98	91	80	51	Q
R	26	49	35	52	17	R
S	66	57	72	10	77	S
T	20	78	61	36	46	T
U	13	24	54	31	18	U
V	89	19	63	70	37	V
W	40	14	34	47	99	W
X	93	56	60	30	64	X
Y	84	73	88	45	25	Y
Z	41	16	95	33	10	Z

119

120

11 <u>14</u> 20 23 25 28 30 35 37
40 42 44 <u>50</u> 58 62 <u>64</u> 69 72
<u>74</u> 77 82 90 <u>92</u> 96 99

14 16 20 22 28 33 35 40 42
<u>48</u> 50 <u>53</u> 56 <u>59</u> 62 65 70 <u>72</u>
75 79 83 87 <u>90</u> 93 97

A	68	95	32	57	41	A
B	92	82	77	44	69	B
C	60	29	84	55	38	C
D	88	80	26	45	54	D
E	11	99	23	30	74	E
F	78	36	47	89	18	F
G	72	35	28	50	42	G
H	31	43	17	71	61	H
I	24	12	51	94	19	I
J	91	46	66	13	85	J
K	10	98	34	76	67	K
L	96	25	64	37	58	L
M	86	81	49	15	21	M

N	73	27	63	52	39	N
O	93	70	59	16	33	O
P	83	79	22	97	53	P
Q	26	54	67	88	46	Q
R	87	48	75	56	65	R
S	36	68	95	17	61	S
T	15	80	66	24	85	T
U	40	14	20	90	62	U
V	98	21	41	73	31	V
W	34	86	63	10	45	W
X	94	12	29	89	76	X
Y	18	60	91	13	51	Y
Z	78	47	52	39	84	Z

121

122

11 13 <u>15</u> 18 20 25 <u>27</u> 32 35
38 41 43 <u>48</u> 50 52 56 63 67
70 <u>73</u> 79 82 <u>88</u> 95 98

13 17 19 <u>23</u> 27 28 30 32 <u>34</u>
37 39 <u>43</u> 49 <u>51</u> 59 61 65 72
75 79 81 84 89 <u>91</u> 99

A	50	88	20	35	18	**A**
B	74	26	14	54	22	**B**
C	69	47	96	92	58	**C**
D	90	42	55	64	24	**D**
E	79	43	13	32	27	**E**
F	21	10	44	62	31	**F**
G	16	46	76	29	85	**G**
H	36	80	57	66	40	**H**
I	94	53	33	77	45	**I**
J	60	78	97	12	93	**J**
K	68	33	76	53	58	**K**
L	38	56	48	63	98	**L**
M	62	42	97	86	77	**M**

N	57	92	68	45	24	**N**
O	31	12	44	60	64	**O**
P	71	40	93	47	87	**P**
Q	85	54	66	22	26	**Q**
R	80	16	94	90	21	**R**
S	65	84	23	59	30	**S**
T	19	72	81	91	39	**T**
U	82	52	70	15	95	**U**
V	73	67	41	25	11	**V**
W	10	14	36	78	55	**W**
X	74	96	83	69	29	**X**
Y	89	75	49	99	34	**Y**
Z	51	37	17	28	61	**Z**

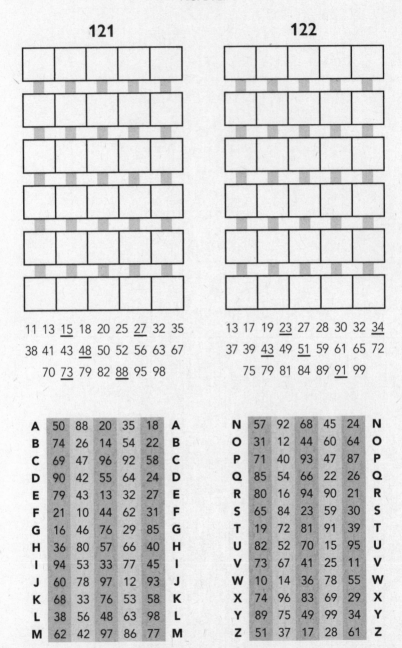

123

124

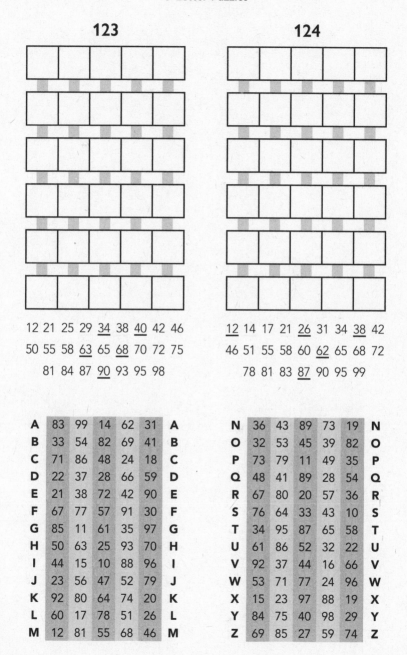

12 21 25 29 <u>34</u> 38 <u>40</u> 42 46
50 55 58 <u>63</u> 65 <u>68</u> 70 72 75
81 84 87 <u>90</u> 93 95 98

<u>12</u> 14 17 21 <u>26</u> 31 34 <u>38</u> 42
46 51 55 58 60 <u>62</u> 65 68 72
78 81 83 <u>87</u> 90 95 99

A	83	99	14	62	31	A	
B	33	54	82	69	41	B	
C	71	86	48	24	18	C	
D	22	37	28	66	59	D	
E	21	38	72	42	90	E	
F	67	77	57	91	30	F	
G	85	11	61	35	97	G	
H	50	63	25	93	70	H	
I	44	15	10	88	96	I	
J	23	56	47	52	79	J	
K	92	80	64	74	20	K	
L	60	17	78	51	26	L	
M	12	81	55	68	46	M	

N	36	43	89	73	19	N	
O	32	53	45	39	82	O	
P	73	79	11	49	35	P	
Q	48	41	89	28	54	Q	
R	67	80	20	57	36	R	
S	76	64	33	43	10	S	
T	34	95	87	65	58	T	
U	61	86	52	32	22	U	
V	92	37	44	16	66	V	
W	53	71	77	24	96	W	
X	15	23	97	88	19	X	
Y	84	75	40	98	29	Y	
Z	69	85	27	59	74	Z	

Word Fall

125

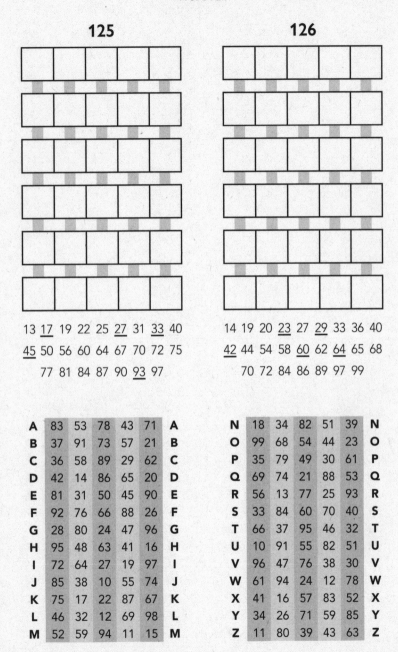

13 <u>17</u> 19 22 25 <u>27</u> 31 <u>33</u> 40
<u>45</u> 50 56 60 64 67 70 72 75
77 81 84 87 90 <u>93</u> 97

126

14 19 20 <u>23</u> 27 <u>29</u> 33 36 40
<u>42</u> 44 54 58 <u>60</u> 62 <u>64</u> 65 68
70 72 84 86 89 97 99

A	83	53	78	43	71	A
B	37	91	73	57	21	B
C	36	58	89	29	62	C
D	42	14	86	65	20	D
E	81	31	50	45	90	E
F	92	76	66	88	26	F
G	28	80	24	47	96	G
H	95	48	63	41	16	H
I	72	64	27	19	97	I
J	85	38	10	55	74	J
K	75	17	22	87	67	K
L	46	32	12	69	98	L
M	52	59	94	11	15	M

N	18	34	82	51	39	N
O	99	68	54	44	23	O
P	35	79	49	30	61	P
Q	69	74	21	88	53	Q
R	56	13	77	25	93	R
S	33	84	60	70	40	S
T	66	37	95	46	32	T
U	10	91	55	82	51	U
V	96	47	76	38	30	V
W	61	94	24	12	78	W
X	41	16	57	83	52	X
Y	34	26	71	59	85	Y
Z	11	80	39	43	63	Z

127

128

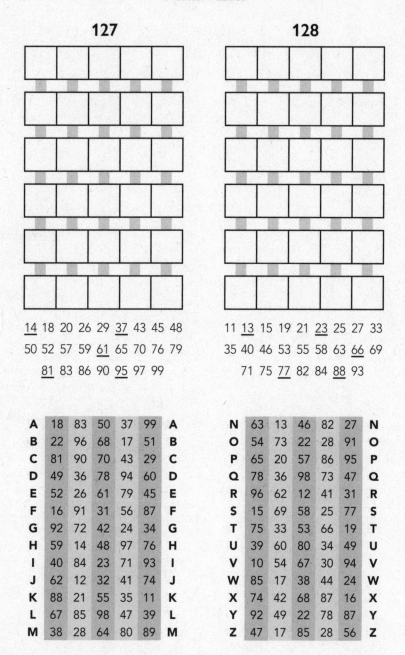

14 18 20 26 29 37 43 45 48
50 52 57 59 61 65 70 76 79
81 83 86 90 95 97 99

11 13 15 19 21 23 25 27 33
35 40 46 53 55 58 63 66 69
71 75 77 82 84 88 93

A	18	83	50	37	99	A
B	22	96	68	17	51	B
C	81	90	70	43	29	C
D	49	36	78	94	60	D
E	52	26	61	79	45	E
F	16	91	31	56	87	F
G	92	72	42	24	34	G
H	59	14	48	97	76	H
I	40	84	23	71	93	I
J	62	12	32	41	74	J
K	88	21	55	35	11	K
L	67	85	98	47	39	L
M	38	28	64	80	89	M

N	63	13	46	82	27	N
O	54	73	22	28	91	O
P	65	20	57	86	95	P
Q	78	36	98	73	47	Q
R	96	62	12	41	31	R
S	15	69	58	25	77	S
T	75	33	53	66	19	T
U	39	60	80	34	49	U
V	10	54	67	30	94	V
W	85	17	38	44	24	W
X	74	42	68	87	16	X
Y	92	49	22	78	87	Y
Z	47	17	85	28	56	Z

Word Fall

129

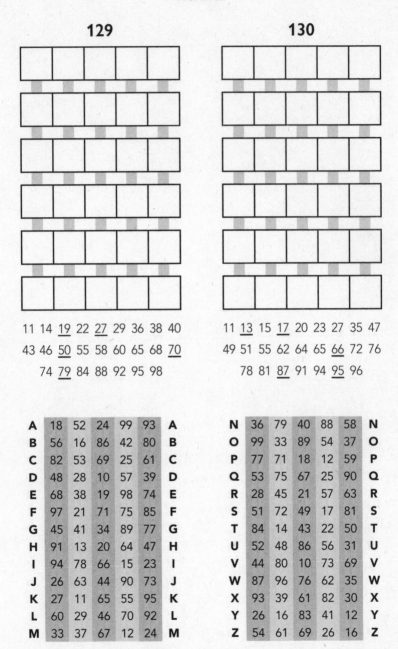

11 14 <u>19</u> 22 <u>27</u> 29 36 38 40
43 46 <u>50</u> 55 58 60 65 68 <u>70</u>
74 <u>79</u> 84 88 92 95 98

130

11 <u>13</u> 15 <u>17</u> 20 23 27 35 47
49 51 55 62 64 65 <u>66</u> 72 76
78 81 <u>87</u> 91 94 <u>95</u> 96

A	18	52	24	99	93	A
B	56	16	86	42	80	B
C	82	53	69	25	61	C
D	48	28	10	57	39	D
E	68	38	19	98	74	E
F	97	21	71	75	85	F
G	45	41	34	89	77	G
H	91	13	20	64	47	H
I	94	78	66	15	23	I
J	26	63	44	90	73	J
K	27	11	65	55	95	K
L	60	29	46	70	92	L
M	33	37	67	12	24	M

N	36	79	40	88	58	N
O	99	33	89	54	37	O
P	77	71	18	12	59	P
Q	53	75	67	25	90	Q
R	28	45	21	57	63	R
S	51	72	49	17	81	S
T	84	14	43	22	50	T
U	52	48	86	56	31	U
V	44	80	10	73	69	V
W	87	96	76	62	35	W
X	93	39	61	82	30	X
Y	26	16	83	41	12	Y
Z	54	61	69	26	16	Z

131

132

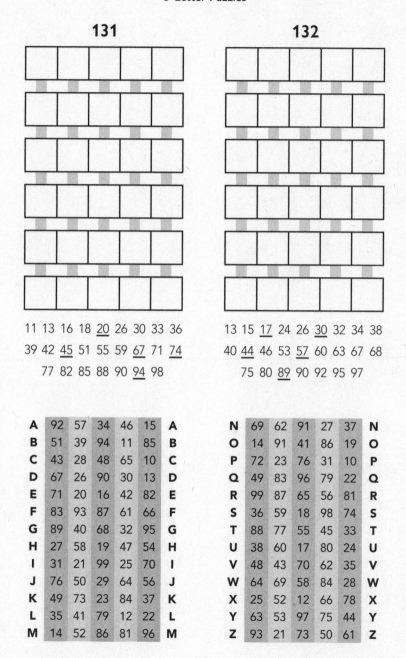

11 13 16 18 <u>20</u> 26 30 33 36
39 42 <u>45</u> 51 55 59 <u>67</u> 71 <u>74</u>
77 82 85 88 90 <u>94</u> 98

13 15 <u>17</u> 24 26 <u>30</u> 32 34 38
40 <u>44</u> 46 53 <u>57</u> 60 63 67 68
75 80 <u>89</u> 90 92 95 97

A	92	57	34	46	15	A
B	51	39	94	11	85	B
C	43	28	48	65	10	C
D	67	26	90	30	13	D
E	71	20	16	42	82	E
F	83	93	87	61	66	F
G	89	40	68	32	95	G
H	27	58	19	47	54	H
I	31	21	99	25	70	I
J	76	50	29	64	56	J
K	49	73	23	84	37	K
L	35	41	79	12	22	L
M	14	52	86	81	96	M

N	69	62	91	27	37	N
O	14	91	41	86	19	O
P	72	23	76	31	10	P
Q	49	83	96	79	22	Q
R	99	87	65	56	81	R
S	36	59	18	98	74	S
T	88	77	55	45	33	T
U	38	60	17	80	24	U
V	48	43	70	62	35	V
W	64	69	58	84	28	W
X	25	52	12	66	78	X
Y	63	53	97	75	44	Y
Z	93	21	73	50	61	Z

133

134

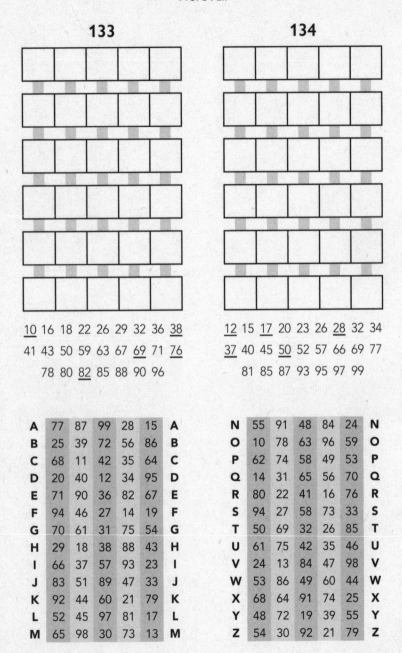

133

<u>10</u> 16 18 22 26 29 32 36 <u>38</u>
41 43 50 59 63 67 <u>69</u> 71 <u>76</u>
78 80 <u>82</u> 85 88 90 96

134

<u>12</u> 15 <u>17</u> 20 23 26 <u>28</u> 32 34
<u>37</u> 40 45 <u>50</u> 52 57 66 69 77
81 85 87 93 95 97 99

A	77	87	99	28	15	A
B	25	39	72	56	86	B
C	68	11	42	35	64	C
D	20	40	12	34	95	D
E	71	90	36	82	67	E
F	94	46	27	14	19	F
G	70	61	31	75	54	G
H	29	18	38	88	43	H
I	66	37	57	93	23	I
J	83	51	89	47	33	J
K	92	44	60	21	79	K
L	52	45	97	81	17	L
M	65	98	30	73	13	M

N	55	91	48	84	24	N
O	10	78	63	96	59	O
P	62	74	58	49	53	P
Q	14	31	65	56	70	Q
R	80	22	41	16	76	R
S	94	27	58	73	33	S
T	50	69	32	26	85	T
U	61	75	42	35	46	U
V	24	13	84	47	98	V
W	53	86	49	60	44	W
X	68	64	91	74	25	X
Y	48	72	19	39	55	Y
Z	54	30	92	21	79	Z

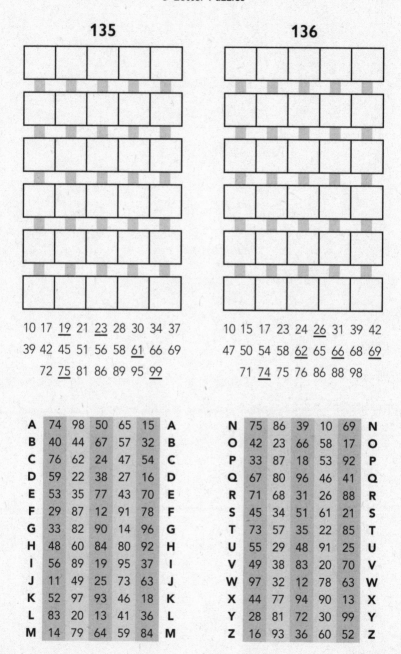

135

10 17 <u>19</u> 21 <u>23</u> 28 30 34 37
39 42 45 51 56 58 <u>61</u> 66 69
72 <u>75</u> 81 86 89 95 <u>99</u>

136

10 15 17 23 24 <u>26</u> 31 39 42
47 50 54 58 <u>62</u> 65 <u>66</u> 68 <u>69</u>
71 <u>74</u> 75 76 86 88 98

A	74	98	50	65	15	A
B	40	44	67	57	32	B
C	76	62	24	47	54	C
D	59	22	38	27	16	D
E	53	35	77	43	70	E
F	29	87	12	91	78	F
G	33	82	90	14	96	G
H	48	60	84	80	92	H
I	56	89	19	95	37	I
J	11	49	25	73	63	J
K	52	97	93	46	18	K
L	83	20	13	41	36	L
M	14	79	64	59	84	M

N	75	86	39	10	69	N
O	42	23	66	58	17	O
P	33	87	18	53	92	P
Q	67	80	96	46	41	Q
R	71	68	31	26	88	R
S	45	34	51	61	21	S
T	73	57	35	22	85	T
U	55	29	48	91	25	U
V	49	38	83	20	70	V
W	97	32	12	78	63	W
X	44	77	94	90	13	X
Y	28	81	72	30	99	Y
Z	16	93	36	60	52	Z

Word Fall

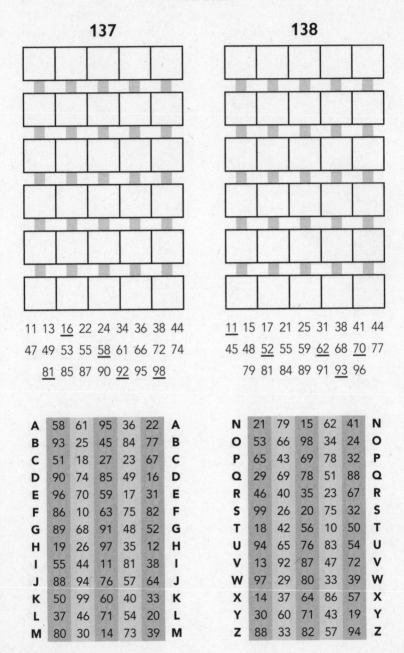

137

11 13 <u>16</u> 22 24 34 36 38 44
47 49 53 55 <u>58</u> 61 66 72 74
<u>81</u> 85 87 90 <u>92</u> 95 <u>98</u>

A	58	61	95	36	22	A
B	93	25	45	84	77	B
C	51	18	27	23	67	C
D	90	74	85	49	16	D
E	96	70	59	17	31	E
F	86	10	63	75	82	F
G	89	68	91	48	52	G
H	19	26	97	35	12	H
I	55	44	11	81	38	I
J	88	94	76	57	64	J
K	50	99	60	40	33	K
L	37	46	71	54	20	L
M	80	30	14	73	39	M

138

<u>11</u> 15 17 21 25 31 38 41 44
45 48 <u>52</u> 55 59 <u>62</u> 68 <u>70</u> 77
79 81 84 89 91 <u>93</u> 96

N	21	79	15	62	41	N
O	53	66	98	34	24	O
P	65	43	69	78	32	P
Q	29	69	78	51	88	Q
R	46	40	35	23	67	R
S	99	26	20	75	32	S
T	18	42	56	10	50	T
U	94	65	76	83	54	U
V	13	92	87	47	72	V
W	97	29	80	33	39	W
X	14	37	64	86	57	X
Y	30	60	71	43	19	Y
Z	88	33	82	57	94	Z

139

140

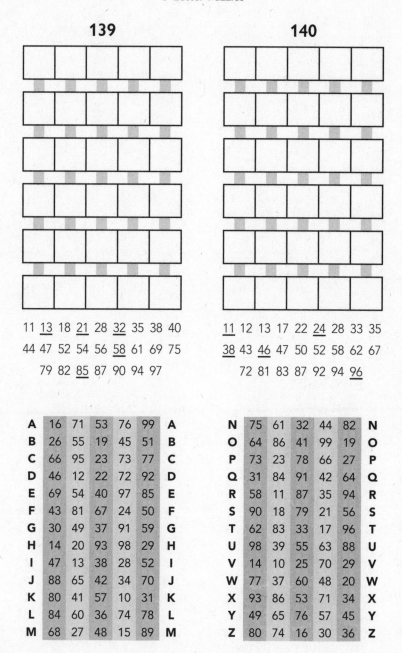

11 <u>13</u> 18 <u>21</u> 28 <u>32</u> 35 38 40
44 47 52 54 56 <u>58</u> 61 69 75
79 82 <u>85</u> 87 90 94 97

<u>11</u> 12 13 17 22 <u>24</u> 28 33 35
<u>38</u> 43 <u>46</u> 47 50 52 58 62 67
72 81 83 87 92 94 <u>96</u>

A	16	71	53	76	99	A
B	26	55	19	45	51	B
C	66	95	23	73	77	C
D	46	12	22	72	92	D
E	69	54	40	97	85	E
F	43	81	67	24	50	F
G	30	49	37	91	59	G
H	14	20	93	98	29	H
I	47	13	38	28	52	I
J	88	65	42	34	70	J
K	80	41	57	10	31	K
L	84	60	36	74	78	L
M	68	27	48	15	89	M

N	75	61	32	44	82	N
O	64	86	41	99	19	O
P	73	23	78	66	27	P
Q	31	84	91	42	64	Q
R	58	11	87	35	94	R
S	90	18	79	21	56	S
T	62	83	33	17	96	T
U	98	39	55	63	88	U
V	14	10	25	70	29	V
W	77	37	60	48	20	W
X	93	86	53	71	34	X
Y	49	65	76	57	45	Y
Z	80	74	16	30	36	Z

141

<u>13</u> 15 17 22 24 27 31 34 36
<u>41</u> 43 48 51 60 64 68 <u>71</u> 73
75 <u>79</u> 82 <u>85</u> 88 94 98

142

<u>10</u> 12 20 27 30 <u>35</u> 38 <u>40</u> 42
44 48 49 <u>52</u> 54 56 62 68 72
<u>73</u> 80 85 87 89 92 97

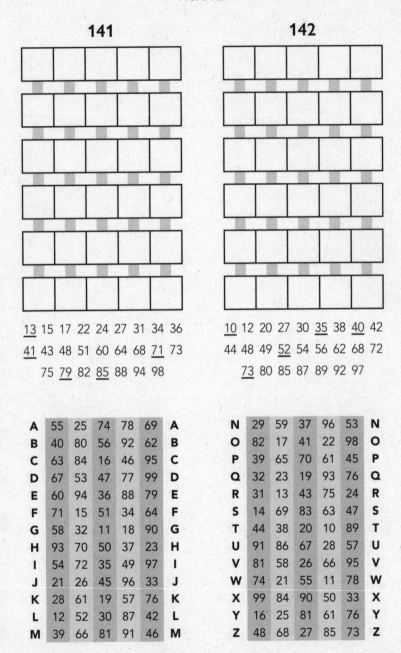

A	55	25	74	78	69	A
B	40	80	56	92	62	B
C	63	84	16	46	95	C
D	67	53	47	77	99	D
E	60	94	36	88	79	E
F	71	15	51	34	64	F
G	58	32	11	18	90	G
H	93	70	50	37	23	H
I	54	72	35	49	97	I
J	21	26	45	96	33	J
K	28	61	19	57	76	K
L	12	52	30	87	42	L
M	39	66	81	91	46	M

N	29	59	37	96	53	N
O	82	17	41	22	98	O
P	39	65	70	61	45	P
Q	32	23	19	93	76	Q
R	31	13	43	75	24	R
S	14	69	83	63	47	S
T	44	38	20	10	89	T
U	91	86	67	28	57	U
V	81	58	26	66	95	V
W	74	21	55	11	78	W
X	99	84	90	50	33	X
Y	16	25	81	61	76	Y
Z	48	68	27	85	73	Z

143

144

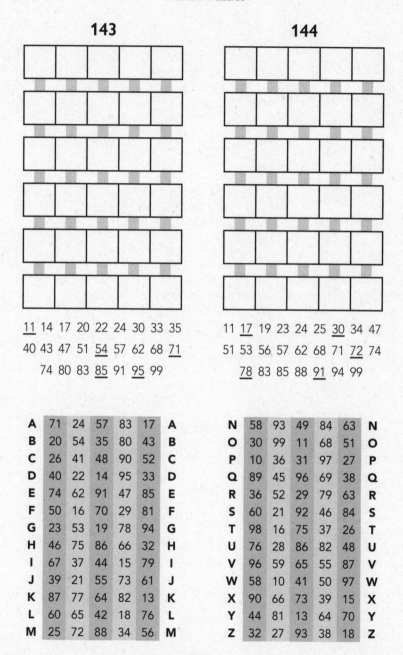

11 14 17 20 22 24 30 33 35
40 43 47 51 54 57 62 68 71
74 80 83 85 91 95 99

11 17 19 23 24 25 30 34 47
51 53 56 57 62 68 71 72 74
78 83 85 88 91 94 99

A	71	24	57	83	17	A
B	20	54	35	80	43	B
C	26	41	48	90	52	C
D	40	22	14	95	33	D
E	74	62	91	47	85	E
F	50	16	70	29	81	F
G	23	53	19	78	94	G
H	46	75	86	66	32	H
I	67	37	44	15	79	I
J	39	21	55	73	61	J
K	87	77	64	82	13	K
L	60	65	42	18	76	L
M	25	72	88	34	56	M

N	58	93	49	84	63	N
O	30	99	11	68	51	O
P	10	36	31	97	27	P
Q	89	45	96	69	38	Q
R	36	52	29	79	63	R
S	60	21	92	46	84	S
T	98	16	75	37	26	T
U	76	28	86	82	48	U
V	96	59	65	55	87	V
W	58	10	41	50	97	W
X	90	66	73	39	15	X
Y	44	81	13	64	70	Y
Z	32	27	93	38	18	Z

145

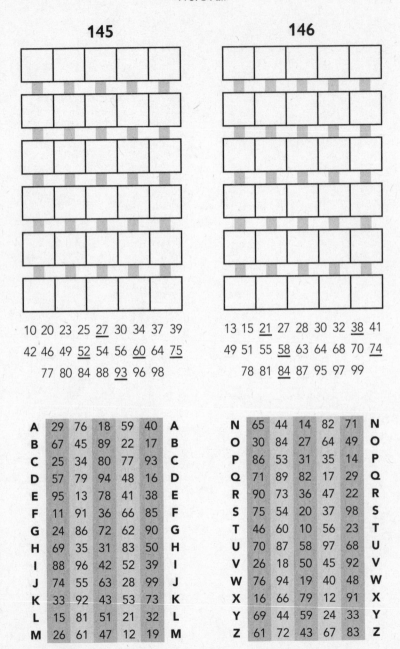

10 20 23 25 <u>27</u> 30 34 37 39
42 46 49 <u>52</u> 54 56 <u>60</u> 64 <u>75</u>
77 80 84 88 <u>93</u> 96 98

146

13 15 <u>21</u> 27 28 30 32 <u>38</u> 41
49 51 55 <u>58</u> 63 64 68 70 <u>74</u>
78 81 <u>84</u> 87 95 97 99

A	29	76	18	59	40	A
B	67	45	89	22	17	B
C	25	34	80	77	93	C
D	57	79	94	48	16	D
E	95	13	78	41	38	E
F	11	91	36	66	85	F
G	24	86	72	62	90	G
H	69	35	31	83	50	H
I	88	96	42	52	39	I
J	74	55	63	28	99	J
K	33	92	43	53	73	K
L	15	81	51	21	32	L
M	26	61	47	12	19	M

N	65	44	14	82	71	N
O	30	84	27	64	49	O
P	86	53	31	35	14	P
Q	71	89	82	17	29	Q
R	90	73	36	47	22	R
S	75	54	20	37	98	S
T	46	60	10	56	23	T
U	70	87	58	97	68	U
V	26	18	50	45	92	V
W	76	94	19	40	48	W
X	16	66	79	12	91	X
Y	69	44	59	24	33	Y
Z	61	72	43	67	83	Z

147

148

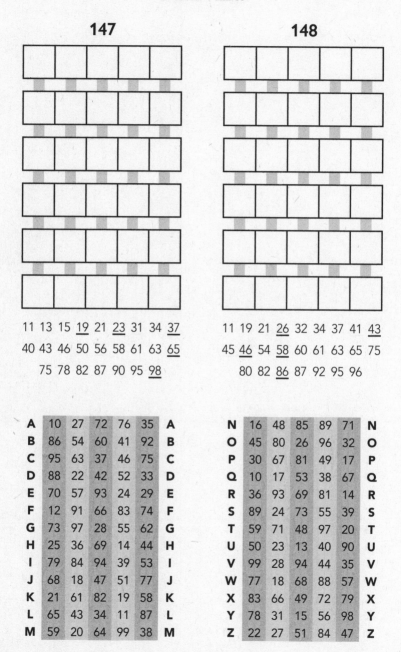

147

11 13 15 <u>19</u> 21 <u>23</u> 31 34 <u>37</u>
40 43 46 50 56 58 61 63 <u>65</u>
75 78 82 87 90 95 <u>98</u>

148

11 19 21 <u>26</u> 32 34 37 41 <u>43</u>
45 <u>46</u> 54 <u>58</u> 60 61 63 65 75
80 82 <u>86</u> 87 92 95 96

A	10	27	72	76	35	A
B	86	54	60	41	92	B
C	95	63	37	46	75	C
D	88	22	42	52	33	D
E	70	57	93	24	29	E
F	12	91	66	83	74	F
G	73	97	28	55	62	G
H	25	36	69	14	44	H
I	79	84	94	39	53	I
J	68	18	47	51	77	J
K	21	61	82	19	58	K
L	65	43	34	11	87	L
M	59	20	64	99	38	M

N	16	48	85	89	71	N
O	45	80	26	96	32	O
P	30	67	81	49	17	P
Q	10	17	53	38	67	Q
R	36	93	69	81	14	R
S	89	24	73	55	39	S
T	59	71	48	97	20	T
U	50	23	13	40	90	U
V	99	28	94	44	35	V
W	77	18	68	88	57	W
X	83	66	49	72	79	X
Y	78	31	15	56	98	Y
Z	22	27	51	84	47	Z

Word Fall

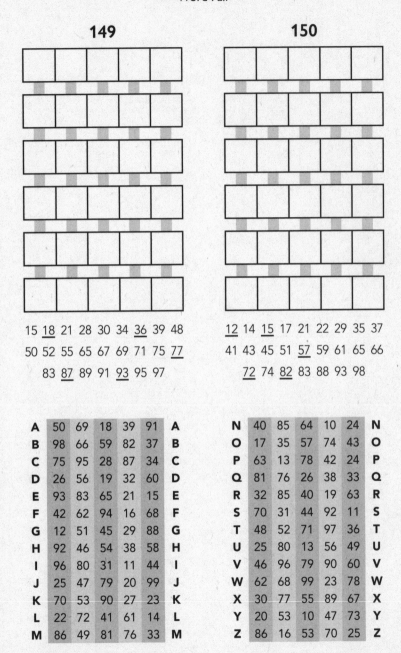

149

15 <u>18</u> 21 28 30 34 <u>36</u> 39 48
50 52 55 65 67 69 71 75 <u>77</u>
83 <u>87</u> 89 91 <u>93</u> 95 97

150

<u>12</u> 14 <u>15</u> 17 21 22 29 35 37
41 43 45 51 <u>57</u> 59 61 65 66
<u>72</u> 74 <u>82</u> 83 88 93 98

A	50	69	18	39	91	A
B	98	66	59	82	37	B
C	75	95	28	87	34	C
D	26	56	19	32	60	D
E	93	83	65	21	15	E
F	42	62	94	16	68	F
G	12	51	45	29	88	G
H	92	46	54	38	58	H
I	96	80	31	11	44	I
J	25	47	79	20	99	J
K	70	53	90	27	23	K
L	22	72	41	61	14	L
M	86	49	81	76	33	M

N	40	85	64	10	24	N
O	17	35	57	74	43	O
P	63	13	78	42	24	P
Q	81	76	26	38	33	Q
R	32	85	40	19	63	R
S	70	31	44	92	11	S
T	48	52	71	97	36	T
U	25	80	13	56	49	U
V	46	96	79	90	60	V
W	62	68	99	23	78	W
X	30	77	55	89	67	X
Y	20	53	10	47	73	Y
Z	86	16	53	70	25	Z

151

152

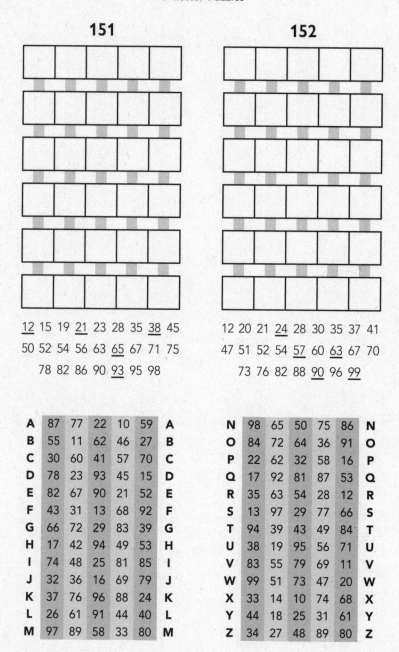

151

<u>12</u> 15 19 <u>21</u> 23 28 35 <u>38</u> 45
50 52 54 56 63 <u>65</u> 67 71 75
78 82 86 90 <u>93</u> 95 98

A	87	77	22	10	59	A
B	55	11	62	46	27	B
C	30	60	41	57	70	C
D	78	23	93	45	15	D
E	82	67	90	21	52	E
F	43	31	13	68	92	F
G	66	72	29	83	39	G
H	17	42	94	49	53	H
I	74	48	25	81	85	I
J	32	36	16	69	79	J
K	37	76	96	88	24	K
L	26	61	91	44	40	L
M	97	89	58	33	80	M

152

12 20 21 <u>24</u> 28 30 35 37 41
47 51 52 54 <u>57</u> 60 <u>63</u> 67 70
73 76 82 88 <u>90</u> 96 <u>99</u>

N	98	65	50	75	86	N
O	84	72	64	36	91	O
P	22	62	32	58	16	P
Q	17	92	81	87	53	Q
R	35	63	54	28	12	R
S	13	97	29	77	66	S
T	94	39	43	49	84	T
U	38	19	95	56	71	U
V	83	55	79	69	11	V
W	99	51	73	47	20	W
X	33	14	10	74	68	X
Y	44	18	25	31	61	Y
Z	34	27	48	89	80	Z

153

154

153: 12 15 17 21 27 29 32 37 43 46 49 55 61 63 69 72 74 76 78 81 86 88 90 94 99

154: 10 12 16 17 21 22 25 27 38 40 43 47 52 58 60 63 69 71 73 74 78 85 88 91 98

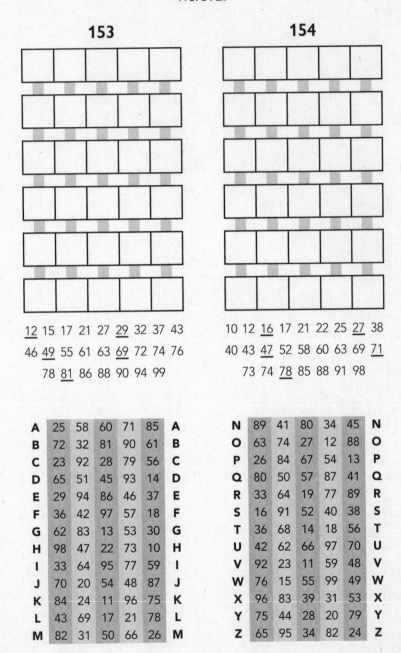

A	25	58	60	71	85	A
B	72	32	81	90	61	B
C	23	92	28	79	56	C
D	65	51	45	93	14	D
E	29	94	86	46	37	E
F	36	42	97	57	18	F
G	62	83	13	53	30	G
H	98	47	22	73	10	H
I	33	64	95	77	59	I
J	70	20	54	48	87	J
K	84	24	11	96	75	K
L	43	69	17	21	78	L
M	82	31	50	66	26	M

N	89	41	80	34	45	N
O	63	74	27	12	88	O
P	26	84	67	54	13	P
Q	80	50	57	87	41	Q
R	33	64	19	77	89	R
S	16	91	52	40	38	S
T	36	68	14	18	56	T
U	42	62	66	97	70	U
V	92	23	11	59	48	V
W	76	15	55	99	49	W
X	96	83	39	31	53	X
Y	75	44	28	20	79	Y
Z	65	95	34	82	24	Z

155

156

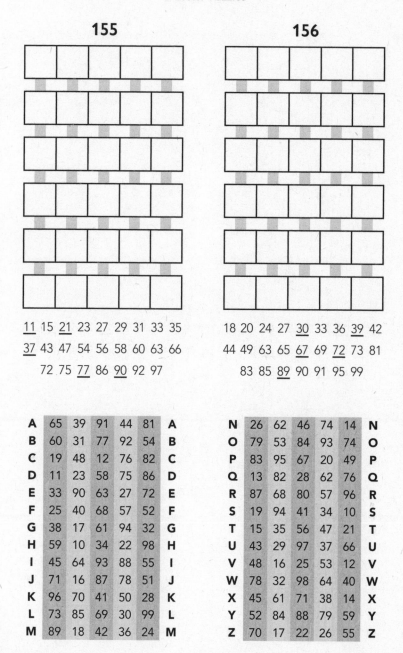

11 15 21 23 27 29 31 33 35
37 43 47 54 56 58 60 63 66
72 75 77 86 90 92 97

18 20 24 27 30 33 36 39 42
44 49 63 65 67 69 72 73 81
83 85 89 90 91 95 99

A	65	39	91	44	81	A
B	60	31	77	92	54	B
C	19	48	12	76	82	C
D	11	23	58	75	86	D
E	33	90	63	27	72	E
F	25	40	68	57	52	F
G	38	17	61	94	32	G
H	59	10	34	22	98	H
I	45	64	93	88	55	I
J	71	16	87	78	51	J
K	96	70	41	50	28	K
L	73	85	69	30	99	L
M	89	18	42	36	24	M

N	26	62	46	74	14	N
O	79	53	84	93	74	O
P	83	95	67	20	49	P
Q	13	82	28	62	76	Q
R	87	68	80	57	96	R
S	19	94	41	34	10	S
T	15	35	56	47	21	T
U	43	29	97	37	66	U
V	48	16	25	53	12	V
W	78	32	98	64	40	W
X	45	61	71	38	14	X
Y	52	84	88	79	59	Y
Z	70	17	22	26	55	Z

157

11 15 <u>17</u> 23 30 38 40 42 45
47 <u>52</u> 55 58 60 63 <u>66</u> 69 73
<u>76</u> 80 <u>85</u> 87 90 96 98

158

13 17 18 20 <u>24</u> 26 28 <u>35</u> 37
39 44 46 50 53 63 67 73 <u>75</u>
77 <u>80</u> 86 89 <u>91</u> 95 98

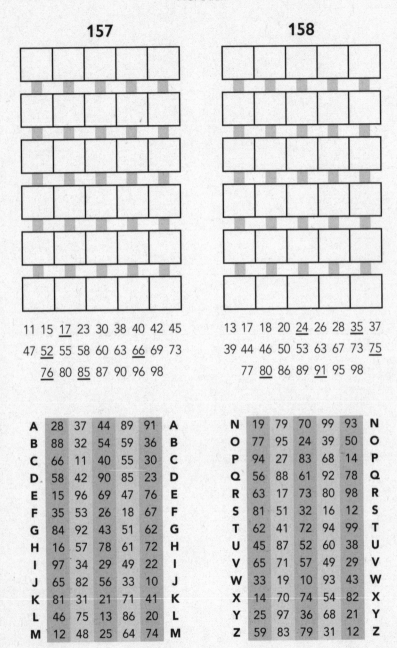

A	28	37	44	89	91	**A**
B	88	32	54	59	36	**B**
C	66	11	40	55	30	**C**
D	58	42	90	85	23	**D**
E	15	96	69	47	76	**E**
F	35	53	26	18	67	**F**
G	84	92	43	51	62	**G**
H	16	57	78	61	72	**H**
I	97	34	29	49	22	**I**
J	65	82	56	33	10	**J**
K	81	31	21	71	41	**K**
L	46	75	13	86	20	**L**
M	12	48	25	64	74	**M**

N	19	79	70	99	93	**N**
O	77	95	24	39	50	**O**
P	94	27	83	68	14	**P**
Q	56	88	61	92	78	**Q**
R	63	17	73	80	98	**R**
S	81	51	32	16	12	**S**
T	62	41	72	94	99	**T**
U	45	87	52	60	38	**U**
V	65	71	57	49	29	**V**
W	33	19	10	93	43	**W**
X	14	70	74	54	82	**X**
Y	25	97	36	68	21	**Y**
Z	59	83	79	31	12	**Z**

159

160

10 14 16 19 25 28 31 33 35
41 43 48 51 54 58 60 65 69
71 74 81 83 89 92 95

10 13 18 21 24 30 33 36 38
47 50 52 58 62 64 65 68 71
72 76 80 85 87 90 94

A	60	41	25	74	51	A
B	34	99	29	39	63	B
C	68	87	76	30	18	C
D	73	17	56	97	61	D
E	83	92	54	19	35	E
F	38	72	64	52	24	F
G	78	84	49	40	57	G
H	96	53	77	32	23	H
I	44	86	91	22	12	I
J	75	15	11	67	20	J
K	90	50	13	47	85	K
L	33	71	58	10	65	L
M	98	42	79	70	37	M

N	26	59	66	93	88	N
O	80	62	94	36	21	O
P	55	45	27	86	96	P
Q	78	91	59	97	42	Q
R	49	63	15	84	70	R
S	37	82	98	67	11	S
T	89	43	14	28	31	T
U	20	27	99	93	12	U
V	56	75	17	22	45	V
W	61	34	29	77	39	W
X	16	48	81	69	95	X
Y	88	66	26	57	40	Y
Z	79	23	55	73	96	Z

161

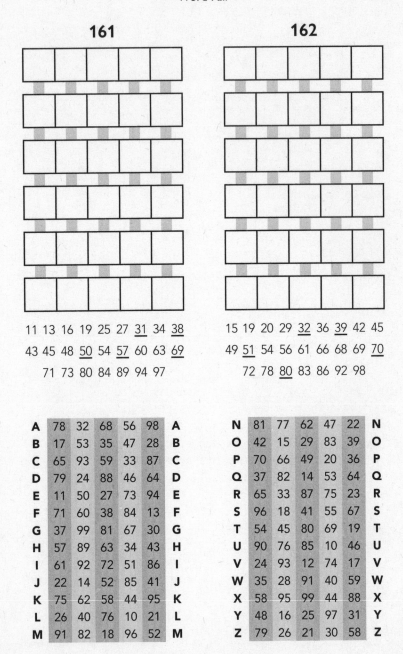

11 13 16 19 25 27 <u>31</u> 34 <u>38</u>
43 45 48 <u>50</u> 54 <u>57</u> 60 63 <u>69</u>
71 73 80 84 89 94 97

162

15 19 20 29 <u>32</u> 36 <u>39</u> 42 45
49 <u>51</u> 54 56 61 66 68 69 <u>70</u>
72 78 <u>80</u> 83 86 92 98

A	78	32	68	56	98	A
B	17	53	35	47	28	B
C	65	93	59	33	87	C
D	79	24	88	46	64	D
E	11	50	27	73	94	E
F	71	60	38	84	13	F
G	37	99	81	67	30	G
H	57	89	63	34	43	H
I	61	92	72	51	86	I
J	22	14	52	85	41	J
K	75	62	58	44	95	K
L	26	40	76	10	21	L
M	91	82	18	96	52	M

N	81	77	62	47	22	N
O	42	15	29	83	39	O
P	70	66	49	20	36	P
Q	37	82	14	53	64	Q
R	65	33	87	75	23	R
S	96	18	41	55	67	S
T	54	45	80	69	19	T
U	90	76	85	10	46	U
V	24	93	12	74	17	V
W	35	28	91	40	59	W
X	58	95	99	44	88	X
Y	48	16	25	97	31	Y
Z	79	26	21	30	58	Z

163

14 17 <u>20</u> 24 27 <u>33</u> 39 41 44
47 50 <u>55</u> 58 63 65 67 69 73
<u>78</u> 82 85 91 94 96 <u>99</u>

164

11 20 <u>24</u> 27 28 33 <u>37</u> 41 42
44 47 48 50 53 61 <u>65</u> 67 69
<u>71</u> 82 85 86 89 <u>94</u> 99

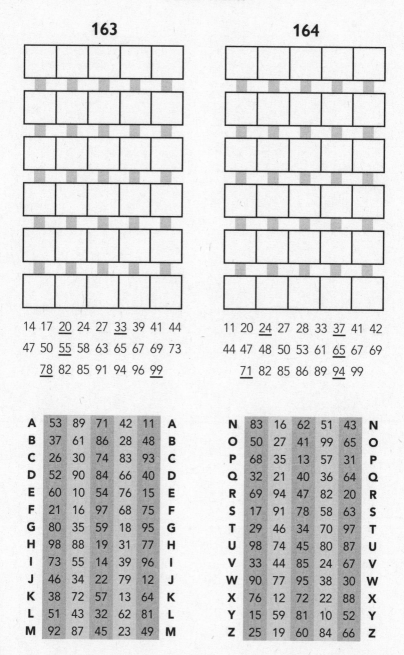

A	53	89	71	42	11	**A**
B	37	61	86	28	48	**B**
C	26	30	74	83	93	**C**
D	52	90	84	66	40	**D**
E	60	10	54	76	15	**E**
F	21	16	97	68	75	**F**
G	80	35	59	18	95	**G**
H	98	88	19	31	77	**H**
I	73	55	14	39	96	**I**
J	46	34	22	79	12	**J**
K	38	72	57	13	64	**K**
L	51	43	32	62	81	**L**
M	92	87	45	23	49	**M**

N	83	16	62	51	43	**N**
O	50	27	41	99	65	**O**
P	68	35	13	57	31	**P**
Q	32	21	40	36	64	**Q**
R	69	94	47	82	20	**R**
S	17	91	78	58	63	**S**
T	29	46	34	70	97	**T**
U	98	74	45	80	87	**U**
V	33	44	85	24	67	**V**
W	90	77	95	38	30	**W**
X	76	12	72	22	88	**X**
Y	15	59	81	10	52	**Y**
Z	25	19	60	84	66	**Z**

165

12 14 17 24 27 30 33 36 39
41 44 47 51 59 62 65 67 72
75 77 80 85 90 97 99

166

11 13 15 20 23 25 29 33 35
37 41 43 48 50 55 60 65 71
74 77 79 81 83 87 97

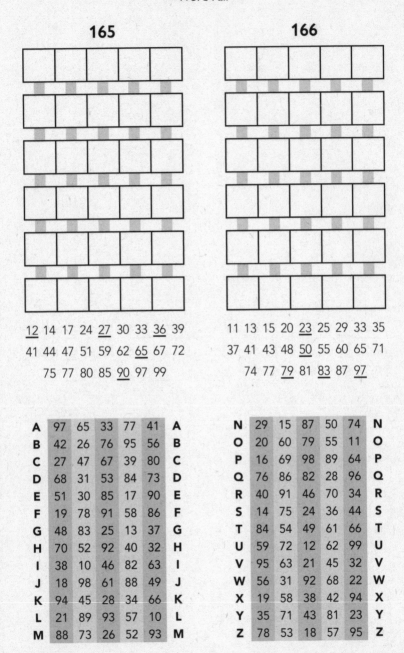

A	97	65	33	77	41	A
B	42	26	76	95	56	B
C	27	47	67	39	80	C
D	68	31	53	84	73	D
E	51	30	85	17	90	E
F	19	78	91	58	86	F
G	48	83	25	13	37	G
H	70	52	92	40	32	H
I	38	10	46	82	63	I
J	18	98	61	88	49	J
K	94	45	28	34	66	K
L	21	89	93	57	10	L
M	88	73	26	52	93	M

N	29	15	87	50	74	N
O	20	60	79	55	11	O
P	16	69	98	89	64	P
Q	76	86	82	28	96	Q
R	40	91	46	70	34	R
S	14	75	24	36	44	S
T	84	54	49	61	66	T
U	59	72	12	62	99	U
V	95	63	21	45	32	V
W	56	31	92	68	22	W
X	19	58	38	42	94	X
Y	35	71	43	81	23	Y
Z	78	53	18	57	95	Z

167

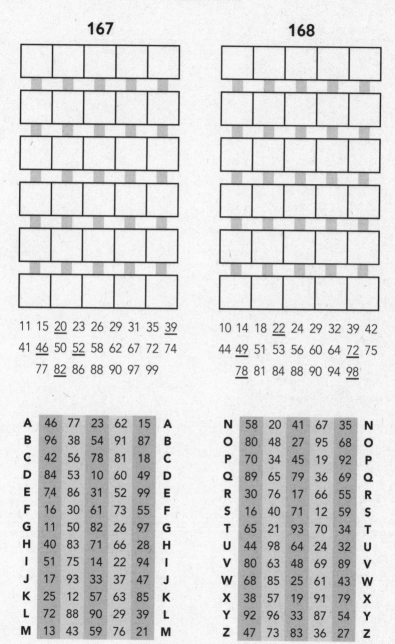

11 15 <u>20</u> 23 26 29 31 35 <u>39</u>
41 <u>46</u> 50 <u>52</u> 58 62 67 72 74
77 <u>82</u> 86 88 90 97 99

168

10 14 18 <u>22</u> 24 29 32 39 42
44 <u>49</u> 51 53 56 60 64 <u>72</u> 75
<u>78</u> 81 84 88 90 94 <u>98</u>

A	46	77	23	62	15	A
B	96	38	54	91	87	B
C	42	56	78	81	18	C
D	84	53	10	60	49	D
E	74	86	31	52	99	E
F	16	30	61	73	55	F
G	11	50	82	26	97	G
H	40	83	71	66	28	H
I	51	75	14	22	94	I
J	17	93	33	37	47	J
K	25	12	57	63	85	K
L	72	88	90	29	39	L
M	13	43	59	76	21	M

N	58	20	41	67	35	N
O	80	48	27	95	68	O
P	70	34	45	19	92	P
Q	89	65	79	36	69	Q
R	30	76	17	66	55	R
S	16	40	71	12	59	S
T	65	21	93	70	34	T
U	44	98	64	24	32	U
V	80	63	48	69	89	V
W	68	85	25	61	43	W
X	38	57	19	91	79	X
Y	92	96	33	87	54	Y
Z	47	73	83	36	27	Z

Word Fall

169

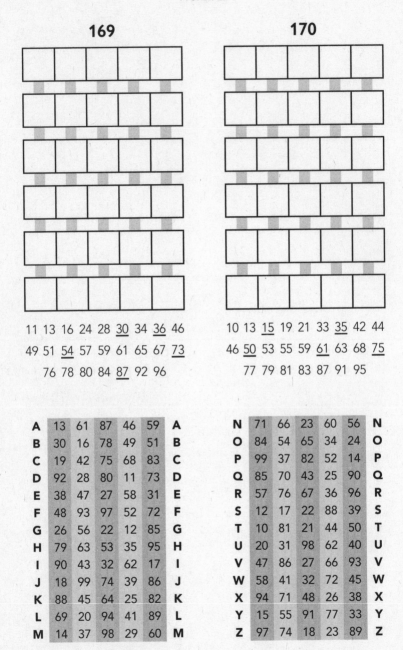

11 13 16 24 28 <u>30</u> 34 <u>36</u> 46
49 51 <u>54</u> 57 59 61 65 67 <u>73</u>
76 78 80 84 <u>87</u> 92 96

170

10 13 <u>15</u> 19 21 33 <u>35</u> 42 44
46 <u>50</u> 53 55 59 <u>61</u> 63 68 <u>75</u>
77 79 81 83 87 91 95

A	13	61	87	46	59	A
B	30	16	78	49	51	B
C	19	42	75	68	83	C
D	92	28	80	11	73	D
E	38	47	27	58	31	E
F	48	93	97	52	72	F
G	26	56	22	12	85	G
H	79	63	53	35	95	H
I	90	43	32	62	17	I
J	18	99	74	39	86	J
K	88	45	64	25	82	K
L	69	20	94	41	89	L
M	14	37	98	29	60	M

N	71	66	23	60	56	N
O	84	54	65	34	24	O
P	99	37	82	52	14	P
Q	85	70	43	25	90	Q
R	57	76	67	36	96	R
S	12	17	22	88	39	S
T	10	81	21	44	50	T
U	20	31	98	62	40	U
V	47	86	27	66	93	V
W	58	41	32	72	45	W
X	94	71	48	26	38	X
Y	15	55	91	77	33	Y
Z	97	74	18	23	89	Z

171

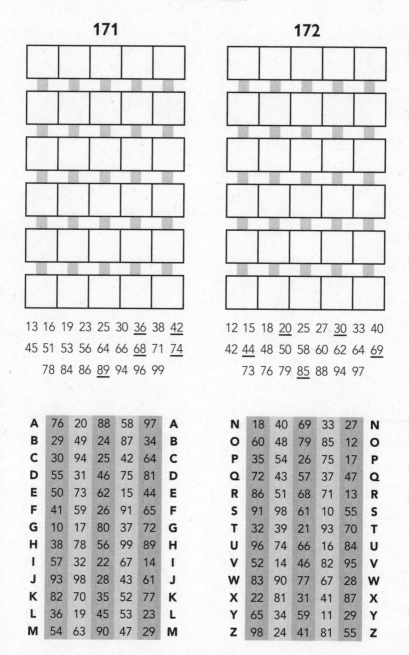

13 16 19 23 25 30 <u>36</u> 38 <u>42</u>
45 51 53 56 64 66 <u>68</u> 71 <u>74</u>
78 84 86 <u>89</u> 94 96 99

172

12 15 18 <u>20</u> 25 27 <u>30</u> 33 40
42 <u>44</u> 48 50 58 60 62 64 <u>69</u>
73 76 79 <u>85</u> 88 94 97

A	76	20	88	58	97	A
B	29	49	24	87	34	B
C	30	94	25	42	64	C
D	55	31	46	75	81	D
E	50	73	62	15	44	E
F	41	59	26	91	65	F
G	10	17	80	37	72	G
H	38	78	56	99	89	H
I	57	32	22	67	14	I
J	93	98	28	43	61	J
K	82	70	35	52	77	K
L	36	19	45	53	23	L
M	54	63	90	47	29	M

N	18	40	69	33	27	N
O	60	48	79	85	12	O
P	35	54	26	75	17	P
Q	72	43	57	37	47	Q
R	86	51	68	71	13	R
S	91	98	61	10	55	S
T	32	39	21	93	70	T
U	96	74	66	16	84	U
V	52	14	46	82	95	V
W	83	90	77	67	28	W
X	22	81	31	41	87	X
Y	65	34	59	11	29	Y
Z	98	24	41	81	55	Z

Word Fall

173

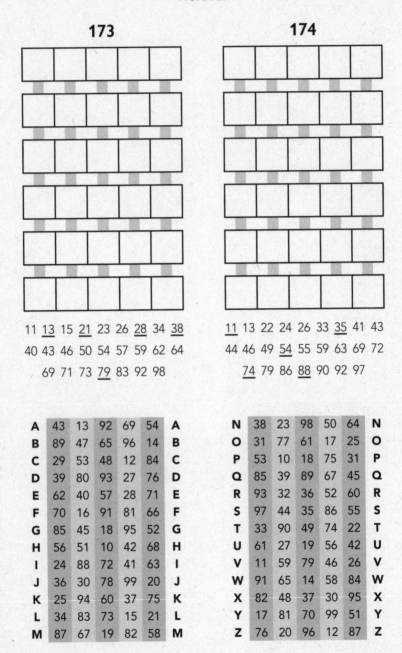

11 <u>13</u> 15 <u>21</u> 23 26 <u>28</u> 34 <u>38</u>
40 43 46 50 54 57 59 62 64
69 71 73 <u>79</u> 83 92 98

174

<u>11</u> 13 22 24 26 33 <u>35</u> 41 43
44 46 49 <u>54</u> 55 59 63 69 72
<u>74</u> 79 86 <u>88</u> 90 92 97

A	43	13	92	69	54	A
B	89	47	65	96	14	B
C	29	53	48	12	84	C
D	39	80	93	27	76	D
E	62	40	57	28	71	E
F	70	16	91	81	66	F
G	85	45	18	95	52	G
H	56	51	10	42	68	H
I	24	88	72	41	63	I
J	36	30	78	99	20	J
K	25	94	60	37	75	K
L	34	83	73	15	21	L
M	87	67	19	82	58	M

N	38	23	98	50	64	N
O	31	77	61	17	25	O
P	53	10	18	75	31	P
Q	85	39	89	67	45	Q
R	93	32	36	52	60	R
S	97	44	35	86	55	S
T	33	90	49	74	22	T
U	61	27	19	56	42	U
V	11	59	79	46	26	V
W	91	65	14	58	84	W
X	82	48	37	30	95	X
Y	17	81	70	99	51	Y
Z	76	20	96	12	87	Z

175

176

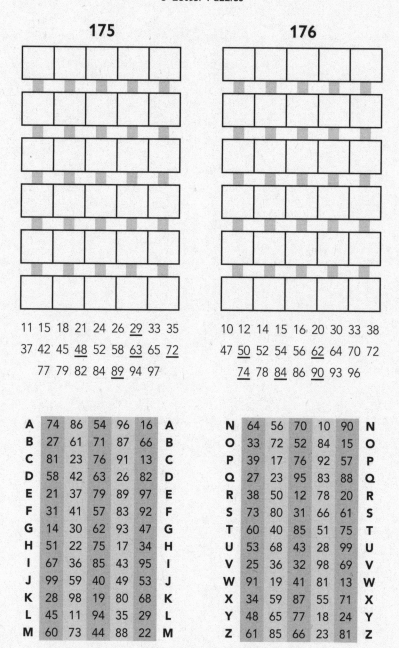

11 15 18 21 24 26 <u>29</u> 33 35
37 42 45 <u>48</u> 52 58 <u>63</u> 65 <u>72</u>
77 79 82 84 <u>89</u> 94 97

10 12 14 15 16 20 30 33 38
47 <u>50</u> 52 54 56 <u>62</u> 64 70 72
<u>74</u> 78 <u>84</u> 86 <u>90</u> 93 96

A	74	86	54	96	16	A
B	27	61	71	87	66	B
C	81	23	76	91	13	C
D	58	42	63	26	82	D
E	21	37	79	89	97	E
F	31	41	57	83	92	F
G	14	30	62	93	47	G
H	51	22	75	17	34	H
I	67	36	85	43	95	I
J	99	59	40	49	53	J
K	28	98	19	80	68	K
L	45	11	94	35	29	L
M	60	73	44	88	22	M

N	64	56	70	10	90	N
O	33	72	52	84	15	O
P	39	17	76	92	57	P
Q	27	23	95	83	88	Q
R	38	50	12	78	20	R
S	73	80	31	66	61	S
T	60	40	85	51	75	T
U	53	68	43	28	99	U
V	25	36	32	98	69	V
W	91	19	41	81	13	W
X	34	59	87	55	71	X
Y	48	65	77	18	24	Y
Z	61	85	66	23	81	Z

Word Fall

177

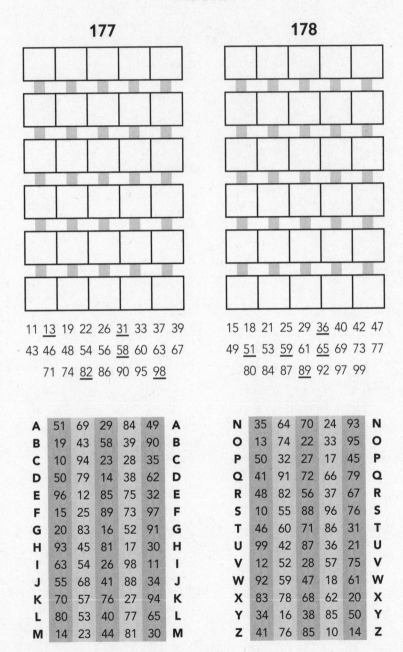

11 <u>13</u> 19 22 26 <u>31</u> 33 37 39
43 46 48 54 56 <u>58</u> 60 63 67
71 74 <u>82</u> 86 90 95 <u>98</u>

178

15 18 21 25 29 <u>36</u> 40 42 47
49 <u>51</u> 53 <u>59</u> 61 <u>65</u> 69 73 77
80 84 87 <u>89</u> 92 97 99

A	51	69	29	84	49	A
B	19	43	58	39	90	B
C	10	94	23	28	35	C
D	50	79	14	38	62	D
E	96	12	85	75	32	E
F	15	25	89	73	97	F
G	20	83	16	52	91	G
H	93	45	81	17	30	H
I	63	54	26	98	11	I
J	55	68	41	88	34	J
K	70	57	76	27	94	K
L	80	53	40	77	65	L
M	14	23	44	81	30	M

N	35	64	70	24	93	N
O	13	74	22	33	95	O
P	50	32	27	17	45	P
Q	41	91	72	66	79	Q
R	48	82	56	37	67	R
S	10	55	88	96	76	S
T	46	60	71	86	31	T
U	99	42	87	36	21	U
V	12	52	28	57	75	V
W	92	59	47	18	61	W
X	83	78	68	62	20	X
Y	34	16	38	85	50	Y
Z	41	76	85	10	14	Z

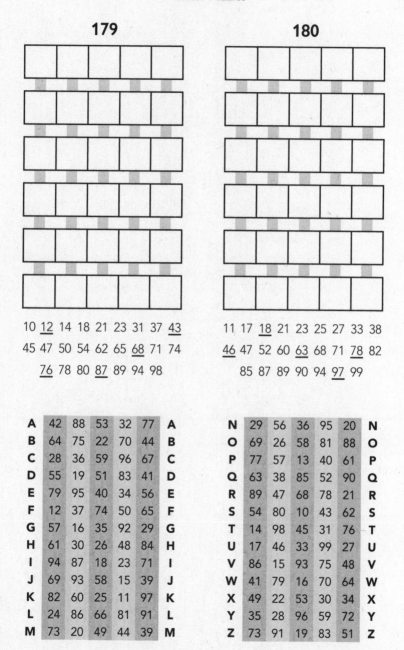

179

10 <u>12</u> 14 18 21 23 31 37 <u>43</u>
45 47 50 54 62 65 <u>68</u> 71 74
<u>76</u> 78 80 <u>87</u> 89 94 98

180

11 17 <u>18</u> 21 23 25 27 33 38
<u>46</u> 47 52 60 <u>63</u> 68 71 <u>78</u> 82
85 87 89 90 94 <u>97</u> 99

A	42	88	53	32	77	A
B	64	75	22	70	44	B
C	28	36	59	96	67	C
D	55	19	51	83	41	D
E	79	95	40	34	56	E
F	12	37	74	50	65	F
G	57	16	35	92	29	G
H	61	30	26	48	84	H
I	94	87	18	23	71	I
J	69	93	58	15	39	J
K	82	60	25	11	97	K
L	24	86	66	81	91	L
M	73	20	49	44	39	M

N	29	56	36	95	20	N
O	69	26	58	81	88	O
P	77	57	13	40	61	P
Q	63	38	85	52	90	Q
R	89	47	68	78	21	R
S	54	80	10	43	62	S
T	14	98	45	31	76	T
U	17	46	33	99	27	U
V	86	15	93	75	48	V
W	41	79	16	70	64	W
X	49	22	53	30	34	X
Y	35	28	96	59	72	Y
Z	73	91	19	83	51	Z

181

12 16 18 20 22 26 35 38 40
43 47 51 53 59 63 66 68 72
79 81 87 89 92 94 97

182

11 12 15 17 22 25 27 36 46
48 51 54 56 60 67 70 78 80
83 86 89 91 93 94 96

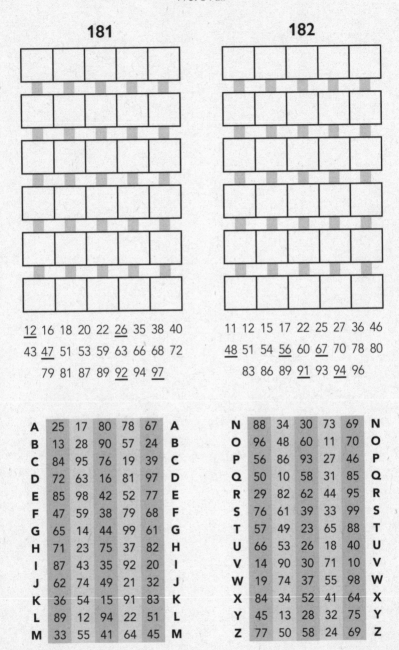

A	25	17	80	78	67	A
B	13	28	90	57	24	B
C	84	95	76	19	39	C
D	72	63	16	81	97	D
E	85	98	42	52	77	E
F	47	59	38	79	68	F
G	65	14	44	99	61	G
H	71	23	75	37	82	H
I	87	43	35	92	20	I
J	62	74	49	21	32	J
K	36	54	15	91	83	K
L	89	12	94	22	51	L
M	33	55	41	64	45	M

N	88	34	30	73	69	N
O	96	48	60	11	70	O
P	56	86	93	27	46	P
Q	50	10	58	31	85	Q
R	29	82	62	44	95	R
S	76	61	39	33	99	S
T	57	49	23	65	88	T
U	66	53	26	18	40	U
V	14	90	30	71	10	V
W	19	74	37	55	98	W
X	84	34	52	41	64	X
Y	45	13	28	32	75	Y
Z	77	50	58	24	69	Z

183

184

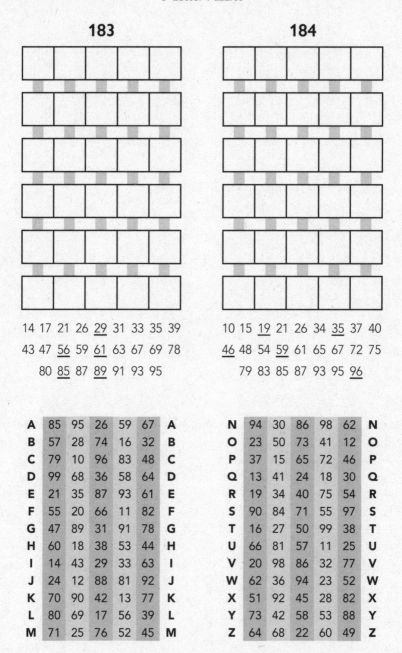

14 17 21 26 <u>29</u> 31 33 35 39
43 47 <u>56</u> 59 <u>61</u> 63 67 69 78
80 <u>85</u> 87 <u>89</u> 91 93 95

10 15 <u>19</u> 21 26 34 <u>35</u> 37 40
<u>46</u> 48 54 <u>59</u> 61 65 67 72 75
79 83 85 87 93 95 <u>96</u>

A	85	95	26	59	67	A		N	94	30	86	98	62	N
B	57	28	74	16	32	B		O	23	50	73	41	12	O
C	79	10	96	83	48	C		P	37	15	65	72	46	P
D	99	68	36	58	64	D		Q	13	41	24	18	30	Q
E	21	35	87	93	61	E		R	19	34	40	75	54	R
F	55	20	66	11	82	F		S	90	84	71	55	97	S
G	47	89	31	91	78	G		T	16	27	50	99	38	T
H	60	18	38	53	44	H		U	66	81	57	11	25	U
I	14	43	29	33	63	I		V	20	98	86	32	77	V
J	24	12	88	81	92	J		W	62	36	94	23	52	W
K	70	90	42	13	77	K		X	51	92	45	28	82	X
L	80	69	17	56	39	L		Y	73	42	58	53	88	Y
M	71	25	76	52	45	M		Z	64	68	22	60	49	Z

Word Fall

185

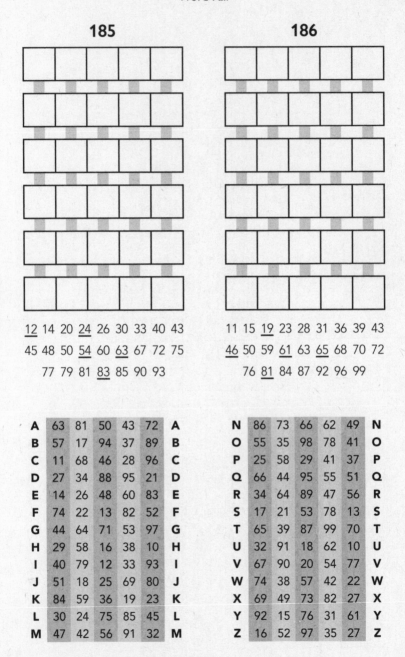

<u>12</u> 14 20 <u>24</u> 26 30 33 40 43
45 48 50 <u>54</u> 60 <u>63</u> 67 72 75
77 79 81 <u>83</u> 85 90 93

186

11 15 <u>19</u> 23 28 31 36 39 43
<u>46</u> 50 59 <u>61</u> 63 <u>65</u> 68 70 72
76 <u>81</u> 84 87 92 96 99

A	63	81	50	43	72	**A**
B	57	17	94	37	89	**B**
C	11	68	46	28	96	**C**
D	27	34	88	95	21	**D**
E	14	26	48	60	83	**E**
F	74	22	13	82	52	**F**
G	44	64	71	53	97	**G**
H	29	58	16	38	10	**H**
I	40	79	12	33	93	**I**
J	51	18	25	69	80	**J**
K	84	59	36	19	23	**K**
L	30	24	75	85	45	**L**
M	47	42	56	91	32	**M**

N	86	73	66	62	49	**N**
O	55	35	98	78	41	**O**
P	25	58	29	41	37	**P**
Q	66	44	95	55	51	**Q**
R	34	64	89	47	56	**R**
S	17	21	53	78	13	**S**
T	65	39	87	99	70	**T**
U	32	91	18	62	10	**U**
V	67	90	20	54	77	**V**
W	74	38	57	42	22	**W**
X	69	49	73	82	27	**X**
Y	92	15	76	31	61	**Y**
Z	16	52	97	35	27	**Z**

187

188

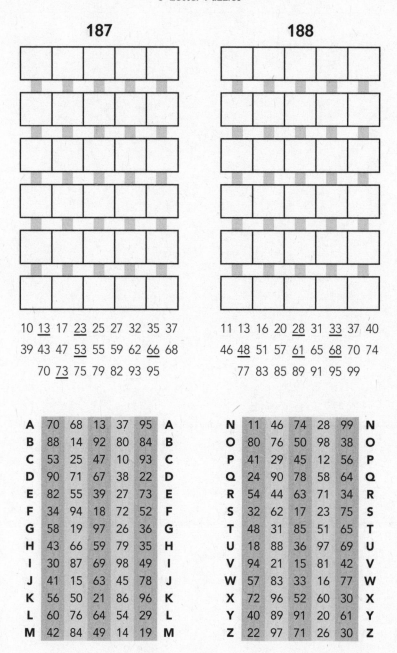

10 <u>13</u> 17 <u>23</u> 25 27 32 35 37
39 43 47 <u>53</u> 55 59 62 <u>66</u> 68
70 <u>73</u> 75 79 82 93 95

11 13 16 20 <u>28</u> 31 <u>33</u> 37 40
46 <u>48</u> 51 57 <u>61</u> 65 <u>68</u> 70 74
77 83 85 89 91 95 99

A	70	68	13	37	95	A
B	88	14	92	80	84	B
C	53	25	47	10	93	C
D	90	71	67	38	22	D
E	82	55	39	27	73	E
F	34	94	18	72	52	F
G	58	19	97	26	36	G
H	43	66	59	79	35	H
I	30	87	69	98	49	I
J	41	15	63	45	78	J
K	56	50	21	86	96	K
L	60	76	64	54	29	L
M	42	84	49	14	19	M

N	11	46	74	28	99	N
O	80	76	50	98	38	O
P	41	29	45	12	56	P
Q	24	90	78	58	64	Q
R	54	44	63	71	34	R
S	32	62	17	23	75	S
T	48	31	85	51	65	T
U	18	88	36	97	69	U
V	94	21	15	81	42	V
W	57	83	33	16	77	W
X	72	96	52	60	30	X
Y	40	89	91	20	61	Y
Z	22	97	71	26	30	Z

Word Fall

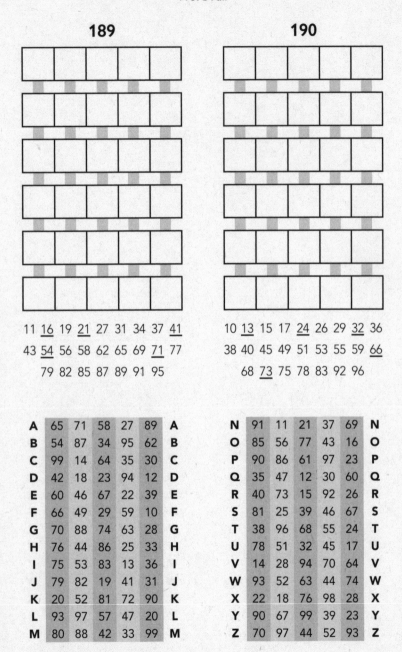

189

11 <u>16</u> 19 <u>21</u> 27 31 34 37 <u>41</u>
43 <u>54</u> 56 58 62 65 69 <u>71</u> 77
79 82 85 87 89 91 95

A	65	71	58	27	89	A
B	54	87	34	95	62	B
C	99	14	64	35	30	C
D	42	18	23	94	12	D
E	60	46	67	22	39	E
F	66	49	29	59	10	F
G	70	88	74	63	28	G
H	76	44	86	25	33	H
I	75	53	83	13	36	I
J	79	82	19	41	31	J
K	20	52	81	72	90	K
L	93	97	57	47	20	L
M	80	88	42	33	99	M

190

10 <u>13</u> 15 17 <u>24</u> 26 29 <u>32</u> 36
38 40 45 49 51 53 55 59 <u>66</u>
68 <u>73</u> 75 78 83 92 96

N	91	11	21	37	69	N
O	85	56	77	43	16	O
P	90	86	61	97	23	P
Q	35	47	12	30	60	Q
R	40	73	15	92	26	R
S	81	25	39	46	67	S
T	38	96	68	55	24	T
U	78	51	32	45	17	U
V	14	28	94	70	64	V
W	93	52	63	44	74	W
X	22	18	76	98	28	X
Y	90	67	99	39	23	Y
Z	70	97	44	52	93	Z

191

192

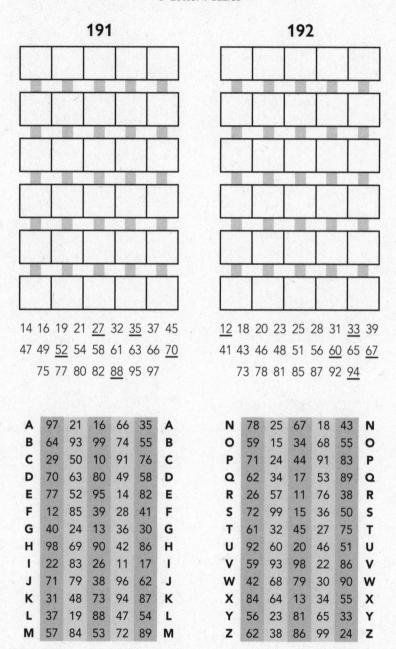

14 16 19 21 <u>27</u> 32 <u>35</u> 37 45
47 49 <u>52</u> 54 58 61 63 66 <u>70</u>
75 77 80 82 <u>88</u> 95 97

<u>12</u> 18 20 23 25 28 31 <u>33</u> 39
41 43 46 48 51 56 <u>60</u> 65 <u>67</u>
73 78 81 85 87 92 <u>94</u>

A	97	21	16	66	35	A
B	64	93	99	74	55	B
C	29	50	10	91	76	C
D	70	63	80	49	58	D
E	77	52	95	14	82	E
F	12	85	39	28	41	F
G	40	24	13	36	30	G
H	98	69	90	42	86	H
I	22	83	26	11	17	I
J	71	79	38	96	62	J
K	31	48	73	94	87	K
L	37	19	88	47	54	L
M	57	84	53	72	89	M

N	78	25	67	18	43	N
O	59	15	34	68	55	O
P	71	24	44	91	83	P
Q	62	34	17	53	89	Q
R	26	57	11	76	38	R
S	72	99	15	36	50	S
T	61	32	45	27	75	T
U	92	60	20	46	51	U
V	59	93	98	22	86	V
W	42	68	79	30	90	W
X	84	64	13	34	55	X
Y	56	23	81	65	33	Y
Z	62	38	86	99	24	Z

Word Fall

193

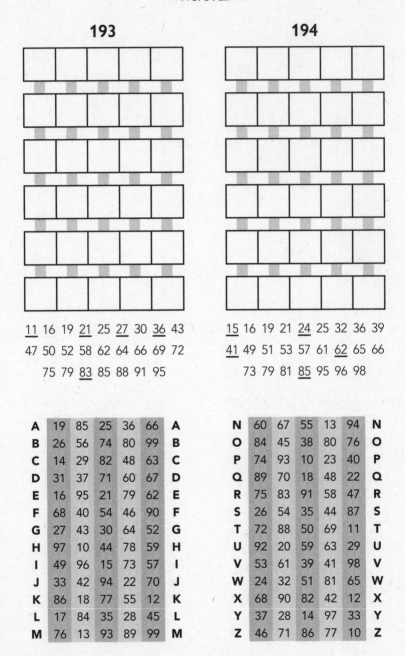

11 16 19 21 25 27 30 36 43
47 50 52 58 62 64 66 69 72
75 79 83 85 88 91 95

194

15 16 19 21 24 25 32 36 39
41 49 51 53 57 61 62 65 66
73 79 81 85 95 96 98

A	19	85	25	36	66	A
B	26	56	74	80	99	B
C	14	29	82	48	63	C
D	31	37	71	60	67	D
E	16	95	21	79	62	E
F	68	40	54	46	90	F
G	27	43	30	64	52	G
H	97	10	44	78	59	H
I	49	96	15	73	57	I
J	33	42	94	22	70	J
K	86	18	77	55	12	K
L	17	84	35	28	45	L
M	76	13	93	89	99	M

N	60	67	55	13	94	N
O	84	45	38	80	76	O
P	74	93	10	23	40	P
Q	89	70	18	48	22	Q
R	75	83	91	58	47	R
S	26	54	35	44	87	S
T	72	88	50	69	11	T
U	92	20	59	63	29	U
V	53	61	39	41	98	V
W	24	32	51	81	65	W
X	68	90	82	42	12	X
Y	37	28	14	97	33	Y
Z	46	71	86	77	10	Z

195

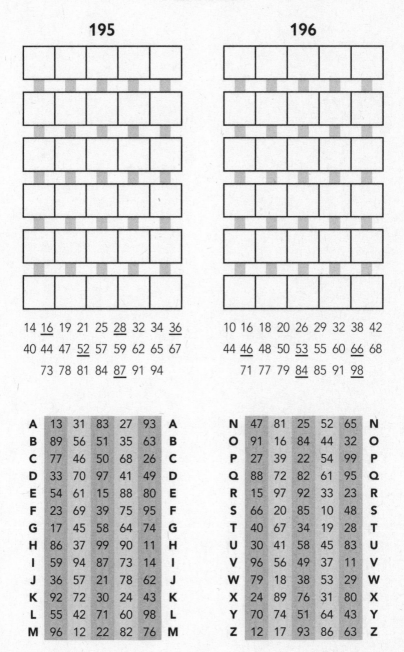

14 <u>16</u> 19 21 25 <u>28</u> 32 34 <u>36</u>
40 44 47 <u>52</u> 57 59 62 65 67
73 78 81 84 <u>87</u> 91 94

196

10 16 18 20 26 29 32 38 42
44 <u>46</u> 48 50 <u>53</u> 55 60 <u>66</u> 68
71 77 79 <u>84</u> 85 91 <u>98</u>

A	13	31	83	27	93	A
B	89	56	51	35	63	B
C	77	46	50	68	26	C
D	33	70	97	41	49	D
E	54	61	15	88	80	E
F	23	69	39	75	95	F
G	17	45	58	64	74	G
H	86	37	99	90	11	H
I	59	94	87	73	14	I
J	36	57	21	78	62	J
K	92	72	30	24	43	K
L	55	42	71	60	98	L
M	96	12	22	82	76	M

N	47	81	25	52	65	N
O	91	16	84	44	32	O
P	27	39	22	54	99	P
Q	88	72	82	61	95	Q
R	15	97	92	33	23	R
S	66	20	85	10	48	S
T	40	67	34	19	28	T
U	30	41	58	45	83	U
V	96	56	49	37	11	V
W	79	18	38	53	29	W
X	24	89	76	31	80	X
Y	70	74	51	64	43	Y
Z	12	17	93	86	63	Z

Word Fall

197

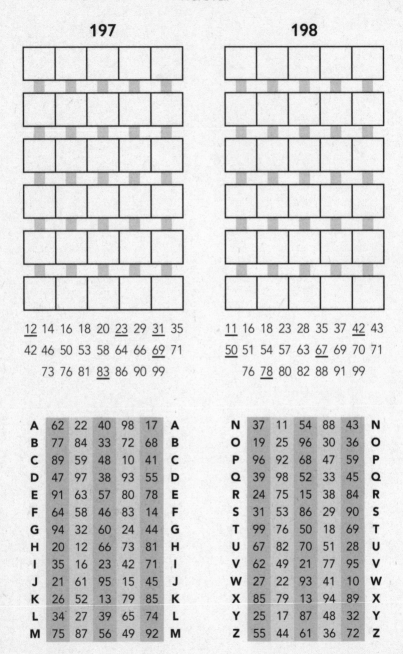

12 14 16 18 20 23 29 31 35
42 46 50 53 58 64 66 69 71
73 76 81 83 86 90 99

198

11 16 18 23 28 35 37 42 43
50 51 54 57 63 67 69 70 71
76 78 80 82 88 91 99

A	62	22	40	98	17	A
B	77	84	33	72	68	B
C	89	59	48	10	41	C
D	47	97	38	93	55	D
E	91	63	57	80	78	E
F	64	58	46	83	14	F
G	94	32	60	24	44	G
H	20	12	66	73	81	H
I	35	16	23	42	71	I
J	21	61	95	15	45	J
K	26	52	13	79	85	K
L	34	27	39	65	74	L
M	75	87	56	49	92	M

N	37	11	54	88	43	N
O	19	25	96	30	36	O
P	96	92	68	47	59	P
Q	39	98	52	33	45	Q
R	24	75	15	38	84	R
S	31	53	86	29	90	S
T	99	76	50	18	69	T
U	67	82	70	51	28	U
V	62	49	21	77	95	V
W	27	22	93	41	10	W
X	85	79	13	94	89	X
Y	25	17	87	48	32	Y
Z	55	44	61	36	72	Z

199

200

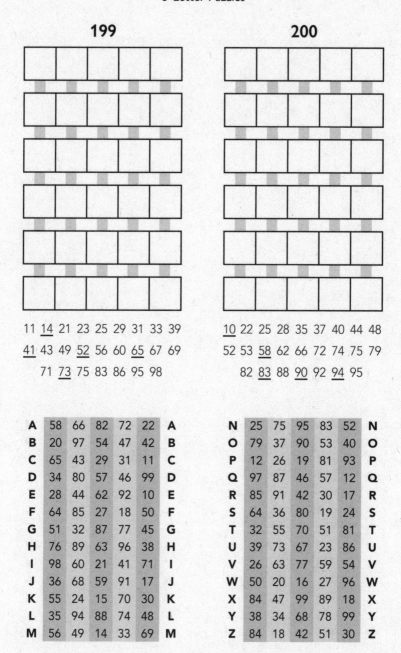

11 <u>14</u> 21 23 25 29 31 33 39
<u>41</u> 43 49 <u>52</u> 56 60 <u>65</u> 67 69
71 <u>73</u> 75 83 86 95 98

<u>10</u> 22 25 28 35 37 40 44 48
52 53 <u>58</u> 62 66 72 74 75 79
82 <u>83</u> 88 <u>90</u> 92 <u>94</u> 95

A	58	66	82	72	22	A
B	20	97	54	47	42	B
C	65	43	29	31	11	C
D	34	80	57	46	99	D
E	28	44	62	92	10	E
F	64	85	27	18	50	F
G	51	32	87	77	45	G
H	76	89	63	96	38	H
I	98	60	21	41	71	I
J	36	68	59	91	17	J
K	55	24	15	70	30	K
L	35	94	88	74	48	L
M	56	49	14	33	69	M

N	25	75	95	83	52	N
O	79	37	90	53	40	O
P	12	26	19	81	93	P
Q	97	87	46	57	12	Q
R	85	91	42	30	17	R
S	64	36	80	19	24	S
T	32	55	70	51	81	T
U	39	73	67	23	86	U
V	26	63	77	59	54	V
W	50	20	16	27	96	W
X	84	47	99	89	18	X
Y	38	34	68	78	99	Y
Z	84	18	42	51	30	Z

Word Fall

201

202

10 18 20 23 <u>26</u> 28 33 36 39
46 48 <u>50</u> 56 59 61 63 <u>70</u> 72
77 80 82 <u>84</u> 90 <u>94</u> 98

10 13 15 17 <u>19</u> 22 24 31 <u>41</u>
43 46 47 52 55 <u>58</u> 62 65 69
73 <u>77</u> 79 84 <u>89</u> 98 99

A	99	41	55	69	17	**A**
B	81	21	75	91	96	**B**
C	30	74	25	11	88	**C**
D	51	83	37	66	97	**D**
E	58	47	13	65	22	**E**
F	32	57	44	53	87	**F**
G	49	27	92	42	38	**G**
H	73	62	43	15	89	**H**
I	70	48	28	90	33	**I**
J	45	16	86	29	95	**J**
K	76	64	12	85	68	**K**
L	71	35	67	14	49	**L**
M	64	75	25	91	11	**M**

N	97	83	34	78	38	**N**
O	72	56	94	20	39	**O**
P	60	30	86	71	35	**P**
Q	66	42	27	85	92	**Q**
R	46	10	77	84	98	**R**
S	16	44	93	37	21	**S**
T	79	24	31	19	52	**T**
U	40	81	76	29	14	**U**
V	80	50	18	23	61	**V**
W	53	12	32	74	95	**W**
X	87	57	67	45	76	**X**
Y	63	59	82	36	26	**Y**
Z	85	38	27	78	67	**Z**

203

204

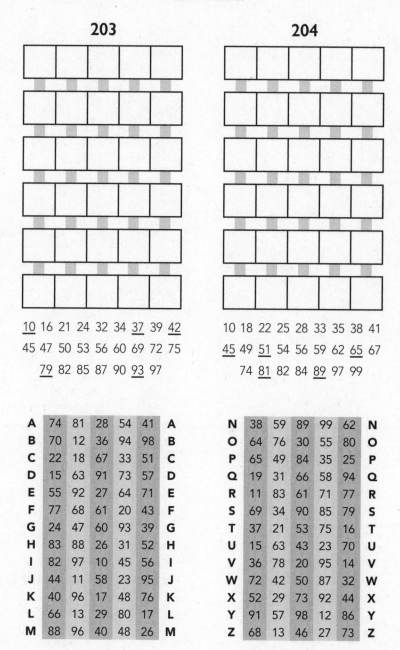

203

<u>10</u> 16 21 24 32 34 <u>37</u> 39 <u>42</u>
45 47 50 53 56 60 69 72 75
<u>79</u> 82 85 87 90 <u>93</u> 97

204

10 18 22 25 28 33 35 38 41
<u>45</u> 49 <u>51</u> 54 56 59 62 <u>65</u> 67
74 <u>81</u> 82 84 <u>89</u> 97 99

A	74	81	28	54	41	A
B	70	12	36	94	98	B
C	22	18	67	33	51	C
D	15	63	91	73	57	D
E	55	92	27	64	71	E
F	77	68	61	20	43	F
G	24	47	60	93	39	G
H	83	88	26	31	52	H
I	82	97	10	45	56	I
J	44	11	58	23	95	J
K	40	96	17	48	76	K
L	66	13	29	80	17	L
M	88	96	40	48	26	M

N	38	59	89	99	62	N
O	64	76	30	55	80	O
P	65	49	84	35	25	P
Q	19	31	66	58	94	Q
R	11	83	61	71	77	R
S	69	34	90	85	79	S
T	37	21	53	75	16	T
U	15	63	43	23	70	U
V	36	78	20	95	14	V
W	72	42	50	87	32	W
X	52	29	73	92	44	X
Y	91	57	98	12	86	Y
Z	68	13	46	27	73	Z

Word Fall

205

_11_ 14 16 _19_ 23 _26_ 28 34 36
39 41 47 52 56 62 65 68 72
74 _77_ 83 90 92 94 _97_

206

11 14 18 21 24 26 _32_ 36 39
44 47 _52_ 54 57 62 65 68 _74_
77 83 85 87 _90_ 92 _96_

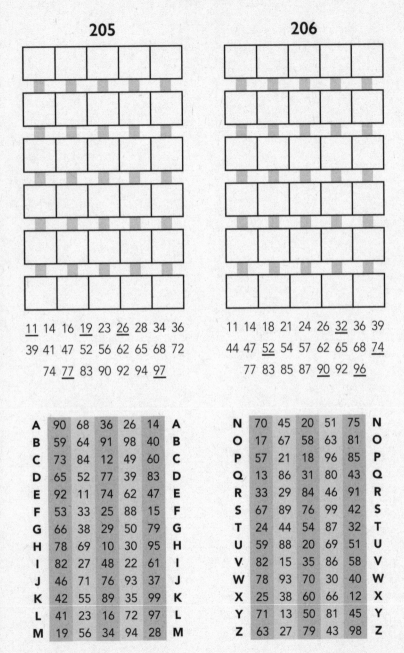

A	90	68	36	26	14	A
B	59	64	91	98	40	B
C	73	84	12	49	60	C
D	65	52	77	39	83	D
E	92	11	74	62	47	E
F	53	33	25	88	15	F
G	66	38	29	50	79	G
H	78	69	10	30	95	H
I	82	27	48	22	61	I
J	46	71	76	93	37	J
K	42	55	89	35	99	K
L	41	23	16	72	97	L
M	19	56	34	94	28	M

N	70	45	20	51	75	N
O	17	67	58	63	81	O
P	57	21	18	96	85	P
Q	13	86	31	80	43	Q
R	33	29	84	46	91	R
S	67	89	76	99	42	S
T	24	44	54	87	32	T
U	59	88	20	69	51	U
V	82	15	35	86	58	V
W	78	93	70	30	40	W
X	25	38	60	66	12	X
Y	71	13	50	81	45	Y
Z	63	27	79	43	98	Z

207

208

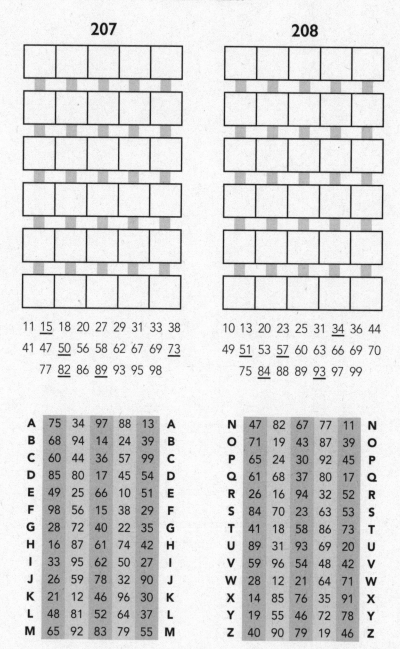

11 <u>15</u> 18 20 27 29 31 33 38
41 47 <u>50</u> 56 58 62 67 69 <u>73</u>
77 <u>82</u> 86 <u>89</u> 93 95 98

10 13 20 23 25 31 <u>34</u> 36 44
49 <u>51</u> 53 <u>57</u> 60 63 66 69 70
75 <u>84</u> 88 89 <u>93</u> 97 99

A	75	34	97	88	13	A
B	68	94	14	24	39	B
C	60	44	36	57	99	C
D	85	80	17	45	54	D
E	49	25	66	10	51	E
F	98	56	15	38	29	F
G	28	72	40	22	35	G
H	16	87	61	74	42	H
I	33	95	62	50	27	I
J	26	59	78	32	90	J
K	21	12	46	96	30	K
L	48	81	52	64	37	L
M	65	92	83	79	55	M

N	47	82	67	77	11	N
O	71	19	43	87	39	O
P	65	24	30	92	45	P
Q	61	68	37	80	17	Q
R	26	16	94	32	52	R
S	84	70	23	63	53	S
T	41	18	58	86	73	T
U	89	31	93	69	20	U
V	59	96	54	48	42	V
W	28	12	21	64	71	W
X	14	85	76	35	91	X
Y	19	55	46	72	78	Y
Z	40	90	79	19	46	Z

Word Fall

209

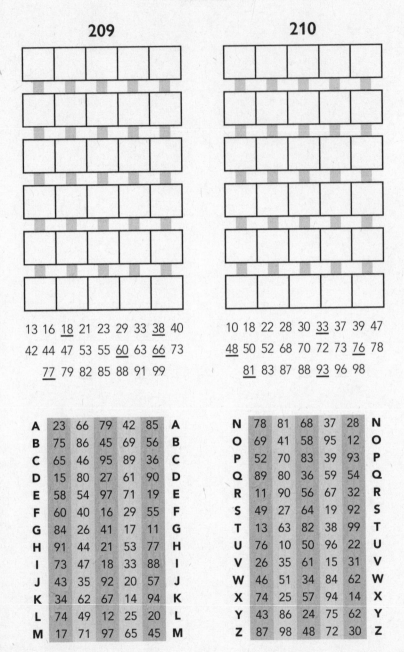

13 16 <u>18</u> 21 23 29 33 <u>38</u> 40
42 44 47 53 55 <u>60</u> 63 <u>66</u> 73
77 79 82 85 88 91 99

210

10 18 22 28 30 <u>33</u> 37 39 47
<u>48</u> 50 52 68 70 72 73 <u>76</u> 78
<u>81</u> 83 87 88 <u>93</u> 96 98

A	23	66	79	42	85	A
B	75	86	45	69	56	B
C	65	46	95	89	36	C
D	15	80	27	61	90	D
E	58	54	97	71	19	E
F	60	40	16	29	55	F
G	84	26	41	17	11	G
H	91	44	21	53	77	H
I	73	47	18	33	88	I
J	43	35	92	20	57	J
K	34	62	67	14	94	K
L	74	49	12	25	20	L
M	17	71	97	65	45	M

N	78	81	68	37	28	N
O	69	41	58	95	12	O
P	52	70	83	39	93	P
Q	89	80	36	59	54	Q
R	11	90	56	67	32	R
S	49	27	64	19	92	S
T	13	63	82	38	99	T
U	76	10	50	96	22	U
V	26	35	61	15	31	V
W	46	51	34	84	62	W
X	74	25	57	94	14	X
Y	43	86	24	75	62	Y
Z	87	98	48	72	30	Z

211

212

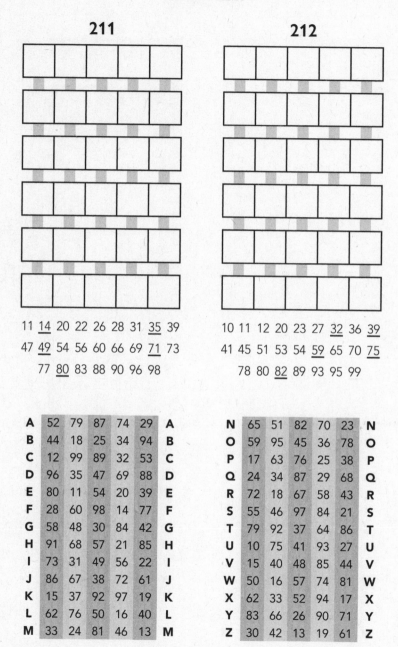

11 <u>14</u> 20 22 26 28 31 <u>35</u> 39
47 <u>49</u> 54 56 60 66 69 <u>71</u> 73
77 <u>80</u> 83 88 90 96 98

10 11 12 20 23 27 <u>32</u> 36 <u>39</u>
41 45 51 53 54 <u>59</u> 65 70 <u>75</u>
78 80 <u>82</u> 89 93 95 99

A	52	79	87	74	29	A
B	44	18	25	34	94	B
C	12	99	89	32	53	C
D	96	35	47	69	88	D
E	80	11	54	20	39	E
F	28	60	98	14	77	F
G	58	48	30	84	42	G
H	91	68	57	21	85	H
I	73	31	49	56	22	I
J	86	67	38	72	61	J
K	15	37	92	97	19	K
L	62	76	50	16	40	L
M	33	24	81	46	13	M

N	65	51	82	70	23	N
O	59	95	45	36	78	O
P	17	63	76	25	38	P
Q	24	34	87	29	68	Q
R	72	18	67	58	43	R
S	55	46	97	84	21	S
T	79	92	37	64	86	T
U	10	75	41	93	27	U
V	15	40	48	85	44	V
W	50	16	57	74	81	W
X	62	33	52	94	17	X
Y	83	66	26	90	71	Y
Z	30	42	13	19	61	Z

213

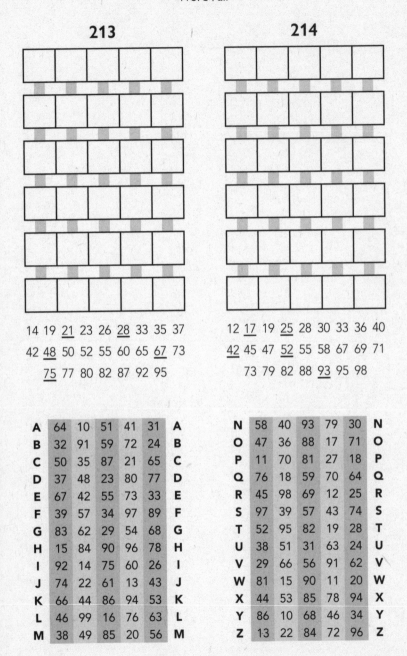

14 19 <u>21</u> 23 26 <u>28</u> 33 35 37

42 <u>48</u> 50 52 55 60 65 <u>67</u> 73

<u>75</u> 77 80 82 87 92 95

214

12 <u>17</u> 19 <u>25</u> 28 30 33 36 40

<u>42</u> 45 47 <u>52</u> 55 58 67 69 71

73 79 82 88 <u>93</u> 95 98

A	64	10	51	41	31	A
B	32	91	59	72	24	B
C	50	35	87	21	65	C
D	37	48	23	80	77	D
E	67	42	55	73	33	E
F	39	57	34	97	89	F
G	83	62	29	54	68	G
H	15	84	90	96	78	H
I	92	14	75	60	26	I
J	74	22	61	13	43	J
K	66	44	86	94	53	K
L	46	99	16	76	63	L
M	38	49	85	20	56	M

N	58	40	93	79	30	N
O	47	36	88	17	71	O
P	11	70	81	27	18	P
Q	76	18	59	70	64	Q
R	45	98	69	12	25	R
S	97	39	57	43	74	S
T	52	95	82	19	28	T
U	38	51	31	63	24	U
V	29	66	56	91	62	V
W	81	15	90	11	20	W
X	44	53	85	78	94	X
Y	86	10	68	46	34	Y
Z	13	22	84	72	96	Z

215

10 14 19 23 25 29 <u>31</u> 34 36
<u>39</u> 41 46 48 57 <u>60</u> 63 65 70
72 74 <u>82</u> 86 89 93 <u>95</u>

216

<u>12</u> 15 <u>17</u> 21 24 28 30 32 38
40 44 47 51 <u>54</u> 59 62 67 <u>69</u>
75 77 80 85 <u>94</u> 96 99

A	50	68	18	83	78	**A**
B	54	38	99	62	44	**B**
C	82	34	14	23	41	**C**
D	55	42	49	33	26	**D**
E	89	36	60	48	93	**E**
F	58	45	35	73	52	**F**
G	64	22	81	92	87	**G**
H	25	95	10	63	70	**H**
I	20	11	76	37	61	**I**
J	97	56	66	90	16	**J**
K	84	43	91	71	55	**K**
L	75	94	15	30	80	**L**
M	64	26	88	73	50	**M**

N	92	68	35	56	43	**N**
O	33	11	83	18	97	**O**
P	53	42	71	37	22	**P**
Q	61	79	98	45	84	**Q**
R	21	85	32	69	40	**R**
S	58	49	91	16	66	**S**
T	28	59	47	77	17	**T**
U	24	96	12	51	67	**U**
V	87	76	81	20	52	**V**
W	72	46	19	31	29	**W**
X	27	90	13	78	53	**X**
Y	74	57	65	86	39	**Y**
Z	26	42	84	58	11	**Z**

Word Fall

217

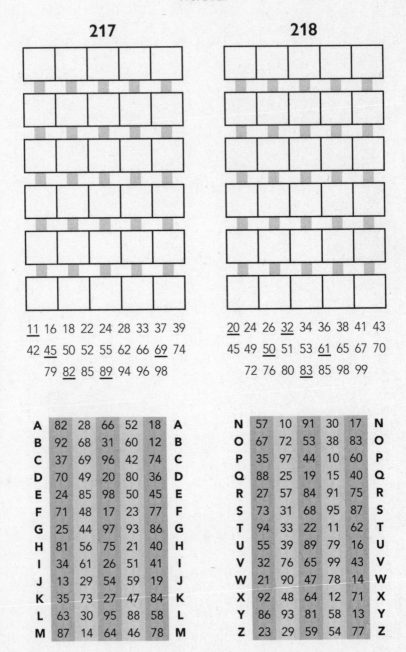

11 16 18 22 24 28 33 37 39
42 45 50 52 55 62 66 69 74
79 82 85 89 94 96 98

A	82	28	66	52	18	A
B	92	68	31	60	12	B
C	37	69	96	42	74	C
D	70	49	20	80	36	D
E	24	85	98	50	45	E
F	71	48	17	23	77	F
G	25	44	97	93	86	G
H	81	56	75	21	40	H
I	34	61	26	51	41	I
J	13	29	54	59	19	J
K	35	73	27	47	84	K
L	63	30	95	88	58	L
M	87	14	64	46	78	M

218

20 24 26 32 34 36 38 41 43
45 49 50 51 53 61 65 67 70
72 76 80 83 85 98 99

N	57	10	91	30	17	N
O	67	72	53	38	83	O
P	35	97	44	10	60	P
Q	88	25	19	15	40	Q
R	27	57	84	91	75	R
S	73	31	68	95	87	S
T	94	33	22	11	62	T
U	55	39	89	79	16	U
V	32	76	65	99	43	V
W	21	90	47	78	14	W
X	92	48	64	12	71	X
Y	86	93	81	58	13	Y
Z	23	29	59	54	77	Z

219

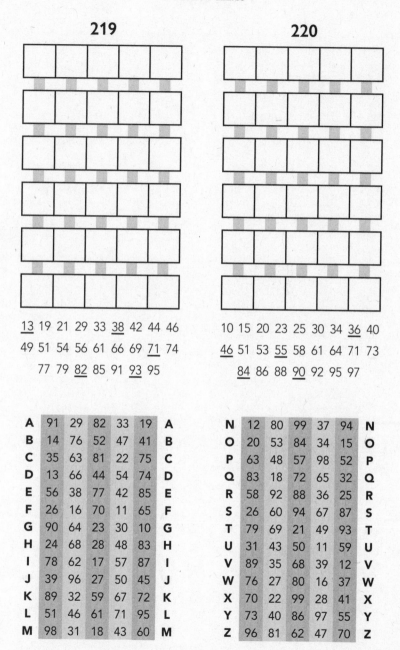

<u>13</u> 19 21 29 33 <u>38</u> 42 44 46
49 51 54 56 61 66 69 <u>71</u> 74
77 79 <u>82</u> 85 91 <u>93</u> 95

220

10 15 20 23 25 30 34 <u>36</u> 40
<u>46</u> 51 53 <u>55</u> 58 61 64 71 73
<u>84</u> 86 88 <u>90</u> 92 95 97

A	91	29	82	33	19	A
B	14	76	52	47	41	B
C	35	63	81	22	75	C
D	13	66	44	54	74	D
E	56	38	77	42	85	E
F	26	16	70	11	65	F
G	90	64	23	30	10	G
H	24	68	28	48	83	H
I	78	62	17	57	87	I
J	39	96	27	50	45	J
K	89	32	59	67	72	K
L	51	46	61	71	95	L
M	98	31	18	43	60	M

N	12	80	99	37	94	N
O	20	53	84	34	15	O
P	63	48	57	98	52	P
Q	83	18	72	65	32	Q
R	58	92	88	36	25	R
S	26	60	94	67	87	S
T	79	69	21	49	93	T
U	31	43	50	11	59	U
V	89	35	68	39	12	V
W	76	27	80	16	37	W
X	70	22	99	28	41	X
Y	73	40	86	97	55	Y
Z	96	81	62	47	70	Z

221

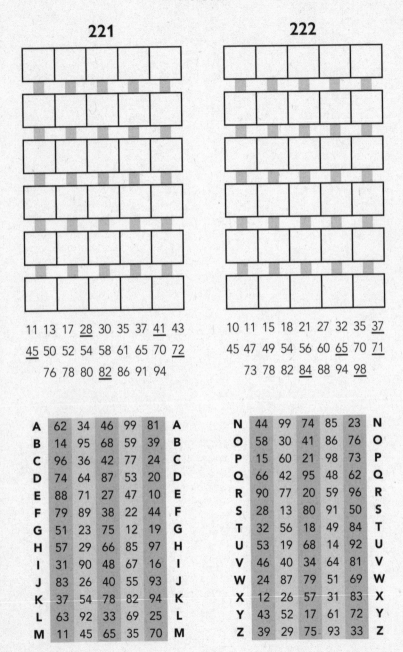

11 13 17 <u>28</u> 30 35 37 <u>41</u> 43
<u>45</u> 50 52 54 58 61 65 70 <u>72</u>
76 78 80 <u>82</u> 86 91 94

222

10 11 15 18 21 27 32 35 <u>37</u>
45 47 49 54 56 60 <u>65</u> 70 <u>71</u>
73 78 82 <u>84</u> 88 94 <u>98</u>

A	62	34	46	99	81	A
B	14	95	68	59	39	B
C	96	36	42	77	24	C
D	74	64	87	53	20	D
E	88	71	27	47	10	E
F	79	89	38	22	44	F
G	51	23	75	12	19	G
H	57	29	66	85	97	H
I	31	90	48	67	16	I
J	83	26	40	55	93	J
K	37	54	78	82	94	K
L	63	92	33	69	25	L
M	11	45	65	35	70	M

N	44	99	74	85	23	N
O	58	30	41	86	76	O
P	15	60	21	98	73	P
Q	66	42	95	48	62	Q
R	90	77	20	59	96	R
S	28	13	80	91	50	S
T	32	56	18	49	84	T
U	53	19	68	14	92	U
V	46	40	34	64	81	V
W	24	87	79	51	69	W
X	12	26	57	31	83	X
Y	43	52	17	61	72	Y
Z	39	29	75	93	33	Z

223

224

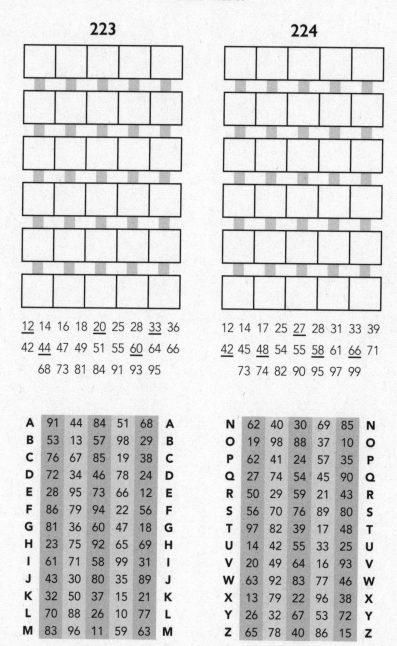

223

12 14 16 18 20 25 28 33 36
42 44 47 49 51 55 60 64 66
68 73 81 84 91 93 95

224

12 14 17 25 27 28 31 33 39
42 45 48 54 55 58 61 66 71
73 74 82 90 95 97 99

A	91	44	84	51	68	A
B	53	13	57	98	29	B
C	76	67	85	19	38	C
D	72	34	46	78	24	D
E	28	95	73	66	12	E
F	86	79	94	22	56	F
G	81	36	60	47	18	G
H	23	75	92	65	69	H
I	61	71	58	99	31	I
J	43	30	80	35	89	J
K	32	50	37	15	21	K
L	70	88	26	10	77	L
M	83	96	11	59	63	M

N	62	40	30	69	85	N
O	19	98	88	37	10	O
P	62	41	24	57	35	P
Q	27	74	54	45	90	Q
R	50	29	59	21	43	R
S	56	70	76	89	80	S
T	97	82	39	17	48	T
U	14	42	55	33	25	U
V	20	49	64	16	93	V
W	63	92	83	77	46	W
X	13	79	22	96	38	X
Y	26	32	67	53	72	Y
Z	65	78	40	86	15	Z

Word Fall

225

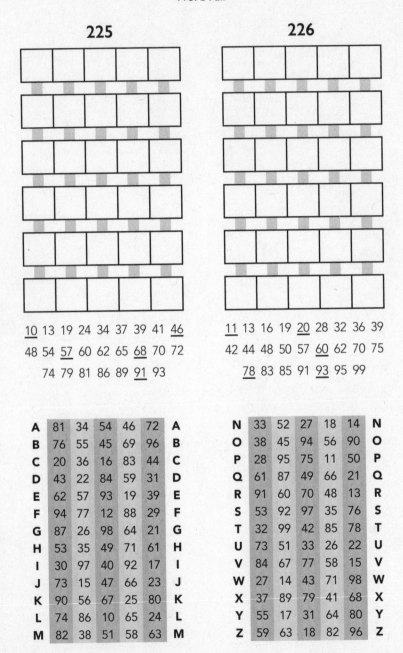

10 13 19 24 34 37 39 41 46
48 54 57 60 62 65 68 70 72
74 79 81 86 89 91 93

226

11 13 16 19 20 28 32 36 39
42 44 48 50 57 60 62 70 75
78 83 85 91 93 95 99

A	81	34	54	46	72	A
B	76	55	45	69	96	B
C	20	36	16	83	44	C
D	43	22	84	59	31	D
E	62	57	93	19	39	E
F	94	77	12	88	29	F
G	87	26	98	64	21	G
H	53	35	49	71	61	H
I	30	97	40	92	17	I
J	73	15	47	66	23	J
K	90	56	67	25	80	K
L	74	86	10	65	24	L
M	82	38	51	58	63	M

N	33	52	27	18	14	N
O	38	45	94	56	90	O
P	28	95	75	11	50	P
Q	61	87	49	66	21	Q
R	91	60	70	48	13	R
S	53	92	97	35	76	S
T	32	99	42	85	78	T
U	73	51	33	26	22	U
V	84	67	77	58	15	V
W	27	14	43	71	98	W
X	37	89	79	41	68	X
Y	55	17	31	64	80	Y
Z	59	63	18	82	96	Z

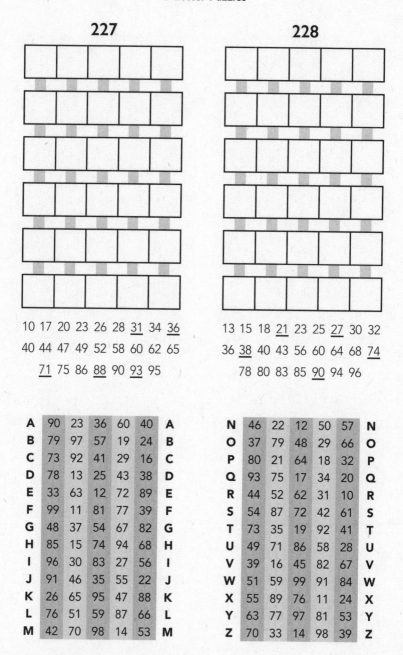

227

10 17 20 23 26 28 <u>31</u> 34 <u>36</u>
40 44 47 49 52 58 60 62 65
<u>71</u> 75 86 <u>88</u> 90 <u>93</u> 95

228

13 15 18 <u>21</u> 23 25 <u>27</u> 30 32
36 <u>38</u> 40 43 56 60 64 68 <u>74</u>
78 80 83 85 <u>90</u> 94 96

A	90	23	36	60	40	**A**
B	79	97	57	19	24	**B**
C	73	92	41	29	16	**C**
D	78	13	25	43	38	**D**
E	33	63	12	72	89	**E**
F	99	11	81	77	39	**F**
G	48	37	54	67	82	**G**
H	85	15	74	94	68	**H**
I	96	30	83	27	56	**I**
J	91	46	35	55	22	**J**
K	26	65	95	47	88	**K**
L	76	51	59	87	66	**L**
M	42	70	98	14	53	**M**

N	46	22	12	50	57	**N**
O	37	79	48	29	66	**O**
P	80	21	64	18	32	**P**
Q	93	75	17	34	20	**Q**
R	44	52	62	31	10	**R**
S	54	87	72	42	61	**S**
T	73	35	19	92	41	**T**
U	49	71	86	58	28	**U**
V	39	16	45	82	67	**V**
W	51	59	99	91	84	**W**
X	55	89	76	11	24	**X**
Y	63	77	97	81	53	**Y**
Z	70	33	14	98	39	**Z**

Word Fall

229

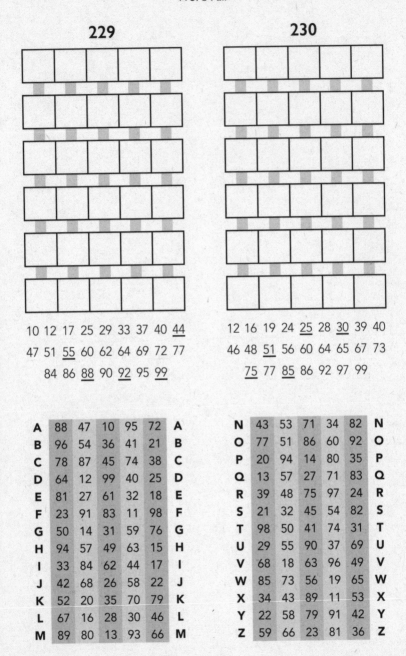

10 12 17 25 29 33 37 40 <u>44</u>
47 51 <u>55</u> 60 62 64 69 72 77
84 86 <u>88</u> 90 <u>92</u> 95 <u>99</u>

A	88	47	10	95	72	A
B	96	54	36	41	21	B
C	78	87	45	74	38	C
D	64	12	99	40	25	D
E	81	27	61	32	18	E
F	23	91	83	11	98	F
G	50	14	31	59	76	G
H	94	57	49	63	15	H
I	33	84	62	44	17	I
J	42	68	26	58	22	J
K	52	20	35	70	79	K
L	67	16	28	30	46	L
M	89	80	13	93	66	M

230

12 16 19 24 <u>25</u> 28 <u>30</u> 39 40
46 48 <u>51</u> 56 60 64 65 67 73
<u>75</u> 77 <u>85</u> 86 92 97 99

N	43	53	71	34	82	N
O	77	51	86	60	92	O
P	20	94	14	80	35	P
Q	13	57	27	71	83	Q
R	39	48	75	97	24	R
S	21	32	45	54	82	S
T	98	50	41	74	31	T
U	29	55	90	37	69	U
V	68	18	63	96	49	V
W	85	73	56	19	65	W
X	34	43	89	11	53	X
Y	22	58	79	91	42	Y
Z	59	66	23	81	36	Z

231

232

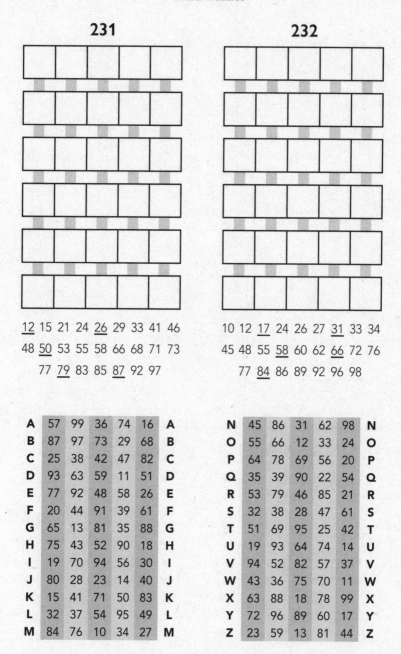

Word Fall

233

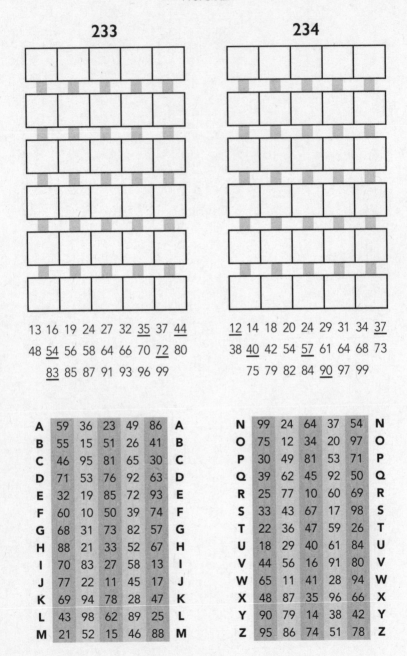

13 16 19 24 27 32 <u>35</u> 37 <u>44</u>
48 <u>54</u> 56 58 64 66 70 <u>72</u> 80
<u>83</u> 85 87 91 93 96 99

234

<u>12</u> 14 18 20 24 29 31 34 <u>37</u>
38 <u>40</u> 42 54 <u>57</u> 61 64 68 73
75 79 82 84 <u>90</u> 97 99

A	59	36	23	49	86	A
B	55	15	51	26	41	B
C	46	95	81	65	30	C
D	71	53	76	92	63	D
E	32	19	85	72	93	E
F	60	10	50	39	74	F
G	68	31	73	82	57	G
H	88	21	33	52	67	H
I	70	83	27	58	13	I
J	77	22	11	45	17	J
K	69	94	78	28	47	K
L	43	98	62	89	25	L
M	21	52	15	46	88	M

N	99	24	64	37	54	N
O	75	12	34	20	97	O
P	30	49	81	53	71	P
Q	39	62	45	92	50	Q
R	25	77	10	60	69	R
S	33	43	67	17	98	S
T	22	36	47	59	26	T
U	18	29	40	61	84	U
V	44	56	16	91	80	V
W	65	11	41	28	94	W
X	48	87	35	96	66	X
Y	90	79	14	38	42	Y
Z	95	86	74	51	78	Z

235

236

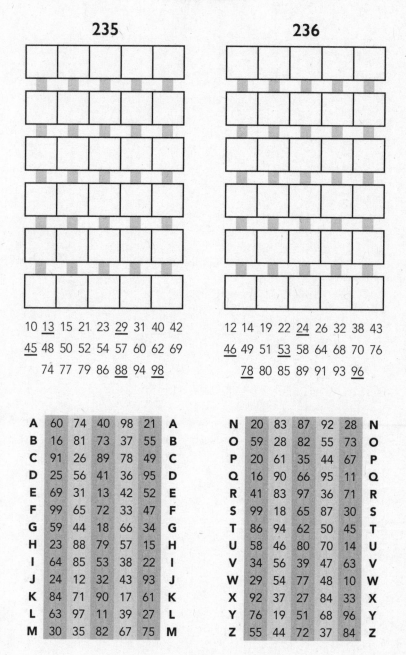

10 <u>13</u> 15 21 23 <u>29</u> 31 40 42
<u>45</u> 48 50 52 54 57 60 62 69
74 77 79 86 <u>88</u> 94 <u>98</u>

12 14 19 22 <u>24</u> 26 32 38 43
<u>46</u> 49 51 <u>53</u> 58 64 68 70 76
<u>78</u> 80 85 89 91 93 <u>96</u>

A	60	74	40	98	21	A
B	16	81	73	37	55	B
C	91	26	89	78	49	C
D	25	56	41	36	95	D
E	69	31	13	42	52	E
F	99	65	72	33	47	F
G	59	44	18	66	34	G
H	23	88	79	57	15	H
I	64	85	53	38	22	I
J	24	12	32	43	93	J
K	84	71	90	17	61	K
L	63	97	11	39	27	L
M	30	35	82	67	75	M

N	20	83	87	92	28	N
O	59	28	82	55	73	O
P	20	61	35	44	67	P
Q	16	90	66	95	11	Q
R	41	83	97	36	71	R
S	99	18	65	87	30	S
T	86	94	62	50	45	T
U	58	46	80	70	14	U
V	34	56	39	47	63	V
W	29	54	77	48	10	W
X	92	37	27	84	33	X
Y	76	19	51	68	96	Y
Z	55	44	72	37	84	Z

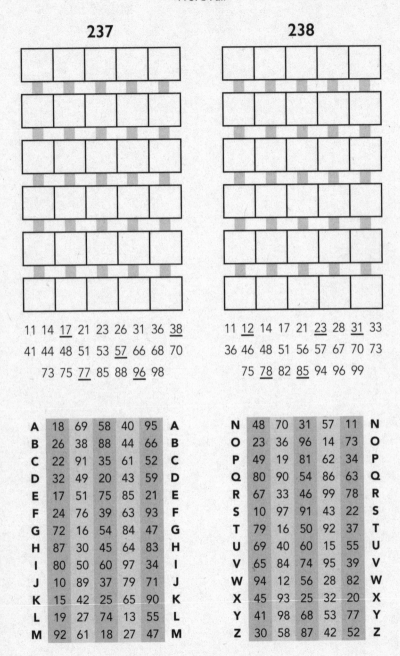

Word Fall

237

238

11 14 <u>17</u> 21 23 26 31 36 <u>38</u>
41 44 48 51 53 <u>57</u> 66 68 70
73 75 <u>77</u> 85 88 <u>96</u> 98

11 <u>12</u> 14 17 21 <u>23</u> 28 <u>31</u> 33
36 46 48 51 56 57 67 70 73
75 <u>78</u> 82 <u>85</u> 94 96 99

A	18	69	58	40	95	A
B	26	38	88	44	66	B
C	22	91	35	61	52	C
D	32	49	20	43	59	D
E	17	51	75	85	21	E
F	24	76	39	63	93	F
G	72	16	54	84	47	G
H	87	30	45	64	83	H
I	80	50	60	97	34	I
J	10	89	37	79	71	J
K	15	42	25	65	90	K
L	19	27	74	13	55	L
M	92	61	18	27	47	M

N	48	70	31	57	11	N
O	23	36	96	14	73	O
P	49	19	81	62	34	P
Q	80	90	54	86	63	Q
R	67	33	46	99	78	R
S	10	97	91	43	22	S
T	79	16	50	92	37	T
U	69	40	60	15	55	U
V	65	84	74	95	39	V
W	94	12	56	28	82	W
X	45	93	25	32	20	X
Y	41	98	68	53	77	Y
Z	30	58	87	42	52	Z

239

240

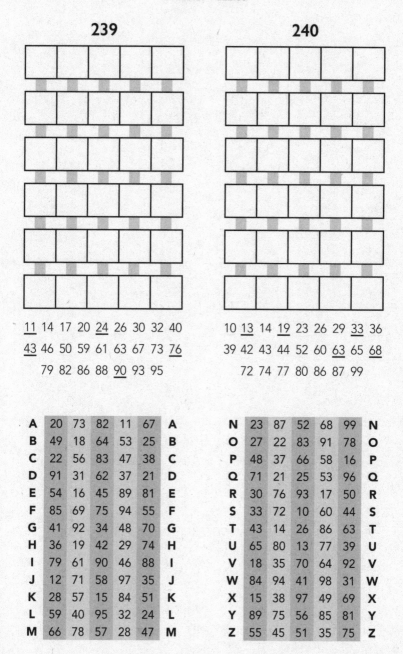

11 14 17 20 24 26 30 32 40
43 46 50 59 61 63 67 73 76
79 82 86 88 90 93 95

10 13 14 19 23 26 29 33 36
39 42 43 44 52 60 63 65 68
72 74 77 80 86 87 99

A	20	73	82	11	67	A
B	49	18	64	53	25	B
C	22	56	83	47	38	C
D	91	31	62	37	21	D
E	54	16	45	89	81	E
F	85	69	75	94	55	F
G	41	92	34	48	70	G
H	36	19	42	29	74	H
I	79	61	90	46	88	I
J	12	71	58	97	35	J
K	28	57	15	84	51	K
L	59	40	95	32	24	L
M	66	78	57	28	47	M

N	23	87	52	68	99	N
O	27	22	83	91	78	O
P	48	37	66	58	16	P
Q	71	21	25	53	96	Q
R	30	76	93	17	50	R
S	33	72	10	60	44	S
T	43	14	26	86	63	T
U	65	80	13	77	39	U
V	18	35	70	64	92	V
W	84	94	41	98	31	W
X	15	38	97	49	69	X
Y	89	75	56	85	81	Y
Z	55	45	51	35	75	Z

Word Fall

241

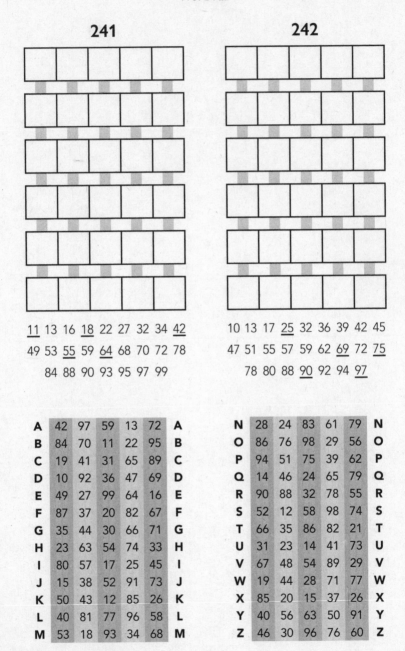

11 13 16 18 22 27 32 34 42
49 53 55 59 64 68 70 72 78
84 88 90 93 95 97 99

242

10 13 17 25 32 36 39 42 45
47 51 55 57 59 62 69 72 75
78 80 88 90 92 94 97

A	42	97	59	13	72	A
B	84	70	11	22	95	B
C	19	41	31	65	89	C
D	10	92	36	47	69	D
E	49	27	99	64	16	E
F	87	37	20	82	67	F
G	35	44	30	66	71	G
H	23	63	54	74	33	H
I	80	57	17	25	45	I
J	15	38	52	91	73	J
K	50	43	12	85	26	K
L	40	81	77	96	58	L
M	53	18	93	34	68	M

N	28	24	83	61	79	N
O	86	76	98	29	56	O
P	94	51	75	39	62	P
Q	14	46	24	65	79	Q
R	90	88	32	78	55	R
S	52	12	58	98	74	S
T	66	35	86	82	21	T
U	31	23	14	41	73	U
V	67	48	54	89	29	V
W	19	44	28	71	77	W
X	85	20	15	37	26	X
Y	40	56	63	50	91	Y
Z	46	30	96	76	60	Z

243

244

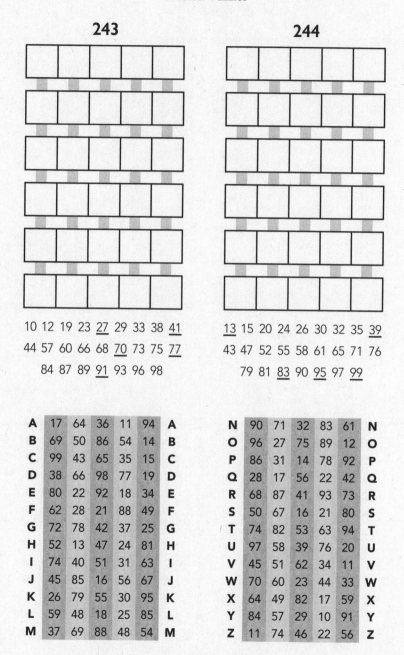

10 12 19 23 <u>27</u> 29 33 38 <u>41</u>
44 57 60 66 68 <u>70</u> 73 75 <u>77</u>
84 87 89 <u>91</u> 93 96 98

<u>13</u> 15 20 24 26 30 32 35 <u>39</u>
43 47 52 55 58 61 65 71 76
79 81 <u>83</u> 90 <u>95</u> 97 <u>99</u>

A	17	64	36	11	94	A
B	69	50	86	54	14	B
C	99	43	65	35	15	C
D	38	66	98	77	19	D
E	80	22	92	18	34	E
F	62	28	21	88	49	F
G	72	78	42	37	25	G
H	52	13	47	24	81	H
I	74	40	51	31	63	I
J	45	85	16	56	67	J
K	26	79	55	30	95	K
L	59	48	18	25	85	L
M	37	69	88	48	54	M

N	90	71	32	83	61	N
O	96	27	75	89	12	O
P	86	31	14	78	92	P
Q	28	17	56	22	42	Q
R	68	87	41	93	73	R
S	50	67	16	21	80	S
T	74	82	53	63	94	T
U	97	58	39	76	20	U
V	45	51	62	34	11	V
W	70	60	23	44	33	W
X	64	49	82	17	59	X
Y	84	57	29	10	91	Y
Z	11	74	46	22	56	Z

245

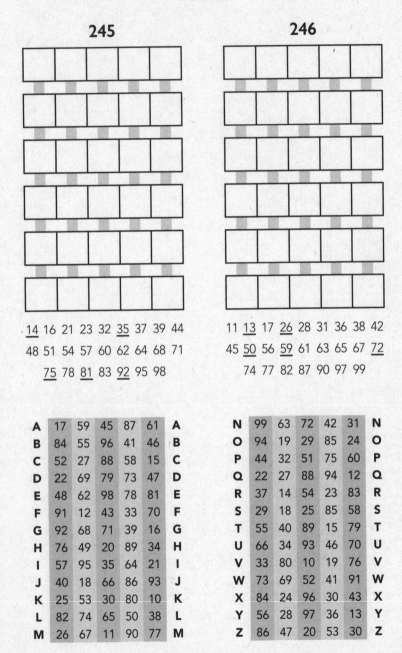

14 16 21 23 32 35 37 39 44
48 51 54 57 60 62 64 68 71
75 78 81 83 92 95 98

246

11 13 17 26 28 31 36 38 42
45 50 56 59 61 63 65 67 72
74 77 82 87 90 97 99

A	17	59	45	87	61	A
B	84	55	96	41	46	B
C	52	27	88	58	15	C
D	22	69	79	73	47	D
E	48	62	98	78	81	E
F	91	12	43	33	70	F
G	92	68	71	39	16	G
H	76	49	20	89	34	H
I	57	95	35	64	21	I
J	40	18	66	86	93	J
K	25	53	30	80	10	K
L	82	74	65	50	38	L
M	26	67	11	90	77	M

N	99	63	72	42	31	N
O	94	19	29	85	24	O
P	44	32	51	75	60	P
Q	22	27	88	94	12	Q
R	37	14	54	23	83	R
S	29	18	25	85	58	S
T	55	40	89	15	79	T
U	66	34	93	46	70	U
V	33	80	10	19	76	V
W	73	69	52	41	91	W
X	84	24	96	30	43	X
Y	56	28	97	36	13	Y
Z	86	47	20	53	30	Z

247

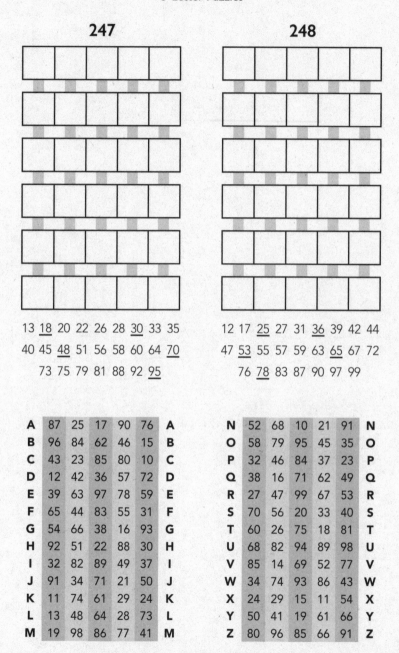

13 <u>18</u> 20 22 26 28 <u>30</u> 33 35
40 45 <u>48</u> 51 56 58 60 64 <u>70</u>
73 75 79 81 88 92 <u>95</u>

248

12 17 <u>25</u> 27 31 <u>36</u> 39 42 44
47 <u>53</u> 55 57 59 63 <u>65</u> 67 72
76 <u>78</u> 83 87 90 97 99

A	87	25	17	90	76	A
B	96	84	62	46	15	B
C	43	23	85	80	10	C
D	12	42	36	57	72	D
E	39	63	97	78	59	E
F	65	44	83	55	31	F
G	54	66	38	16	93	G
H	92	51	22	88	30	H
I	32	82	89	49	37	I
J	91	34	71	21	50	J
K	11	74	61	29	24	K
L	13	48	64	28	73	L
M	19	98	86	77	41	M

N	52	68	10	21	91	N
O	58	79	95	45	35	O
P	32	46	84	37	23	P
Q	38	16	71	62	49	Q
R	27	47	99	67	53	R
S	70	56	20	33	40	S
T	60	26	75	18	81	T
U	68	82	94	89	98	U
V	85	14	69	52	77	V
W	34	74	93	86	43	W
X	24	29	15	11	54	X
Y	50	41	19	61	66	Y
Z	80	96	85	66	91	Z

Word Fall

249

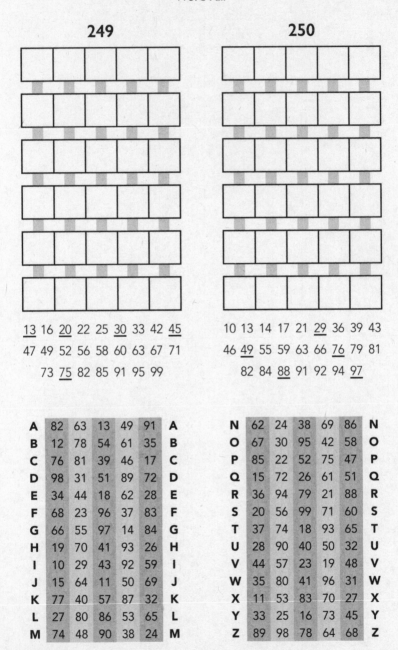

13 16 20 22 25 30 33 42 45

47 49 52 56 58 60 63 67 71

73 75 82 85 91 95 99

250

10 13 14 17 21 29 36 39 43

46 49 55 59 63 66 76 79 81

82 84 88 91 92 94 97

A	82	63	13	49	91	A
B	12	78	54	61	35	B
C	76	81	39	46	17	C
D	98	31	51	89	72	D
E	34	44	18	62	28	E
F	68	23	96	37	83	F
G	66	55	97	14	84	G
H	19	70	41	93	26	H
I	10	29	43	92	59	I
J	15	64	11	50	69	J
K	77	40	57	87	32	K
L	27	80	86	53	65	L
M	74	48	90	38	24	M

N	62	24	38	69	86	N
O	67	30	95	42	58	O
P	85	22	52	75	47	P
Q	15	72	26	61	51	Q
R	36	94	79	21	88	R
S	20	56	99	71	60	S
T	37	74	18	93	65	T
U	28	90	40	50	32	U
V	44	57	23	19	48	V
W	35	80	41	96	31	W
X	11	53	83	70	27	X
Y	33	25	16	73	45	Y
Z	89	98	78	64	68	Z

251

252

10 14 19 21 24 <u>26</u> 30 <u>33</u> 36
<u>39</u> 42 44 48 52 55 63 65 69
72 76 <u>80</u> 86 89 91 <u>93</u>

<u>10</u> 13 17 <u>21</u> 22 26 <u>28</u> 36 <u>40</u>
42 47 52 54 58 63 68 70 72
73 77 84 86 <u>92</u> 93 95

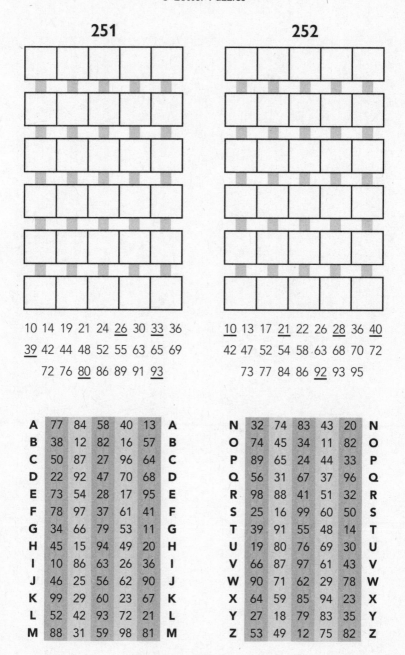

A	77	84	58	40	13	A
B	38	12	82	16	57	B
C	50	87	27	96	64	C
D	22	92	47	70	68	D
E	73	54	28	17	95	E
F	78	97	37	61	41	F
G	34	66	79	53	11	G
H	45	15	94	49	20	H
I	10	86	63	26	36	I
J	46	25	56	62	90	J
K	99	29	60	23	67	K
L	52	42	93	72	21	L
M	88	31	59	98	81	M

N	32	74	83	43	20	N
O	74	45	34	11	82	O
P	89	65	24	44	33	P
Q	56	31	67	37	96	Q
R	98	88	41	51	32	R
S	25	16	99	60	50	S
T	39	91	55	48	14	T
U	19	80	76	69	30	U
V	66	87	97	61	43	V
W	90	71	62	29	78	W
X	64	59	85	94	23	X
Y	27	18	79	83	35	Y
Z	53	49	12	75	82	Z

253

10 13 16 18 20 <u>23</u> 26 <u>28</u> 31
37 40 44 54 <u>58</u> 61 63 <u>66</u> 70
72 76 <u>83</u> 85 89 93 95

254

19 <u>21</u> 24 27 30 32 34 36 42
45 47 <u>49</u> 51 <u>56</u> 59 62 64 67
<u>69</u> 73 78 81 94 96 <u>99</u>

A	78	96	67	42	21	A
B	27	34	56	81	62	B
C	69	24	94	45	30	C
D	57	38	50	74	25	D
E	72	16	63	20	58	E
F	48	33	15	60	68	F
G	80	29	97	35	11	G
H	43	22	53	87	91	H
I	18	89	23	54	76	I
J	71	39	75	84	12	J
K	79	46	90	98	65	K
L	52	17	82	86	41	L
M	88	97	17	25	80	M

N	85	31	13	28	70	N
O	51	99	47	73	36	O
P	82	39	65	53	43	P
Q	92	79	33	71	38	Q
R	19	59	32	49	64	R
S	74	11	48	98	35	S
T	83	37	61	95	40	T
U	57	90	75	46	22	U
V	68	29	12	60	91	V
W	44	66	26	10	93	W
X	84	77	14	52	41	X
Y	53	29	75	33	57	Y
Z	14	98	87	25	48	Z

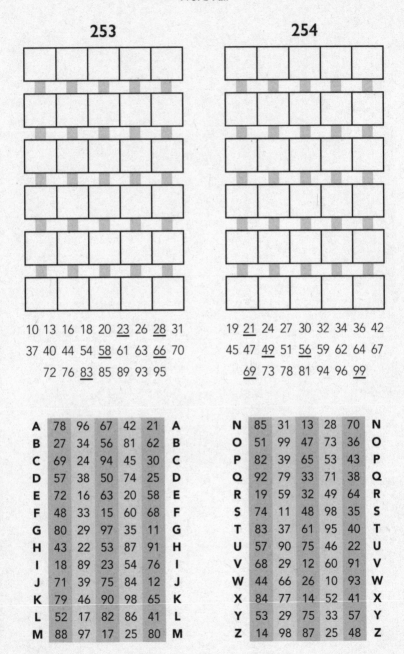

255

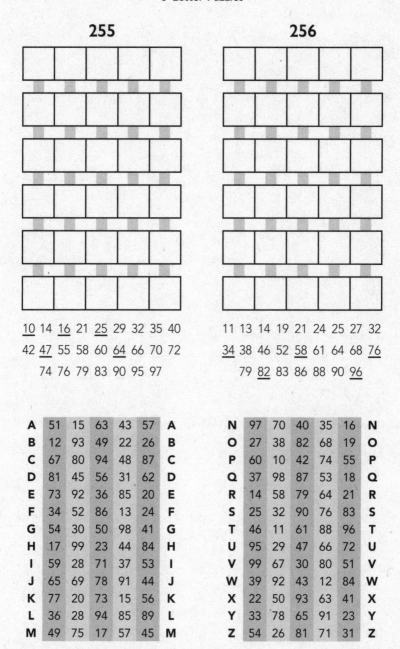

10 14 16 21 25 29 32 35 40
42 47 55 58 60 64 66 70 72
74 76 79 83 90 95 97

A	51	15	63	43	57	A
B	12	93	49	22	26	B
C	67	80	94	48	87	C
D	81	45	56	31	62	D
E	73	92	36	85	20	E
F	34	52	86	13	24	F
G	54	30	50	98	41	G
H	17	99	23	44	84	H
I	59	28	71	37	53	I
J	65	69	78	91	44	J
K	77	20	73	15	56	K
L	36	28	94	85	89	L
M	49	75	17	57	45	M

256

11 13 14 19 21 24 25 27 32
34 38 46 52 58 61 64 68 76
79 82 83 86 88 90 96

N	97	70	40	35	16	N
O	27	38	82	68	19	O
P	60	10	42	74	55	P
Q	37	98	87	53	18	Q
R	14	58	79	64	21	R
S	25	32	90	76	83	S
T	46	11	61	88	96	T
U	95	29	47	66	72	U
V	99	67	30	80	51	V
W	39	92	43	12	84	W
X	22	50	93	63	41	X
Y	33	78	65	91	23	Y
Z	54	26	81	71	31	Z

Word Fall

257

10 12 18 20 24 26 33 35 37
40 45 48 50 53 59 62 68 72
78 80 83 88 94 96 98

258

11 12 18 22 26 33 36 39 43
45 46 50 52 53 54 56 62 65
70 73 77 84 88 92 96

A	63	71	21	57	97	**A**
B	49	64	76	25	42	**B**
C	90	28	69	19	34	**C**
D	51	14	81	91	30	**D**
E	40	35	72	80	20	**E**
F	95	15	67	55	82	**F**
G	17	87	29	41	58	**G**
H	22	39	70	65	56	**H**
I	36	54	77	43	11	**I**
J	44	23	13	85	32	**J**
K	16	38	47	99	66	**K**
L	12	33	62	53	88	**L**
M	59	48	24	94	83	**M**

N	93	75	60	27	89	**N**
O	31	79	86	61	74	**O**
P	51	32	75	16	58	**P**
Q	67	81	28	61	91	**Q**
R	26	18	45	96	50	**R**
S	30	14	49	55	41	**S**
T	34	85	76	93	17	**T**
U	98	10	37	68	78	**U**
V	89	25	64	21	71	**V**
W	46	92	52	73	84	**W**
X	60	13	90	27	23	**X**
Y	66	79	97	44	19	**Y**
Z	82	15	87	29	74	**Z**

259

260

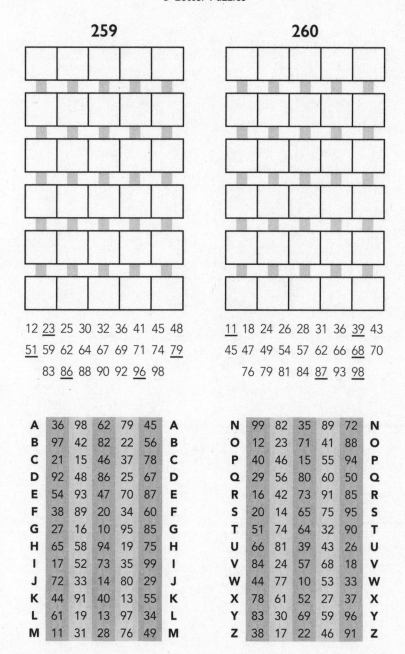

12 <u>23</u> 25 30 32 36 41 45 48
<u>51</u> 59 62 64 67 69 71 74 <u>79</u>
83 <u>86</u> 88 90 92 <u>96</u> 98

<u>11</u> 18 24 26 28 31 36 <u>39</u> 43
45 47 49 54 57 62 66 <u>68</u> 70
76 79 81 84 <u>87</u> 93 <u>98</u>

A	36	98	62	79	45	A
B	97	42	82	22	56	B
C	21	15	46	37	78	C
D	92	48	86	25	67	D
E	54	93	47	70	87	E
F	38	89	20	34	60	F
G	27	16	10	95	85	G
H	65	58	94	19	75	H
I	17	52	73	35	99	I
J	72	33	14	80	29	J
K	44	91	40	13	55	K
L	61	19	13	97	34	L
M	11	31	28	76	49	M

N	99	82	35	89	72	N
O	12	23	71	41	88	O
P	40	46	15	55	94	P
Q	29	56	80	60	50	Q
R	16	42	73	91	85	R
S	20	14	65	75	95	S
T	51	74	64	32	90	T
U	66	81	39	43	26	U
V	84	24	57	68	18	V
W	44	77	10	53	33	W
X	78	61	52	27	37	X
Y	83	30	69	59	96	Y
Z	38	17	22	46	91	Z

Word Fall

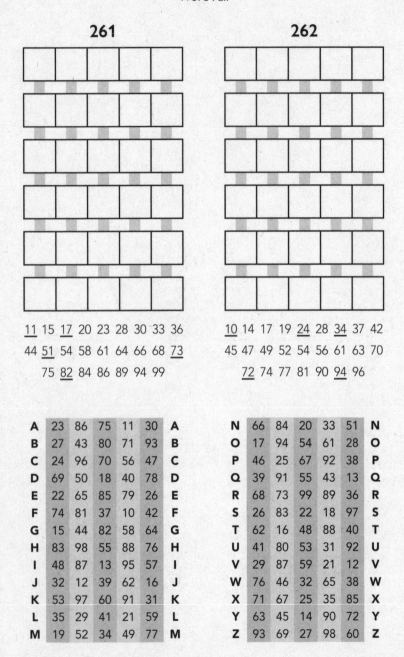

261

11 15 17 20 23 28 30 33 36
44 51 54 58 61 64 66 68 73
75 82 84 86 89 94 99

262

10 14 17 19 24 28 34 37 42
45 47 49 52 54 56 61 63 70
72 74 77 81 90 94 96

A	23	86	75	11	30	A
B	27	43	80	71	93	B
C	24	96	70	56	47	C
D	69	50	18	40	78	D
E	22	65	85	79	26	E
F	74	81	37	10	42	F
G	15	44	82	58	64	G
H	83	98	55	88	76	H
I	48	87	13	95	57	I
J	32	12	39	62	16	J
K	53	97	60	91	31	K
L	35	29	41	21	59	L
M	19	52	34	49	77	M

N	66	84	20	33	51	N
O	17	94	54	61	28	O
P	46	25	67	92	38	P
Q	39	91	55	43	13	Q
R	68	73	99	89	36	R
S	26	83	22	18	97	S
T	62	16	48	88	40	T
U	41	80	53	31	92	U
V	29	87	59	21	12	V
W	76	46	32	65	38	W
X	71	67	25	35	85	X
Y	63	45	14	90	72	Y
Z	93	69	27	98	60	Z

263

264

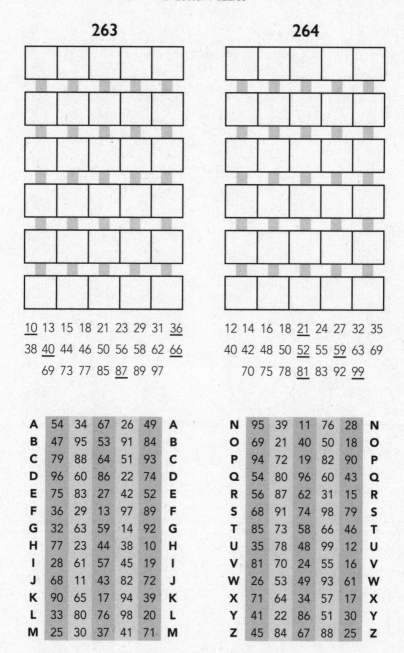

263

10 13 15 18 21 23 29 31 36
38 40 44 46 50 56 58 62 66
69 73 77 85 87 89 97

264

12 14 16 18 21 24 27 32 35
40 42 48 50 52 55 59 63 69
70 75 78 81 83 92 99

A	54	34	67	26	49	A
B	47	95	53	91	84	B
C	79	88	64	51	93	C
D	96	60	86	22	74	D
E	75	83	27	42	52	E
F	36	29	13	97	89	F
G	32	63	59	14	92	G
H	77	23	44	38	10	H
I	28	61	57	45	19	I
J	68	11	43	82	72	J
K	90	65	17	94	39	K
L	33	80	76	98	20	L
M	25	30	37	41	71	M

N	95	39	11	76	28	N
O	69	21	40	50	18	O
P	94	72	19	82	90	P
Q	54	80	96	60	43	Q
R	56	87	62	31	15	R
S	68	91	74	98	79	S
T	85	73	58	66	46	T
U	35	78	48	99	12	U
V	81	70	24	55	16	V
W	26	53	49	93	61	W
X	71	64	34	57	17	X
Y	41	22	86	51	30	Y
Z	45	84	67	88	25	Z

265

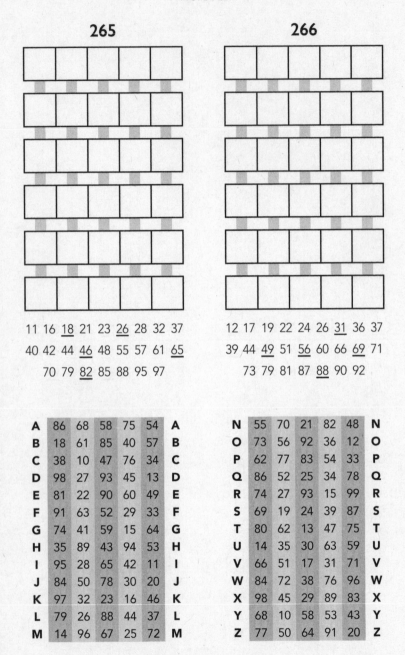

11 16 <u>18</u> 21 23 <u>26</u> 28 32 37
40 42 44 <u>46</u> 48 55 57 61 <u>65</u>
70 79 <u>82</u> 85 88 95 97

266

12 17 19 22 24 26 <u>31</u> 36 37
39 44 <u>49</u> 51 <u>56</u> 60 66 <u>69</u> 71
73 79 81 87 <u>88</u> 90 92

A	86	68	58	75	54	A
B	18	61	85	40	57	B
C	38	10	47	76	34	C
D	98	27	93	45	13	D
E	81	22	90	60	49	E
F	91	63	52	29	33	F
G	74	41	59	15	64	G
H	35	89	43	94	53	H
I	95	28	65	42	11	I
J	84	50	78	30	20	J
K	97	32	23	16	46	K
L	79	26	88	44	37	L
M	14	96	67	25	72	M

N	55	70	21	82	48	N
O	73	56	92	36	12	O
P	62	77	83	54	33	P
Q	86	52	25	34	78	Q
R	74	27	93	15	99	R
S	69	19	24	39	87	S
T	80	62	13	47	75	T
U	14	35	30	63	59	U
V	66	51	17	31	71	V
W	84	72	38	76	96	W
X	98	45	29	89	83	X
Y	68	10	58	53	43	Y
Z	77	50	64	91	20	Z

267

268

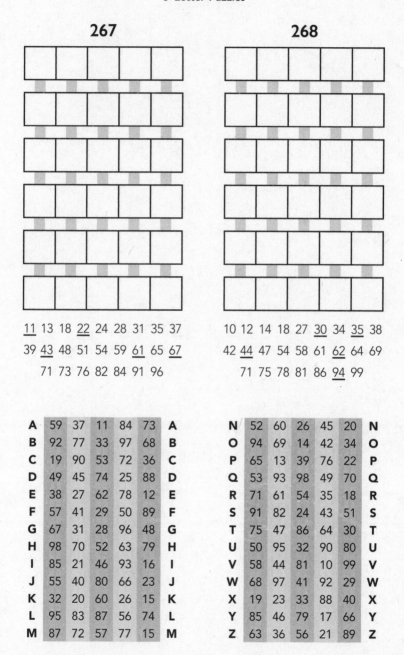

267

<u>11</u> 13 18 <u>22</u> 24 28 31 35 37
39 <u>43</u> 48 51 54 59 <u>61</u> 65 <u>67</u>
71 73 76 82 84 91 96

268

10 12 14 18 27 <u>30</u> 34 <u>35</u> 38
42 <u>44</u> 47 54 58 61 <u>62</u> 64 69
71 75 78 81 86 <u>94</u> 99

A	59	37	11	84	73	A
B	92	77	33	97	68	B
C	19	90	53	72	36	C
D	49	45	74	25	88	D
E	38	27	62	78	12	E
F	57	41	29	50	89	F
G	67	31	28	96	48	G
H	98	70	52	63	79	H
I	85	21	46	93	16	I
J	55	40	80	66	23	J
K	32	20	60	26	15	K
L	95	83	87	56	74	L
M	87	72	57	77	15	M

N	52	60	26	45	20	N
O	94	69	14	42	34	O
P	65	13	39	76	22	P
Q	53	93	98	49	70	Q
R	71	61	54	35	18	R
S	91	82	24	43	51	S
T	75	47	86	64	30	T
U	50	95	32	90	80	U
V	58	44	81	10	99	V
W	68	97	41	92	29	W
X	19	23	33	88	40	X
Y	85	46	79	17	66	Y
Z	63	36	56	21	89	Z

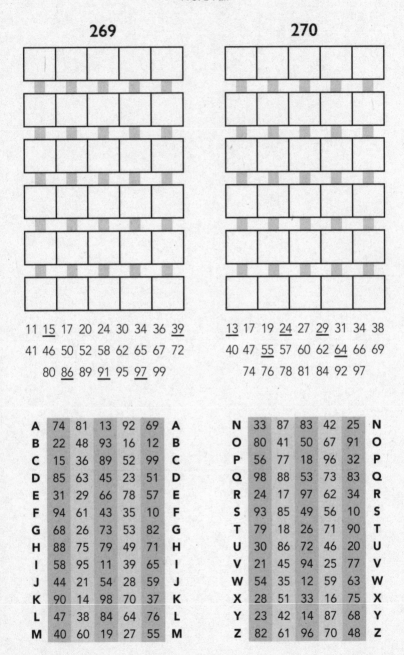

Word Fall

269

270

11 <u>15</u> 17 20 24 30 34 36 <u>39</u>
41 46 50 52 58 62 65 67 72
80 <u>86</u> 89 <u>91</u> 95 <u>97</u> 99

<u>13</u> 17 19 <u>24</u> 27 <u>29</u> 31 34 38
40 47 <u>55</u> 57 60 62 <u>64</u> 66 69
74 76 78 81 84 92 97

A	74	81	13	92	69	A
B	22	48	93	16	12	B
C	15	36	89	52	99	C
D	85	63	45	23	51	D
E	31	29	66	78	57	E
F	94	61	43	35	10	F
G	68	26	73	53	82	G
H	88	75	79	49	71	H
I	58	95	11	39	65	I
J	44	21	54	28	59	J
K	90	14	98	70	37	K
L	47	38	84	64	76	L
M	40	60	19	27	55	M

N	33	87	83	42	25	N
O	80	41	50	67	91	O
P	56	77	18	96	32	P
Q	98	88	53	73	83	Q
R	24	17	97	62	34	R
S	93	85	49	56	10	S
T	79	18	26	71	90	T
U	30	86	72	46	20	U
V	21	45	94	25	77	V
W	54	35	12	59	63	W
X	28	51	33	16	75	X
Y	23	42	14	87	68	Y
Z	82	61	96	70	48	Z

271

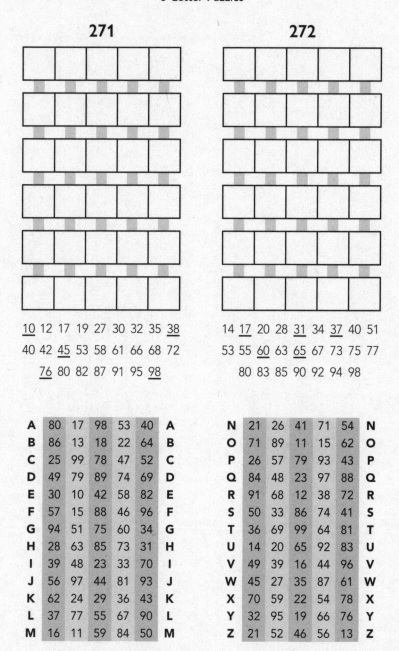

10 12 17 19 27 30 32 35 38
40 42 45 53 58 61 66 68 72
76 80 82 87 91 95 98

272

14 17 20 28 31 34 37 40 51
53 55 60 63 65 67 73 75 77
80 83 85 90 92 94 98

A	80	17	98	53	40	A
B	86	13	18	22	64	B
C	25	99	78	47	52	C
D	49	79	89	74	69	D
E	30	10	42	58	82	E
F	57	15	88	46	96	F
G	94	51	75	60	34	G
H	28	63	85	73	31	H
I	39	48	23	33	70	I
J	56	97	44	81	93	J
K	62	24	29	36	43	K
L	37	77	55	67	90	L
M	16	11	59	84	50	M

N	21	26	41	71	54	N
O	71	89	11	15	62	O
P	26	57	79	93	43	P
Q	84	48	23	97	88	Q
R	91	68	12	38	72	R
S	50	33	86	74	41	S
T	36	69	99	64	81	T
U	14	20	65	92	83	U
V	49	39	16	44	96	V
W	45	27	35	87	61	W
X	70	59	22	54	78	X
Y	32	95	19	66	76	Y
Z	21	52	46	56	13	Z

Word Fall

273

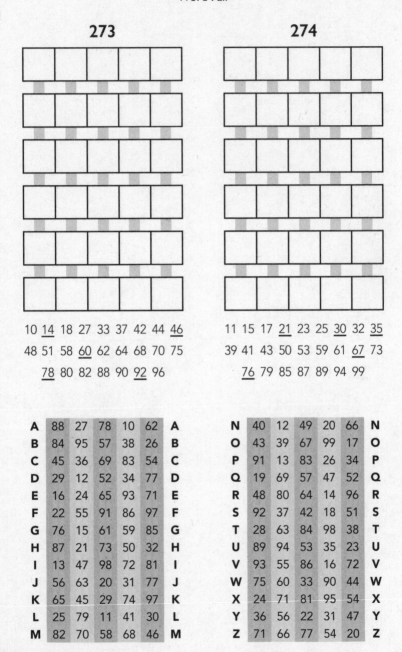

10 <u>14</u> 18 27 33 37 42 44 <u>46</u>
48 51 58 <u>60</u> 62 64 68 70 75
<u>78</u> 80 82 88 90 <u>92</u> 96

274

11 15 17 <u>21</u> 23 25 <u>30</u> 32 <u>35</u>
39 41 43 50 53 59 61 <u>67</u> 73
<u>76</u> 79 85 87 89 94 99

A	88	27	78	10	62	A
B	84	95	57	38	26	B
C	45	36	69	83	54	C
D	29	12	52	34	77	D
E	16	24	65	93	71	E
F	22	55	91	86	97	F
G	76	15	61	59	85	G
H	87	21	73	50	32	H
I	13	47	98	72	81	I
J	56	63	20	31	77	J
K	65	45	29	74	97	K
L	25	79	11	41	30	L
M	82	70	58	68	46	M

N	40	12	49	20	66	N
O	43	39	67	99	17	O
P	91	13	83	26	34	P
Q	19	69	57	47	52	Q
R	48	80	64	14	96	R
S	92	37	42	18	51	S
T	28	63	84	98	38	T
U	89	94	53	35	23	U
V	93	55	86	16	72	V
W	75	60	33	90	44	W
X	24	71	81	95	54	X
Y	36	56	22	31	47	Y
Z	71	66	77	54	20	Z

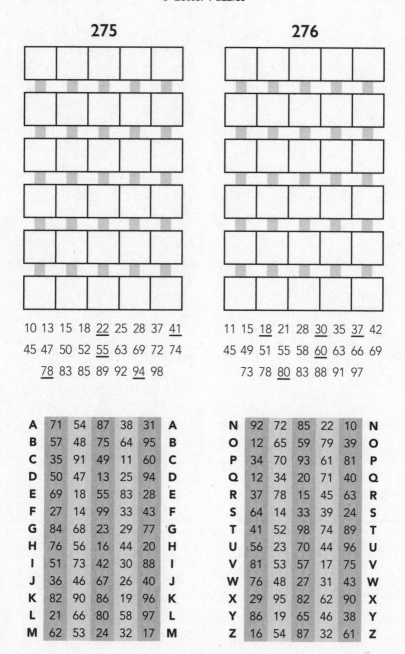

275

10 13 15 18 <u>22</u> 25 28 37 <u>41</u>
45 47 50 52 <u>55</u> 63 69 72 74
<u>78</u> 83 85 89 92 <u>94</u> 98

276

11 15 <u>18</u> 21 28 <u>30</u> 35 <u>37</u> 42
45 49 51 55 58 <u>60</u> 63 66 69
73 78 <u>80</u> 83 88 91 97

A	71	54	87	38	31	A
B	57	48	75	64	95	B
C	35	91	49	11	60	C
D	50	47	13	25	94	D
E	69	18	55	83	28	E
F	27	14	99	33	43	F
G	84	68	23	29	77	G
H	76	56	16	44	20	H
I	51	73	42	30	88	I
J	36	46	67	26	40	J
K	82	90	86	19	96	K
L	21	66	80	58	97	L
M	62	53	24	32	17	M

N	92	72	85	22	10	N
O	12	65	59	79	39	O
P	34	70	93	61	81	P
Q	12	34	20	71	40	Q
R	37	78	15	45	63	R
S	64	14	33	39	24	S
T	41	52	98	74	89	T
U	56	23	70	44	96	U
V	81	53	57	17	75	V
W	76	48	27	31	43	W
X	29	95	82	62	90	X
Y	86	19	65	46	38	Y
Z	16	54	87	32	61	Z

Word Fall

277

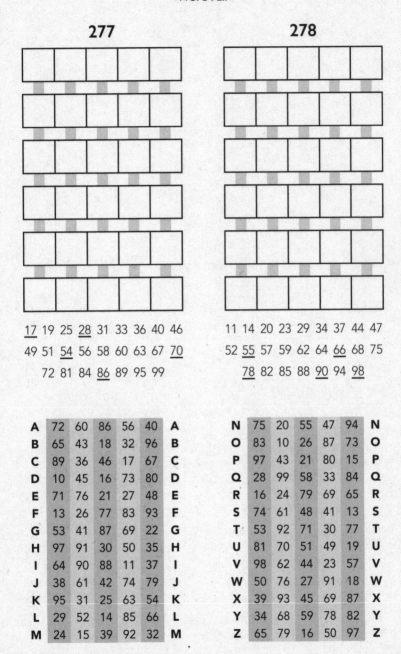

17 19 25 28 31 33 36 40 46
49 51 54 56 58 60 63 67 70
72 81 84 86 89 95 99

278

11 14 20 23 29 34 37 44 47
52 55 57 59 62 64 66 68 75
78 82 85 88 90 94 98

A	72	60	86	56	40	A
B	65	43	18	32	96	B
C	89	36	46	17	67	C
D	10	45	16	73	80	D
E	71	76	21	27	48	E
F	13	26	77	83	93	F
G	53	41	87	69	22	G
H	97	91	30	50	35	H
I	64	90	88	11	37	I
J	38	61	42	74	79	J
K	95	31	25	63	54	K
L	29	52	14	85	66	L
M	24	15	39	92	32	M

N	75	20	55	47	94	N
O	83	10	26	87	73	O
P	97	43	21	80	15	P
Q	28	99	58	33	84	Q
R	16	24	79	69	65	R
S	74	61	48	41	13	S
T	53	92	71	30	77	T
U	81	70	51	49	19	U
V	98	62	44	23	57	V
W	50	76	27	91	18	W
X	39	93	45	69	87	X
Y	34	68	59	78	82	Y
Z	65	79	16	50	97	Z

279

280

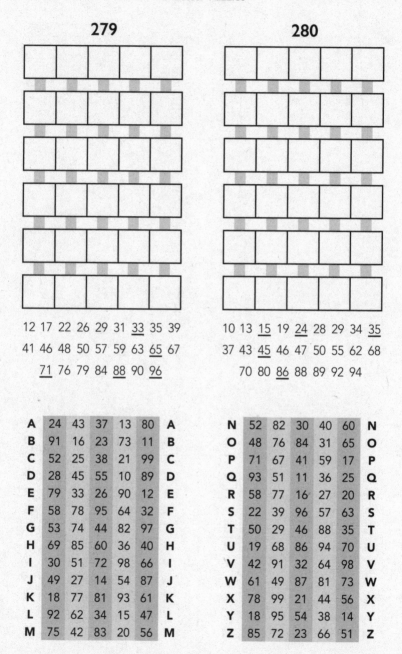

12 17 22 26 29 31 <u>33</u> 35 39
41 46 48 50 57 59 63 <u>65</u> 67
    <u>71</u> 76 79 84 <u>88</u> 90 <u>96</u>

10 13 <u>15</u> 19 <u>24</u> 28 29 34 <u>35</u>
37 43 <u>45</u> 46 47 50 55 62 68
    70 80 <u>86</u> 88 89 92 94

A	24	43	37	13	80	A
B	91	16	23	73	11	B
C	52	25	38	21	99	C
D	28	45	55	10	89	D
E	79	33	26	90	12	E
F	58	78	95	64	32	F
G	53	74	44	82	97	G
H	69	85	60	36	40	H
I	30	51	72	98	66	I
J	49	27	14	54	87	J
K	18	77	81	93	61	K
L	92	62	34	15	47	L
M	75	42	83	20	56	M

N	52	82	30	40	60	N
O	48	76	84	31	65	O
P	71	67	41	59	17	P
Q	93	51	11	36	25	Q
R	58	77	16	27	20	R
S	22	39	96	57	63	S
T	50	29	46	88	35	T
U	19	68	86	94	70	U
V	42	91	32	64	98	V
W	61	49	87	81	73	W
X	78	99	21	44	56	X
Y	18	95	54	38	14	Y
Z	85	72	23	66	51	Z

Word Fall

281

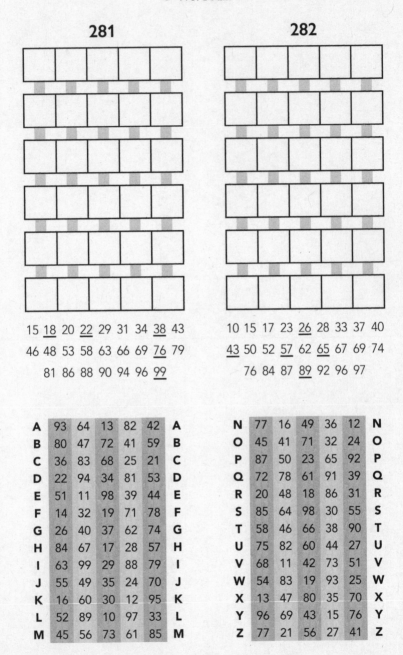

15 <u>18</u> 20 <u>22</u> 29 31 34 <u>38</u> 43
46 48 53 58 63 66 69 <u>76</u> 79
81 86 88 90 94 96 <u>99</u>

282

10 15 17 23 <u>26</u> 28 33 37 40
<u>43</u> 50 52 <u>57</u> 62 <u>65</u> 67 69 74
76 84 87 <u>89</u> 92 96 97

A	93	64	13	82	42	A
B	80	47	72	41	59	B
C	36	83	68	25	21	C
D	22	94	34	81	53	D
E	51	11	98	39	44	E
F	14	32	19	71	78	F
G	26	40	37	62	74	G
H	84	67	17	28	57	H
I	63	99	29	88	79	I
J	55	49	35	24	70	J
K	16	60	30	12	95	K
L	52	89	10	97	33	L
M	45	56	73	61	85	M

N	77	16	49	36	12	N
O	45	41	71	32	24	O
P	87	50	23	65	92	P
Q	72	78	61	91	39	Q
R	20	48	18	86	31	R
S	85	64	98	30	55	S
T	58	46	66	38	90	T
U	75	82	60	44	27	U
V	68	11	42	73	51	V
W	54	83	19	93	25	W
X	13	47	80	35	70	X
Y	96	69	43	15	76	Y
Z	77	21	56	27	41	Z

283

284

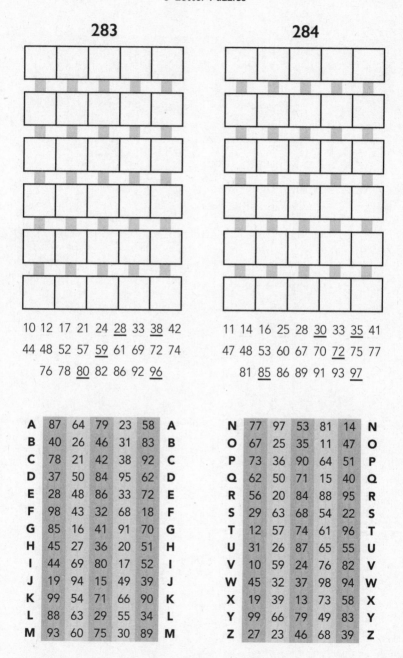

10 12 17 21 24 <u>28</u> 33 <u>38</u> 42
44 48 52 57 <u>59</u> 61 69 72 74
76 78 <u>80</u> 82 86 92 <u>96</u>

11 14 16 25 28 <u>30</u> 33 <u>35</u> 41
47 48 53 60 67 70 <u>72</u> 75 77
81 <u>85</u> 86 89 91 93 <u>97</u>

A	87	64	79	23	58	A
B	40	26	46	31	83	B
C	78	21	42	38	92	C
D	37	50	84	95	62	D
E	28	48	86	33	72	E
F	98	43	32	68	18	F
G	85	16	41	91	70	G
H	45	27	36	20	51	H
I	44	69	80	17	52	I
J	19	94	15	49	39	J
K	99	54	71	66	90	K
L	88	63	29	55	34	L
M	93	60	75	30	89	M

N	77	97	53	81	14	N
O	67	25	35	11	47	O
P	73	36	90	64	51	P
Q	62	50	71	15	40	Q
R	56	20	84	88	95	R
S	29	63	68	54	22	S
T	12	57	74	61	96	T
U	31	26	87	65	55	U
V	10	59	24	76	82	V
W	45	32	37	98	94	W
X	19	39	13	73	58	X
Y	99	66	79	49	83	Y
Z	27	23	46	68	39	Z

285

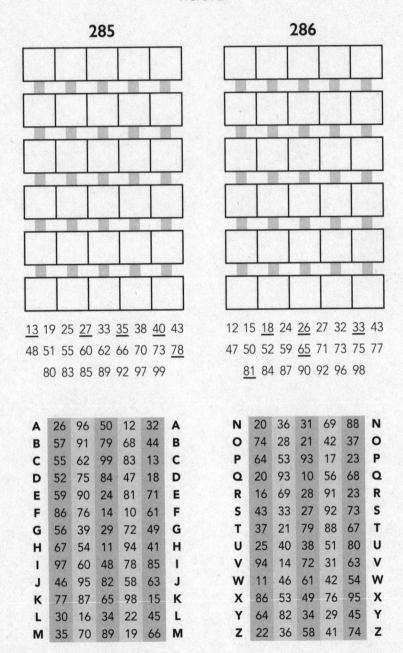

13 19 25 27 33 35 38 40 43
48 51 55 60 62 66 70 73 78
80 83 85 89 92 97 99

286

12 15 18 24 26 27 32 33 43
47 50 52 59 65 71 73 75 77
81 84 87 90 92 96 98

A	26	96	50	12	32	A
B	57	91	79	68	44	B
C	55	62	99	83	13	C
D	52	75	84	47	18	D
E	59	90	24	81	71	E
F	86	76	14	10	61	F
G	56	39	29	72	49	G
H	67	54	11	94	41	H
I	97	60	48	78	85	I
J	46	95	82	58	63	J
K	77	87	65	98	15	K
L	30	16	34	22	45	L
M	35	70	89	19	66	M

N	20	36	31	69	88	N
O	74	28	21	42	37	O
P	64	53	93	17	23	P
Q	20	93	10	56	68	Q
R	16	69	28	91	23	R
S	43	33	27	92	73	S
T	37	21	79	88	67	T
U	25	40	38	51	80	U
V	94	14	72	31	63	V
W	11	46	61	42	54	W
X	86	53	49	76	95	X
Y	64	82	34	29	45	Y
Z	22	36	58	41	74	Z

5-Letter Puzzles

287

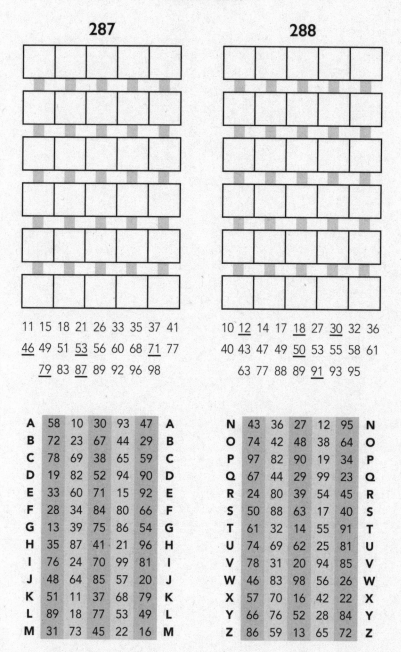

11 15 18 21 26 33 35 37 41
<u>46</u> 49 51 <u>53</u> 56 60 68 <u>71</u> 77
<u>79</u> 83 <u>87</u> 89 92 96 98

288

10 <u>12</u> 14 17 <u>18</u> 27 <u>30</u> 32 36
40 43 47 49 <u>50</u> 53 55 58 61
63 77 88 89 <u>91</u> 93 95

A	58	10	30	93	47	**A**
B	72	23	67	44	29	**B**
C	78	69	38	65	59	**C**
D	19	82	52	94	90	**D**
E	33	60	71	15	92	**E**
F	28	34	84	80	66	**F**
G	13	39	75	86	54	**G**
H	35	87	41	21	96	**H**
I	76	24	70	99	81	**I**
J	48	64	85	57	20	**J**
K	51	11	37	68	79	**K**
L	89	18	77	53	49	**L**
M	31	73	45	22	16	**M**

N	43	36	27	12	95	**N**
O	74	42	48	38	64	**O**
P	97	82	90	19	34	**P**
Q	67	44	29	99	23	**Q**
R	24	80	39	54	45	**R**
S	50	88	63	17	40	**S**
T	61	32	14	55	91	**T**
U	74	69	62	25	81	**U**
V	78	31	20	94	85	**V**
W	46	83	98	56	26	**W**
X	57	70	16	42	22	**X**
Y	66	76	52	28	84	**Y**
Z	86	59	13	65	72	**Z**

289

13 17 22 25 33 35 37 41 43
52 54 57 60 63 67 70 72 74
77 79 83 86 88 90 98

290

13 17 19 23 25 35 36 38 40
43 46 48 51 52 60 62 69 70
73 75 79 82 86 89 95

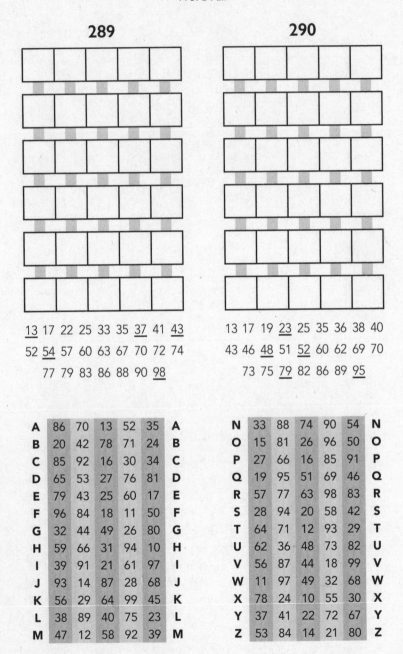

A	86	70	13	52	35	A
B	20	42	78	71	24	B
C	85	92	16	30	34	C
D	65	53	27	76	81	D
E	79	43	25	60	17	E
F	96	84	18	11	50	F
G	32	44	49	26	80	G
H	59	66	31	94	10	H
I	39	91	21	61	97	I
J	93	14	87	28	68	J
K	56	29	64	99	45	K
L	38	89	40	75	23	L
M	47	12	58	92	39	M

N	33	88	74	90	54	N
O	15	81	26	96	50	O
P	27	66	16	85	91	P
Q	19	95	51	69	46	Q
R	57	77	63	98	83	R
S	28	94	20	58	42	S
T	64	71	12	93	29	T
U	62	36	48	73	82	U
V	56	87	44	18	99	V
W	11	97	49	32	68	W
X	78	24	10	55	30	X
Y	37	41	22	72	67	Y
Z	53	84	14	21	80	Z

291

292

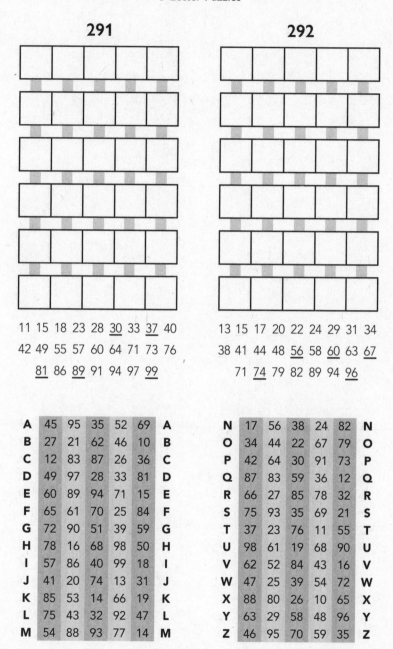

11 15 18 23 28 <u>30</u> 33 <u>37</u> 40
42 49 55 57 60 64 71 73 76
<u>81</u> 86 <u>89</u> 91 94 97 <u>99</u>

13 15 17 20 22 24 29 31 34
38 41 44 48 <u>56</u> 58 <u>60</u> 63 <u>67</u>
71 <u>74</u> 79 82 89 94 <u>96</u>

A	45	95	35	52	69	A
B	27	21	62	46	10	B
C	12	83	87	26	36	C
D	49	97	28	33	81	D
E	60	89	94	71	15	E
F	65	61	70	25	84	F
G	72	90	51	39	59	G
H	78	16	68	98	50	H
I	57	86	40	99	18	I
J	41	20	74	13	31	J
K	85	53	14	66	19	K
L	75	43	32	92	47	L
M	54	88	93	77	14	M

N	17	56	38	24	82	N
O	34	44	22	67	79	O
P	42	64	30	91	73	P
Q	87	83	59	36	12	Q
R	66	27	85	78	32	R
S	75	93	35	69	21	S
T	37	23	76	11	55	T
U	98	61	19	68	90	U
V	62	52	84	43	16	V
W	47	25	39	54	72	W
X	88	80	26	10	65	X
Y	63	29	58	48	96	Y
Z	46	95	70	59	35	Z

293

294

17 19 <u>21</u> 23 32 <u>36</u> 40 <u>45</u> 47
49 53 56 58 62 67 72 78 <u>81</u>
83 85 <u>87</u> 92 94 97 99

10 <u>16</u> 22 25 28 31 <u>33</u> 38 44
46 51 54 57 61 63 <u>69</u> 71 77
<u>82</u> 84 86 <u>88</u> 93 96 98

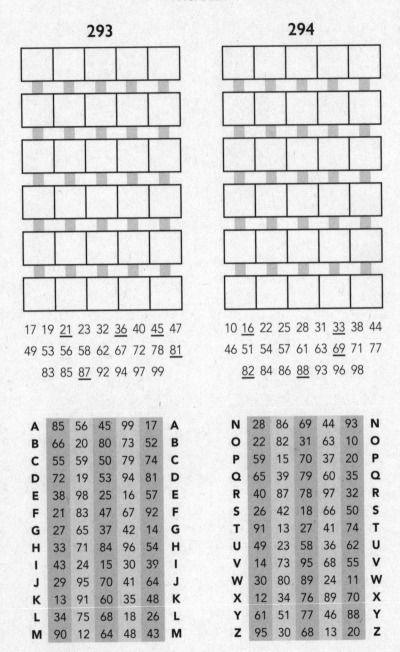

A	85	56	45	99	17	A
B	66	20	80	73	52	B
C	55	59	50	79	74	C
D	72	19	53	94	81	D
E	38	98	25	16	57	E
F	21	83	47	67	92	F
G	27	65	37	42	14	G
H	33	71	84	96	54	H
I	43	24	15	30	39	I
J	29	95	70	41	64	J
K	13	91	60	35	48	K
L	34	75	68	18	26	L
M	90	12	64	48	43	M

N	28	86	69	44	93	N
O	22	82	31	63	10	O
P	59	15	70	37	20	P
Q	65	39	79	60	35	Q
R	40	87	78	97	32	R
S	26	42	18	66	50	S
T	91	13	27	41	74	T
U	49	23	58	36	62	U
V	14	73	95	68	55	V
W	30	80	89	24	11	W
X	12	34	76	89	70	X
Y	61	51	77	46	88	Y
Z	95	30	68	13	20	Z

295

296

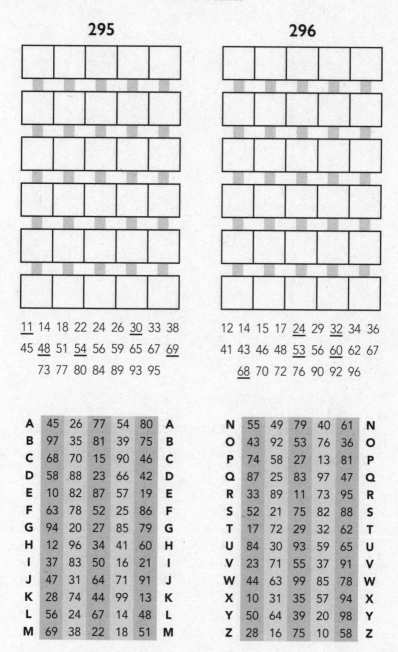

11 14 18 22 24 26 30 33 38
45 48 51 54 56 59 65 67 69
73 77 80 84 89 93 95

12 14 15 17 24 29 32 34 36
41 43 46 48 53 56 60 62 67
68 70 72 76 90 92 96

A	45	26	77	54	80	A
B	97	35	81	39	75	B
C	68	70	15	90	46	C
D	58	88	23	66	42	D
E	10	82	87	57	19	E
F	63	78	52	25	86	F
G	94	20	27	85	79	G
H	12	96	34	41	60	H
I	37	83	50	16	21	I
J	47	31	64	71	91	J
K	28	74	44	99	13	K
L	56	24	67	14	48	L
M	69	38	22	18	51	M

N	55	49	79	40	61	N
O	43	92	53	76	36	O
P	74	58	27	13	81	P
Q	87	25	83	97	47	Q
R	33	89	11	73	95	R
S	52	21	75	82	88	S
T	17	72	29	32	62	T
U	84	30	93	59	65	U
V	23	71	55	37	91	V
W	44	63	99	85	78	W
X	10	31	35	57	94	X
Y	50	64	39	20	98	Y
Z	28	16	75	10	58	Z

Word Fall

297

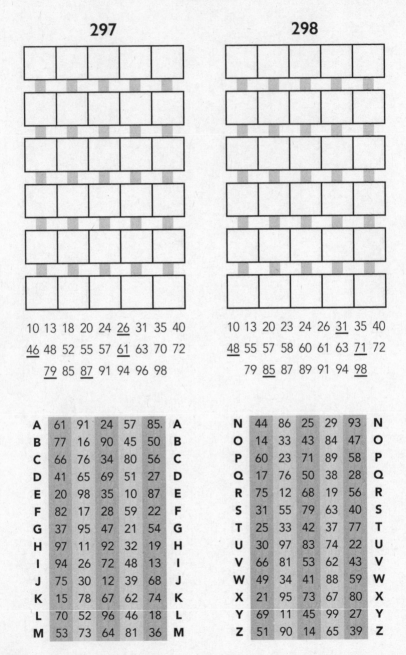

10 13 18 20 24 <u>26</u> 31 35 40
<u>46</u> 48 52 55 57 <u>61</u> 63 70 72
<u>79</u> 85 <u>87</u> 91 94 96 98

A	61	91	24	57	85.	**A**
B	77	16	90	45	50	**B**
C	66	76	34	80	56	**C**
D	41	65	69	51	27	**D**
E	20	98	35	10	87	**E**
F	82	17	28	59	22	**F**
G	37	95	47	21	54	**G**
H	97	11	92	32	19	**H**
I	94	26	72	48	13	**I**
J	75	30	12	39	68	**J**
K	15	78	67	62	74	**K**
L	70	52	96	46	18	**L**
M	53	73	64	81	36	**M**

298

10 13 20 23 24 26 <u>31</u> 35 40
<u>48</u> 55 57 58 60 61 63 <u>71</u> 72
79 <u>85</u> 87 89 91 94 <u>98</u>

N	44	86	25	29	93	**N**
O	14	33	43	84	47	**O**
P	60	23	71	89	58	**P**
Q	17	76	50	38	28	**Q**
R	75	12	68	19	56	**R**
S	31	55	79	63	40	**S**
T	25	33	42	37	77	**T**
U	30	97	83	74	22	**U**
V	66	81	53	62	43	**V**
W	49	34	41	88	59	**W**
X	21	95	73	67	80	**X**
Y	69	11	45	99	27	**Y**
Z	51	90	14	65	39	**Z**

5-Letter Puzzles

299

300

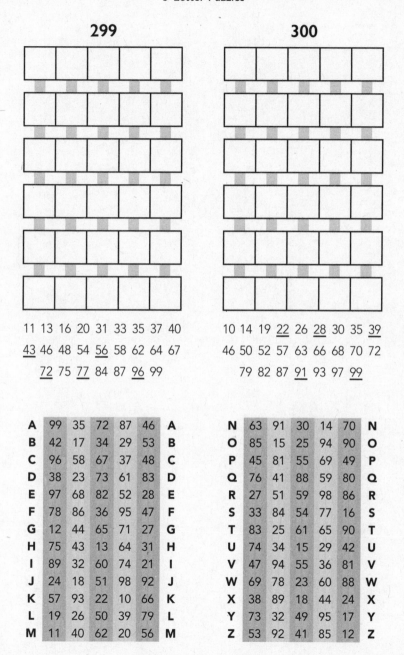

11 13 16 20 31 33 35 37 40
<u>43</u> 46 48 54 <u>56</u> 58 62 64 67
<u>72</u> 75 <u>77</u> 84 87 <u>96</u> 99

10 14 19 <u>22</u> 26 <u>28</u> 30 35 <u>39</u>
46 50 52 57 63 66 68 70 72
79 82 87 <u>91</u> 93 97 <u>99</u>

A	99	35	72	87	46	A
B	42	17	34	29	53	B
C	96	58	67	37	48	C
D	38	23	73	61	83	D
E	97	68	82	52	28	E
F	78	86	36	95	47	F
G	12	44	65	71	27	G
H	75	43	13	64	31	H
I	89	32	60	74	21	I
J	24	18	51	98	92	J
K	57	93	22	10	66	K
L	19	26	50	39	79	L
M	11	40	62	20	56	M

N	63	91	30	14	70	N
O	85	15	25	94	90	O
P	45	81	55	69	49	P
Q	76	41	88	59	80	Q
R	27	51	59	98	86	R
S	33	84	54	77	16	S
T	83	25	61	65	90	T
U	74	34	15	29	42	U
V	47	94	55	36	81	V
W	69	78	23	60	88	W
X	38	89	18	44	24	X
Y	73	32	49	95	17	Y
Z	53	92	41	85	12	Z

6-LETTER
PUZZLES

Word Fall

301

10 13 16 18 20 23 <u>25</u> 28 <u>32</u>

35 37 <u>39</u> 42 <u>44</u> 46 49 51 53

55 58 60 63 <u>66</u> 68 70 72 74

<u>78</u> 82 84 86 89 91 93 96 98

302

10 <u>12</u> 13 17 <u>19</u> 21 25 27 29

<u>31</u> 35 38 <u>42</u> 43 46 48 50 <u>53</u>

55 56 59 62 64 66 69 70 71

76 79 81 82 <u>83</u> 87 94 96 99

A	23	78	18	63	49	89	A	N	85	36	80	45	15	30	N
B	75	67	24	11	95	61	B	O	35	96	53	46	25	13	O
C	79	87	59	94	17	31	C	P	15	67	22	52	97	73	P
D	92	34	97	80	57	47	D	Q	45	40	11	57	61	92	Q
E	19	43	38	81	21	64	E	R	93	16	68	37	72	44	R
F	45	30	73	54	40	22	F	S	39	86	58	20	91	60	S
G	36	41	88	26	14	65	G	T	69	27	50	83	71	48	T
H	77	90	33	52	85	15	H	U	65	90	85	34	95	80	U
I	70	10	66	82	42	55	I	V	30	36	77	88	24	41	V
J	47	24	14	90	65	34	J	W	47	75	26	14	54	33	W
K	73	54	88	40	97	67	K	X	62	12	29	76	56	99	X
L	74	28	98	32	84	51	L	Y	80	47	41	36	22	67	Y
M	95	61	26	11	52	22	M	Z	90	73	61	26	33	54	Z

303

304

11 13 15 17 20 23 26 29 32
35 39 41 43 46 48 50 53 55
57 59 61 64 67 69 71 75 77
79 81 85 89 91 93 95 97 99

11 15 21 25 27 30 32 34 36
38 42 45 46 47 50 52 54 57
58 60 63 66 67 70 72 74 77
79 81 84 86 88 90 92 95 97

A	37	51	28	10	14	22	A
B	94	76	44	65	40	98	B
C	43	85	39	26	61	55	C
D	24	56	83	62	19	96	D
E	67	77	46	11	50	97	E
F	78	33	73	82	12	49	F
G	68	87	18	31	96	37	G
H	98	14	33	94	24	19	H
I	93	41	20	69	17	59	I
J	56	51	68	10	83	16	J
K	80	40	73	62	31	22	K
L	53	64	13	71	99	29	L
M	87	28	18	65	44	49	M

N	23	75	91	48	89	35	N
O	34	66	58	86	45	74	O
P	21	47	84	30	52	70	P
Q	12	78	16	82	65	37	Q
R	60	27	36	92	72	88	R
S	14	80	56	51	44	28	S
T	79	32	81	57	95	15	T
U	31	22	68	12	73	40	U
V	83	98	24	78	94	33	V
W	49	62	96	44	37	68	W
X	98	51	87	14	73	10	X
Y	90	38	63	54	25	42	Y
Z	49	16	33	28	78	22	Z

305

11 13 15 <u>17</u> 19 <u>21</u> 23 26 29
33 35 38 41 <u>43</u> 45 <u>47</u> 49 51
54 <u>57</u> 60 64 67 69 71 73 76
79 82 84 <u>86</u> 88 91 94 97 99

306

10 12 15 18 22 24 26 28 29
<u>30</u> 32 36 38 41 43 <u>44</u> 46 48
51 <u>55</u> 58 <u>60</u> 63 66 68 70 74
77 <u>79</u> 80 86 89 91 <u>93</u> 94 96

A	60	91	86	15	26	41	A
B	37	78	42	61	92	16	B
C	35	13	71	88	21	97	C
D	56	95	40	72	31	27	D
E	54	17	69	45	82	73	E
F	90	39	52	34	20	14	F
G	25	65	85	53	98	59	G
H	67	76	19	33	84	47	H
I	81	92	72	56	16	37	I
J	65	53	14	25	31	95	J
K	40	59	78	20	50	34	K
L	28	30	10	46	89	70	L
M	32	80	44	24	66	12	M

N	85	61	52	75	98	90	N
O	63	48	74	93	58	18	O
P	39	83	27	78	90	52	P
Q	16	87	42	98	59	65	Q
R	11	99	49	57	64	23	R
S	43	94	38	51	79	29	S
T	36	77	68	96	22	55	T
U	85	25	20	53	95	40	U
V	75	81	14	27	34	50	V
W	31	92	39	56	61	78	W
X	92	87	34	27	39	83	X
Y	59	14	85	81	98	75	Y
Z	65	50	72	90	37	31	Z

307

308

10 13 <u>15</u> 17 20 22 27 29 <u>32</u>
34 37 39 42 <u>44</u> 46 <u>48</u> 50 52
<u>54</u> 56 61 64 66 69 71 73 76
78 81 83 85 87 89 <u>92</u> 95 97

10 16 21 22 24 <u>27</u> 31 34 35
37 <u>39</u> 40 46 48 52 53 54 <u>55</u>
57 <u>60</u> 61 62 <u>64</u> 65 69 71 73
74 <u>79</u> 82 83 86 89 92 93 98

A	34	52	61	92	27	73	A
B	44	29	81	56	17	78	B
C	83	46	69	39	54	10	C
D	45	51	41	26	58	30	D
E	97	13	32	42	85	76	E
F	79	40	93	82	62	53	F
G	63	72	84	18	90	25	G
H	50	95	20	87	66	15	H
I	57	60	16	24	35	86	I
J	70	94	99	36	80	28	J
K	23	14	77	59	19	33	K
L	22	48	71	89	37	64	L
M	49	12	67	96	43	38	M

N	68	59	43	30	96	80	N
O	33	47	88	67	75	38	O
P	94	19	84	28	41	11	P
Q	14	58	70	23	91	99	Q
R	26	18	63	77	49	68	R
S	98	31	55	74	21	65	S
T	36	72	45	90	12	25	T
U	51	91	84	18	41	14	U
V	80	72	45	38	96	26	V
W	99	30	58	23	19	67	W
X	88	75	68	11	25	63	X
Y	43	49	94	33	59	90	Y
Z	70	77	12	28	47	51	Z

Word Fall

309

<table>
<tr><td></td><td></td><td></td><td></td><td></td><td></td></tr>
<tr><td></td><td></td><td></td><td></td><td></td><td></td></tr>
<tr><td></td><td></td><td></td><td></td><td></td><td></td></tr>
<tr><td></td><td></td><td></td><td></td><td></td><td></td></tr>
<tr><td></td><td></td><td></td><td></td><td></td><td></td></tr>
<tr><td></td><td></td><td></td><td></td><td></td><td></td></tr>
</table>

10 12 14 17 19 22 25 <u>27</u> 29
<u>31</u> 33 36 38 <u>40</u> 42 44 46 <u>48</u>
51 54 57 60 62 64 66 70 72
74 <u>76</u> 79 <u>82</u> 84 87 95 97 99

310

<table>
<tr><td></td><td></td><td></td><td></td><td></td><td></td></tr>
<tr><td></td><td></td><td></td><td></td><td></td><td></td></tr>
<tr><td></td><td></td><td></td><td></td><td></td><td></td></tr>
<tr><td></td><td></td><td></td><td></td><td></td><td></td></tr>
<tr><td></td><td></td><td></td><td></td><td></td><td></td></tr>
<tr><td></td><td></td><td></td><td></td><td></td><td></td></tr>
</table>

12 15 20 22 24 28 31 32 35
37 39 42 44 47 49 <u>51</u> 52 <u>55</u>
57 58 <u>61</u> 66 <u>69</u> 71 <u>75</u> 76 78
<u>79</u> 80 84 86 88 90 93 95 98

A	98	24	35	15	55	71	A
B	13	41	65	81	92	59	B
C	77	53	34	26	67	85	C
D	29	19	99	82	46	70	D
E	97	64	87	33	14	27	E
F	11	91	96	83	45	18	F
G	38	62	72	25	40	17	G
H	30	68	21	63	56	73	H
I	49	69	37	78	88	52	I
J	94	50	43	23	16	89	J
K	21	30	63	53	11	41	K
L	47	86	20	93	39	61	L
M	36	48	10	60	74	54	M

N	26	43	94	13	65	73	N
O	81	23	85	56	45	77	O
P	68	59	96	18	89	34	P
Q	50	91	63	13	23	18	Q
R	21	81	85	92	96	50	R
S	76	42	51	84	66	22	S
T	53	77	34	26	45	11	T
U	95	12	31	79	57	44	U
V	75	32	58	90	28	80	V
W	30	43	73	59	65	94	W
X	91	16	67	45	50	56	X
Y	65	91	96	81	26	13	Y
Z	30	41	23	68	53	34	Z

311

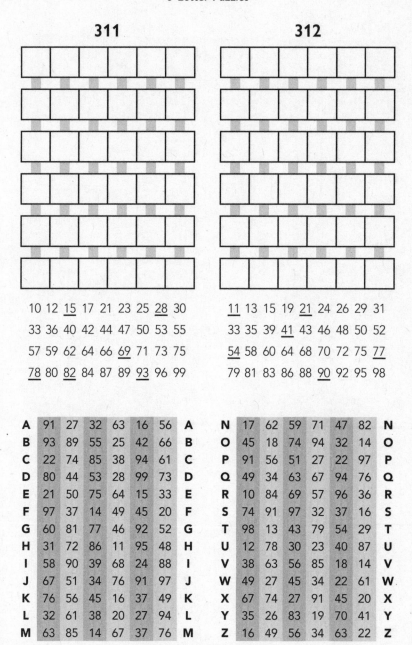

10 12 <u>15</u> 17 21 23 25 <u>28</u> 30
33 36 40 42 44 47 50 53 55
57 59 62 64 66 <u>69</u> 71 73 75
<u>78</u> 80 <u>82</u> 84 87 89 <u>93</u> 96 99

312

<u>11</u> 13 15 19 <u>21</u> 24 26 29 31
33 35 39 <u>41</u> 43 46 48 50 52
<u>54</u> 58 60 64 68 70 72 75 <u>77</u>
79 81 83 86 88 <u>90</u> 92 95 98

A	91	27	32	63	16	56	A
B	93	89	55	25	42	66	B
C	22	74	85	38	94	61	C
D	80	44	53	28	99	73	D
E	21	50	75	64	15	33	E
F	97	37	14	49	45	20	F
G	60	81	77	46	92	52	G
H	31	72	86	11	95	48	H
I	58	90	39	68	24	88	I
J	67	51	34	76	91	97	J
K	76	56	45	16	37	49	K
L	32	61	38	20	27	94	L
M	63	85	14	67	37	76	M

N	17	62	59	71	47	82	N
O	45	18	74	94	32	14	O
P	91	56	51	27	22	97	P
Q	49	34	63	67	94	76	Q
R	10	84	69	57	96	36	R
S	74	91	97	32	37	16	S
T	98	13	43	79	54	29	T
U	12	78	30	23	40	87	U
V	38	63	56	85	18	14	V
W	49	27	45	34	22	61	W
X	67	74	27	91	45	20	X
Y	35	26	83	19	70	41	Y
Z	16	49	56	34	63	22	Z

313

10 <u>12</u> 14 16 <u>20</u> 25 27 <u>29</u> 32
34 36 39 <u>42</u> 44 47 50 54 56
58 60 62 <u>64</u> 68 70 72 75 77
79 81 <u>83</u> 86 88 92 95 97 99

314

10 13 15 17 <u>19</u> 22 24 26 28
30 32 33 35 37 <u>40</u> 42 <u>45</u> 49
52 55 58 61 66 69 <u>72</u> 76 78
80 82 <u>84</u> 86 89 91 <u>94</u> 96 98

A	91	19	52	82	35	76	**A**
B	63	48	41	90	53	18	**B**
C	51	67	11	23	73	59	**C**
D	39	99	29	54	77	81	**D**
E	96	30	24	49	84	61	**E**
F	62	56	44	88	12	75	**F**
G	71	65	85	31	38	57	**G**
H	93	43	59	23	51	65	**H**
I	58	86	72	42	32	10	**I**
J	63	18	31	53	67	74	**J**
K	43	90	73	38	85	11	**K**
L	87	41	48	93	57	21	**L**
M	20	70	36	95	16	68	**M**

N	71	46	65	31	11	38	**N**
O	47	64	92	34	27	79	**O**
P	51	87	21	67	93	46	**P**
Q	23	41	74	57	85	90	**Q**
R	22	69	15	37	98	40	**R**
S	73	43	63	48	53	18	**S**
T	89	28	17	94	66	55	**T**
U	59	71	38	67	43	51	**U**
V	85	21	93	53	63	59	**V**
W	45	78	26	13	80	33	**W**
X	23	46	74	31	18	57	**X**
Y	97	25	60	50	14	83	**Y**
Z	65	73	41	90	18	11	**Z**

6-Letter Puzzles

315

316

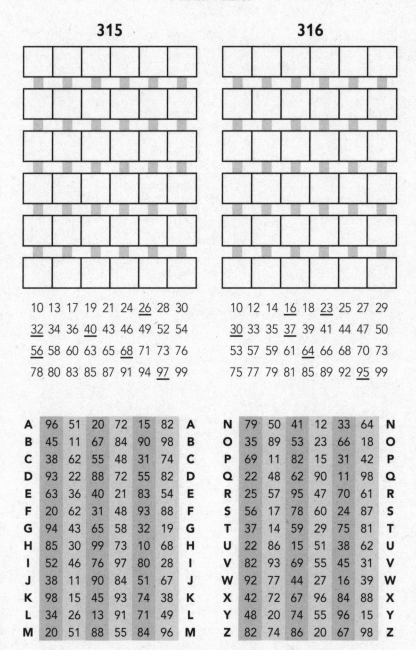

10 13 17 19 21 24 <u>26</u> 28 30
<u>32</u> 34 36 <u>40</u> 43 46 49 52 54
<u>56</u> 58 60 63 65 <u>68</u> 71 73 76
78 80 83 85 87 91 94 <u>97</u> 99

10 12 14 <u>16</u> 18 <u>23</u> 25 27 29
<u>30</u> 33 35 <u>37</u> 39 41 44 47 50
53 57 59 61 <u>64</u> 66 68 70 73
75 77 79 81 85 89 92 <u>95</u> 99

A	96	51	20	72	15	82	A
B	45	11	67	84	90	98	B
C	38	62	55	48	31	74	C
D	93	22	88	72	55	82	D
E	63	36	40	21	83	54	E
F	20	62	31	48	93	88	F
G	94	43	65	58	32	19	G
H	85	30	99	73	10	68	H
I	52	46	76	97	80	28	I
J	38	11	90	84	51	67	J
K	98	15	45	93	74	38	K
L	34	26	13	91	71	49	L
M	20	51	88	55	84	96	M

N	79	50	41	12	33	64	N
O	35	89	53	23	66	18	O
P	69	11	82	15	31	42	P
Q	22	48	62	90	11	98	Q
R	25	57	95	47	70	61	R
S	56	17	78	60	24	87	S
T	37	14	59	29	75	81	T
U	22	86	15	51	38	62	U
V	82	93	69	55	45	31	V
W	92	77	44	27	16	39	W
X	42	72	67	96	84	88	X
Y	48	20	74	55	96	15	Y
Z	82	74	86	20	67	98	Z

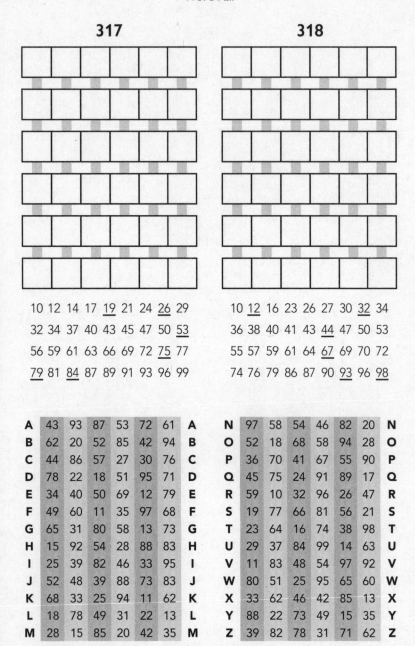

Word Fall

317

318

10 12 14 17 <u>19</u> 21 24 <u>26</u> 29
32 34 37 40 43 45 47 50 <u>53</u>
56 59 61 63 66 69 72 <u>75</u> 77
<u>79</u> 81 <u>84</u> 87 89 91 93 96 99

10 <u>12</u> 16 23 26 27 30 <u>32</u> 34
36 38 40 41 43 <u>44</u> 47 50 53
55 57 59 61 64 <u>67</u> 69 70 72
74 76 79 86 87 90 <u>93</u> 96 <u>98</u>

A	43	93	87	53	72	61	**A**
B	62	20	52	85	42	94	**B**
C	44	86	57	27	30	76	**C**
D	78	22	18	51	95	71	**D**
E	34	40	50	69	12	79	**E**
F	49	60	11	35	97	68	**F**
G	65	31	80	58	13	73	**G**
H	15	92	54	28	88	83	**H**
I	25	39	82	46	33	95	**I**
J	52	48	39	88	73	83	**J**
K	68	33	25	94	11	62	**K**
L	18	78	49	31	22	13	**L**
M	28	15	85	20	42	35	**M**

N	97	58	54	46	82	20	**N**
O	52	18	68	58	94	28	**O**
P	36	70	41	67	55	90	**P**
Q	45	75	24	91	89	17	**Q**
R	59	10	32	96	26	47	**R**
S	19	77	66	81	56	21	**S**
T	23	64	16	74	38	98	**T**
U	29	37	84	99	14	63	**U**
V	11	83	48	54	97	92	**V**
W	80	51	25	95	65	60	**W**
X	33	62	46	42	85	13	**X**
Y	88	22	73	49	15	35	**Y**
Z	39	82	78	31	71	62	**Z**

319

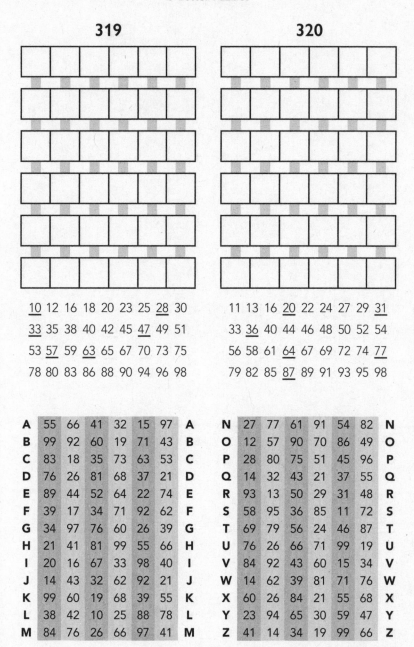

<u>10</u> 12 16 18 20 23 25 <u>28</u> 30
<u>33</u> 35 38 40 42 45 <u>47</u> 49 51
53 <u>57</u> 59 <u>63</u> 65 67 70 73 75
78 80 83 86 88 90 94 96 98

320

11 13 16 <u>20</u> 22 24 27 29 <u>31</u>
33 <u>36</u> 40 44 46 48 50 52 54
56 58 61 <u>64</u> 67 69 72 74 <u>77</u>
79 82 85 <u>87</u> 89 91 93 95 98

A	55	66	41	32	15	97	A
B	99	92	60	19	71	43	B
C	83	18	35	73	63	53	C
D	76	26	81	68	37	21	D
E	89	44	52	64	22	74	E
F	39	17	34	71	92	62	F
G	34	97	76	60	26	39	G
H	21	41	81	99	55	66	H
I	20	16	67	33	98	40	I
J	14	43	32	62	92	21	J
K	99	60	19	68	39	55	K
L	38	42	10	25	88	78	L
M	84	76	26	66	97	41	M

N	27	77	61	91	54	82	N
O	12	57	90	70	86	49	O
P	28	80	75	51	45	96	P
Q	14	32	43	21	37	55	Q
R	93	13	50	29	31	48	R
S	58	95	36	85	11	72	S
T	69	79	56	24	46	87	T
U	76	26	66	71	99	19	U
V	84	92	43	60	15	34	V
W	14	62	39	81	71	76	W
X	60	26	84	21	55	68	X
Y	23	94	65	30	59	47	Y
Z	41	14	34	19	99	66	Z

Word Fall

321

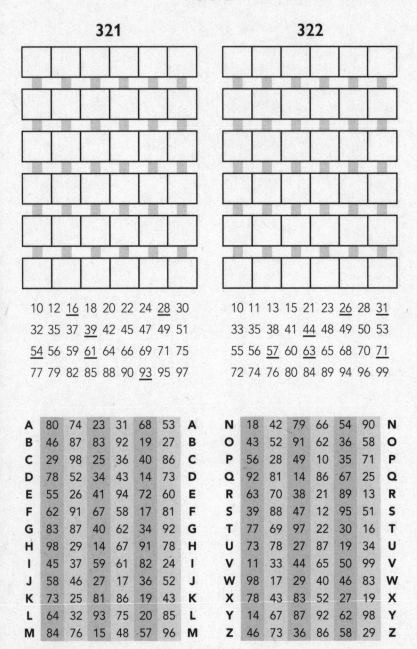

10 12 <u>16</u> 18 20 22 24 <u>28</u> 30
32 35 37 <u>39</u> 42 45 47 49 51
<u>54</u> 56 59 <u>61</u> 64 66 69 71 75
77 79 82 85 88 90 <u>93</u> 95 97

322

10 11 13 15 21 23 <u>26</u> 28 <u>31</u>
33 35 38 41 <u>44</u> 48 49 50 53
55 56 <u>57</u> 60 <u>63</u> 65 68 70 <u>71</u>
72 74 76 80 84 89 94 96 99

A	80	74	23	31	68	53	**A**
B	46	87	83	92	19	27	**B**
C	29	98	25	36	40	86	**C**
D	78	52	34	43	14	73	**D**
E	55	26	41	94	72	60	**E**
F	62	91	67	58	17	81	**F**
G	83	87	40	62	34	92	**G**
H	98	29	14	67	91	78	**H**
I	45	37	59	61	82	24	**I**
J	58	46	27	17	36	52	**J**
K	73	25	81	86	19	43	**K**
L	64	32	93	75	20	85	**L**
M	84	76	15	48	57	96	**M**

N	18	42	79	66	54	90	**N**
O	43	52	91	62	36	58	**O**
P	56	28	49	10	35	71	**P**
Q	92	81	14	86	67	25	**Q**
R	63	70	38	21	89	13	**R**
S	39	88	47	12	95	51	**S**
T	77	69	97	22	30	16	**T**
U	73	78	27	87	19	34	**U**
V	11	33	44	65	50	99	**V**
W	98	17	29	40	46	83	**W**
X	78	43	83	52	27	19	**X**
Y	14	67	87	92	62	98	**Y**
Z	46	73	36	86	58	29	**Z**

323

324

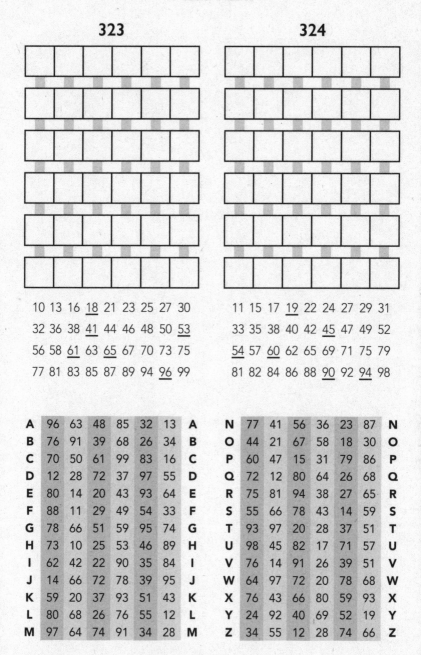

10 13 16 <u>18</u> 21 23 25 27 30
32 36 38 <u>41</u> 44 46 48 50 <u>53</u>
56 58 <u>61</u> 63 <u>65</u> 67 70 73 75
77 81 83 85 87 89 94 <u>96</u> 99

11 15 17 <u>19</u> 22 24 27 29 31
33 35 38 40 42 <u>45</u> 47 49 52
<u>54</u> 57 <u>60</u> 62 65 69 71 75 79
81 82 84 86 88 <u>90</u> 92 <u>94</u> 98

A	96	63	48	85	32	13	A
B	76	91	39	68	26	34	B
C	70	50	61	99	83	16	C
D	12	28	72	37	97	55	D
E	80	14	20	43	93	64	E
F	88	11	29	49	54	33	F
G	78	66	51	59	95	74	G
H	73	10	25	53	46	89	H
I	62	42	22	90	35	84	I
J	14	66	72	78	39	95	J
K	59	20	37	93	51	43	K
L	80	68	26	76	55	12	L
M	97	64	74	91	34	28	M

N	77	41	56	36	23	87	N
O	44	21	67	58	18	30	O
P	60	47	15	31	79	86	P
Q	72	12	80	64	26	68	Q
R	75	81	94	38	27	65	R
S	55	66	78	43	14	59	S
T	93	97	20	28	37	51	T
U	98	45	82	17	71	57	U
V	76	14	91	26	39	51	V
W	64	97	72	20	78	68	W
X	76	43	66	80	59	93	X
Y	24	92	40	69	52	19	Y
Z	34	55	12	28	74	66	Z

Word Fall

325

<table>
<tr><td></td><td></td><td></td><td></td><td></td><td></td></tr>
<tr><td></td><td></td><td></td><td></td><td></td><td></td></tr>
<tr><td></td><td></td><td></td><td></td><td></td><td></td></tr>
<tr><td></td><td></td><td></td><td></td><td></td><td></td></tr>
<tr><td></td><td></td><td></td><td></td><td></td><td></td></tr>
<tr><td></td><td></td><td></td><td></td><td></td><td></td></tr>
</table>

<u>11</u> 13 16 18 20 <u>23</u> 25 27 30
32 36 39 41 44 46 48 50 <u>53</u>
59 61 63 <u>65</u> 67 69 72 75 <u>77</u>
79 81 84 <u>86</u> 88 91 94 96 99

326

<table>
<tr><td></td><td></td><td></td><td></td><td></td><td></td></tr>
<tr><td></td><td></td><td></td><td></td><td></td><td></td></tr>
<tr><td></td><td></td><td></td><td></td><td></td><td></td></tr>
<tr><td></td><td></td><td></td><td></td><td></td><td></td></tr>
<tr><td></td><td></td><td></td><td></td><td></td><td></td></tr>
<tr><td></td><td></td><td></td><td></td><td></td><td></td></tr>
</table>

12 14 <u>16</u> 19 22 24 26 <u>28</u> 30
31 <u>33</u> 35 37 40 43 45 50 52
54 57 60 62 64 <u>66</u> 69 71 <u>74</u>
76 80 83 85 86 90 93 96 <u>98</u>

A	63	23	18	99	32	44	A
B	97	49	58	34	89	73	B
C	53	13	39	84	79	48	C
D	72	94	81	11	67	27	D
E	69	16	50	30	96	86	E
F	21	55	38	47	15	42	F
G	40	26	37	98	19	83	G
H	54	93	22	62	74	35	H
I	60	76	33	52	43	14	I
J	51	68	10	82	95	56	J
K	87	42	58	78	21	92	K
L	75	91	59	41	65	25	L
M	51	34	29	87	97	82	M

N	61	36	77	88	20	46	N
O	70	17	10	56	89	95	O
P	47	55	87	73	82	10	P
Q	89	38	49	68	42	78	Q
R	15	95	34	58	21	29	R
S	56	47	70	97	92	51	S
T	80	64	71	12	45	28	T
U	17	82	47	95	10	73	U
V	56	87	38	21	42	68	V
W	66	31	90	24	57	85	W
X	51	70	34	92	78	97	X
Y	29	17	68	87	56	21	Y
Z	95	47	15	29	73	78	Z

327

328

10 12 15 <u>17</u> 20 <u>22</u> 24 27 30
<u>32</u> 35 37 41 <u>43</u> 47 50 52 54
56 58 60 62 64 <u>66</u> 68 70 73
76 <u>79</u> 81 84 87 90 92 94 98

14 17 19 <u>20</u> 24 29 31 32 33
36 40 42 45 47 53 55 56 59
64 <u>67</u> 68 <u>71</u> 73 74 <u>76</u> 78 80
82 84 <u>86</u> 89 91 93 94 <u>96</u> 99

A	17	64	20	47	94	73	A
B	63	49	75	85	23	69	B
C	67	74	82	93	33	45	C
D	72	46	57	13	83	65	D
E	55	89	99	31	71	14	E
F	11	26	39	44	21	34	F
G	97	88	77	18	51	61	G
H	42	96	80	36	19	53	H
I	30	92	58	79	87	12	I
J	25	49	88	38	57	75	J
K	97	25	63	72	11	46	K
L	29	40	78	86	91	59	L
M	60	37	54	81	10	22	M

N	69	16	44	95	34	85	N
O	77	65	51	39	13	61	O
P	28	18	83	61	95	75	P
Q	69	13	57	48	28	63	Q
R	90	41	66	50	15	70	R
S	77	72	23	34	39	44	S
T	24	32	84	56	68	76	T
U	98	27	52	35	43	62	U
V	65	51	85	97	26	38	V
W	16	21	46	11	88	25	W
X	49	28	18	57	23	65	X
Y	85	97	48	13	61	38	Y
Z	63	72	39	46	34	77	Z

Word Fall

329

11 13 16 18 20 24 29 31 33
35 38 40 42 46 48 51 54 56
59 61 64 66 68 71 73 75 79
82 84 87 89 91 93 95 97 99

330

10 12 14 18 23 28 32 34 37
38 39 43 45 47 50 51 55 57
63 65 67 69 72 74 75 77 81
82 83 85 88 90 92 93 94 96

	1	2	3	4	5	6	
A	81	96	39	69	12	77	A
B	92	28	67	85	50	43	B
C	26	17	98	53	30	58	C
D	47	34	57	74	63	94	D
E	83	55	10	90	37	45	E
F	60	25	41	15	19	36	F
G	14	32	72	23	65	88	G
H	62	78	86	44	27	21	H
I	49	70	41	22	53	80	I
J	76	86	17	49	62	21	J
K	15	36	26	19	44	70	K
L	27	58	98	76	86	62	L
M	44	36	21	80	30	49	M

	1	2	3	4	5	6	
N	19	98	70	53	26	15	N
O	24	99	42	59	61	33	O
P	31	46	13	54	87	64	P
Q	27	58	17	78	41	53	Q
R	75	82	38	18	93	51	R
S	16	79	91	84	35	66	S
T	89	29	71	56	40	97	T
U	68	95	20	48	11	73	U
V	78	86	30	21	15	98	V
W	52	70	41	27	58	36	W
X	80	62	26	17	22	76	X
Y	25	49	44	70	76	21	Y
Z	78	19	30	25	58	62	Z

331

332

10 12 <u>14</u> 16 18 <u>20</u> 23 25 <u>27</u>
29 31 34 37 41 43 46 49 <u>51</u>
57 59 61 63 65 <u>67</u> 70 <u>72</u> 74
77 80 82 86 89 91 94 96 98

16 17 19 21 24 25 28 <u>33</u> 35
37 <u>38</u> 40 43 45 48 50 58 <u>59</u>
62 64 <u>65</u> 66 67 70 72 73 <u>76</u>
78 83 85 86 89 90 <u>92</u> 96 97

A	42	52	60	87	79	99	A
B	78	58	90	38	21	85	B
C	95	11	53	47	69	81	C
D	92	73	48	28	50	62	D
E	37	43	86	25	72	65	E
F	55	88	22	75	15	32	F
G	26	68	36	13	30	54	G
H	84	44	55	26	95	71	H
I	10	27	61	49	80	91	I
J	56	13	68	30	93	44	J
K	88	32	54	99	69	75	K
L	89	70	67	16	59	96	L
M	11	52	36	60	81	22	M

N	47	79	42	53	15	87	N
O	19	33	97	64	83	45	O
P	39	84	53	26	44	13	P
Q	99	95	88	56	79	71	Q
R	77	82	23	63	34	14	R
S	51	18	94	31	41	29	S
T	84	69	39	75	15	22	T
U	40	17	76	66	35	24	U
V	74	46	98	20	57	12	V
W	36	68	93	11	42	30	W
X	87	55	47	81	99	22	X
Y	93	11	39	71	79	32	Y
Z	75	54	30	13	69	36	Z

Word Fall

333

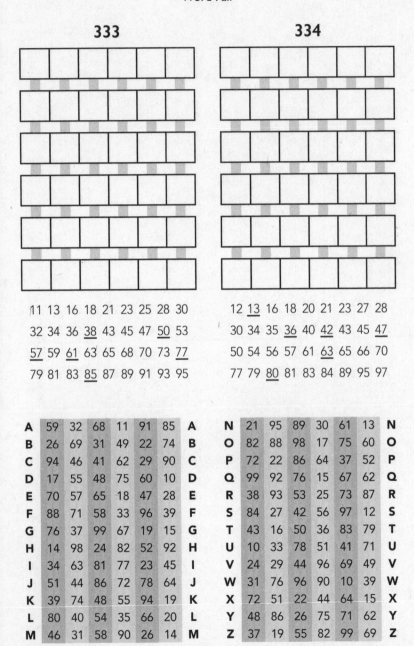

11 13 16 18 21 23 25 28 30
32 34 36 <u>38</u> 43 45 47 <u>50</u> 53
<u>57</u> 59 <u>61</u> 63 65 68 70 73 <u>77</u>
79 81 83 <u>85</u> 87 89 91 93 95

334

12 <u>13</u> 16 18 20 21 23 27 28
30 34 35 <u>36</u> 40 <u>42</u> 43 45 <u>47</u>
50 54 56 57 61 <u>63</u> 65 66 70
77 79 <u>80</u> 81 83 84 89 95 97

A	59	32	68	11	91	85	A
B	26	69	31	49	22	74	B
C	94	46	41	62	29	90	C
D	17	55	48	75	60	10	D
E	70	57	65	18	47	28	E
F	88	71	58	33	96	39	F
G	76	37	99	67	19	15	G
H	14	98	24	82	52	92	H
I	34	63	81	77	23	45	I
J	51	44	86	72	78	64	J
K	39	74	48	55	94	19	K
L	80	40	54	35	66	20	L
M	46	31	58	90	26	14	M

N	21	95	89	30	61	13	N
O	82	88	98	17	75	60	O
P	72	22	86	64	37	52	P
Q	99	92	76	15	67	62	Q
R	38	93	53	25	73	87	R
S	84	27	42	56	97	12	S
T	43	16	50	36	83	79	T
U	10	33	78	51	41	71	U
V	24	29	44	96	69	49	V
W	31	76	96	90	10	39	W
X	72	51	22	44	64	15	X
Y	48	86	26	75	71	62	Y
Z	37	19	55	82	99	69	Z

335

10 <u>15</u> 18 21 24 <u>26</u> 29 31 33
<u>35</u> 37 <u>39</u> 41 43 45 47 50 52
56 58 61 63 <u>65</u> 68 <u>70</u> 72 75
78 81 83 86 88 91 94 97 99

336

12 14 16 <u>18</u> 20 <u>23</u> 26 27 29
33 35 40 45 49 51 <u>53</u> 57 61
64 66 <u>68</u> 71 73 75 77 78 <u>80</u>
82 84 87 88 <u>90</u> 91 93 96 98

A	23	16	87	66	77	93	A
B	42	85	60	30	55	38	B
C	92	11	34	67	46	54	C
D	21	37	15	81	52	94	D
E	97	43	72	39	56	83	E
F	48	22	76	62	89	17	F
G	79	44	95	28	32	13	G
H	51	82	12	90	40	20	H
I	69	36	59	19	25	74	I
J	59	55	74	92	67	17	J
K	28	11	34	38	42	46	K
L	79	32	48	19	89	85	L
M	13	54	95	69	62	25	M

N	45	68	75	29	35	88	N
O	61	26	91	33	18	78	O
P	36	76	44	25	89	13	P
Q	19	62	48	79	67	95	Q
R	65	99	86	58	31	41	R
S	92	17	60	11	38	34	S
T	50	10	63	47	24	70	T
U	22	44	54	74	28	59	U
V	55	85	32	36	76	22	V
W	73	64	96	49	57	80	W
X	48	74	67	95	30	36	X
Y	98	27	53	84	71	14	Y
Z	89	69	59	55	19	79	Z

337

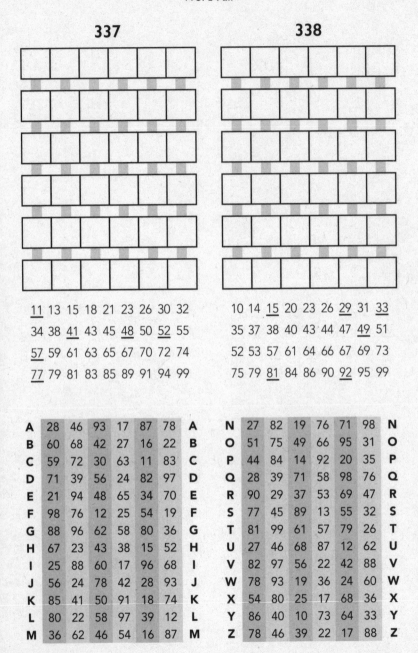

<u>11</u> 13 15 18 21 23 26 30 32
34 38 <u>41</u> 43 45 <u>48</u> 50 <u>52</u> 55
<u>57</u> 59 61 63 65 67 70 72 74
<u>77</u> 79 81 83 85 89 91 94 99

338

10 14 <u>15</u> 20 23 26 <u>29</u> 31 <u>33</u>
35 37 38 40 43 44 47 <u>49</u> 51
52 53 57 61 64 66 67 69 73
75 79 <u>81</u> 84 86 90 <u>92</u> 95 99

A	28	46	93	17	87	78	A
B	60	68	42	27	16	22	B
C	59	72	30	63	11	83	C
D	71	39	56	24	82	97	D
E	21	94	48	65	34	70	E
F	98	76	12	25	54	19	F
G	88	96	62	58	80	36	G
H	67	23	43	38	15	52	H
I	25	88	60	17	96	68	I
J	56	24	78	42	28	93	J
K	85	41	50	91	18	74	K
L	80	22	58	97	39	12	L
M	36	62	46	54	16	87	M

N	27	82	19	76	71	98	N
O	51	75	49	66	95	31	O
P	44	84	14	92	20	35	P
Q	28	39	71	58	98	76	Q
R	90	29	37	53	69	47	R
S	77	45	89	13	55	32	S
T	81	99	61	57	79	26	T
U	27	46	68	87	12	62	U
V	82	97	56	22	42	88	V
W	78	93	19	36	24	60	W
X	54	80	25	17	68	36	X
Y	86	40	10	73	64	33	Y
Z	78	46	39	22	17	88	Z

339

340

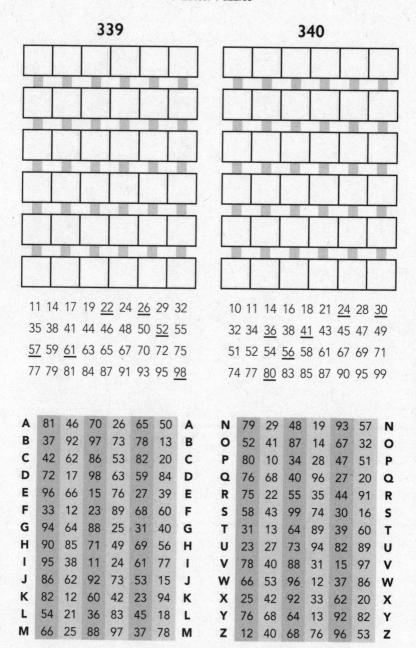

11 14 17 19 22 24 26 29 32

35 38 41 44 46 48 50 52 55

57 59 61 63 65 67 70 72 75

77 79 81 84 87 91 93 95 98

10 11 14 16 18 21 24 28 30

32 34 36 38 41 43 45 47 49

51 52 54 56 58 61 67 69 71

74 77 80 83 85 87 90 95 99

A	81	46	70	26	65	50	A
B	37	92	97	73	78	13	B
C	42	62	86	53	82	20	C
D	72	17	98	63	59	84	D
E	96	66	15	76	27	39	E
F	33	12	23	89	68	60	F
G	94	64	88	25	31	40	G
H	90	85	71	49	69	56	H
I	95	38	11	24	61	77	I
J	86	62	92	73	53	15	J
K	82	12	60	42	23	94	K
L	54	21	36	83	45	18	L
M	66	25	88	97	37	78	M

N	79	29	48	19	93	57	N
O	52	41	87	14	67	32	O
P	80	10	34	28	47	51	P
Q	76	68	40	96	27	20	Q
R	75	22	55	35	44	91	R
S	58	43	99	74	30	16	S
T	31	13	64	89	39	60	T
U	23	27	73	94	82	89	U
V	78	40	88	31	15	97	V
W	66	53	96	12	37	86	W
X	25	42	92	33	62	20	X
Y	76	68	64	13	92	82	Y
Z	12	40	68	76	96	53	Z

Word Fall

341

342

10 12 14 17 20 22 24 27 29
31 <u>33</u> 36 39 41 <u>44</u> 46 48 52
56 58 61 <u>63</u> 65 67 <u>69</u> 71 <u>73</u>
76 <u>79</u> 81 84 87 90 92 96 99

10 11 13 14 17 <u>20</u> 22 24 <u>26</u>
28 31 35 <u>38</u> 39 40 42 44 46
<u>48</u> 51 54 <u>58</u> 59 61 69 72 <u>75</u>
79 81 83 86 89 91 94 96 99

A	78	25	88	74	55	45	**A**
B	57	77	47	16	70	98	**B**
C	79	17	20	46	61	39	**C**
D	93	30	50	64	82	19	**D**
E	22	99	81	10	44	58	**E**
F	95	43	37	53	62	66	**F**
G	36	67	73	90	84	27	**G**
H	85	18	49	60	32	23	**H**
I	38	28	89	51	40	13	**I**
J	80	97	68	21	15	34	**J**
K	68	18	74	93	53	88	**K**
L	43	78	97	60	82	32	**L**
M	83	54	72	91	26	11	**M**

N	96	48	24	69	31	14	**N**
O	59	42	86	75	94	35	**O**
P	64	98	25	49	37	55	**P**
Q	85	23	66	57	80	70	**Q**
R	45	19	15	62	34	30	**R**
S	95	50	60	74	80	55	**S**
T	92	71	56	12	29	63	**T**
U	77	37	66	43	95	57	**U**
V	16	85	78	47	34	25	**V**
W	68	23	88	30	93	50	**W**
X	82	97	53	15	32	62	**X**
Y	52	33	41	87	76	65	**Y**
Z	45	98	64	49	18	30	**Z**

343

344

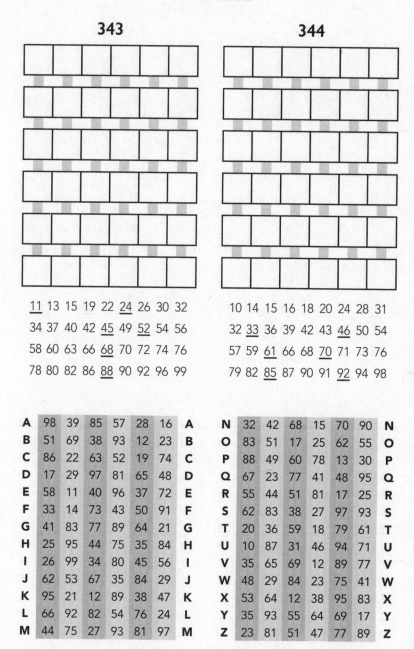

Word Fall

345

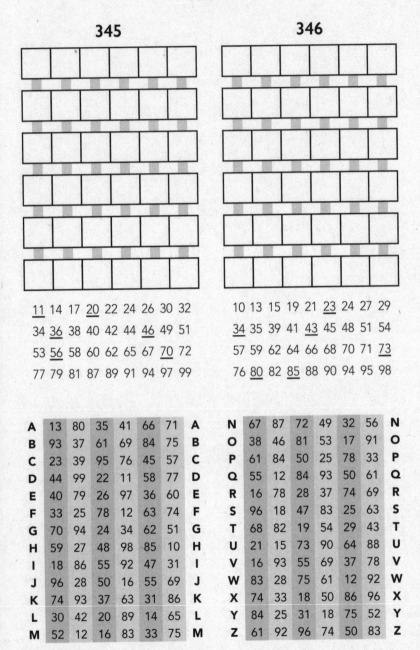

11 14 17 20 22 24 26 30 32
34 36 38 40 42 44 46 49 51
53 56 58 60 62 65 67 70 72
77 79 81 87 89 91 94 97 99

346

10 13 15 19 21 23 24 27 29
34 35 39 41 43 45 48 51 54
57 59 62 64 66 68 70 71 73
76 80 82 85 88 90 94 95 98

A	13	80	35	41	66	71	A
B	93	37	61	69	84	75	B
C	23	39	95	76	45	57	C
D	44	99	22	11	58	77	D
E	40	79	26	97	36	60	E
F	33	25	78	12	63	74	F
G	70	94	24	34	62	51	G
H	59	27	48	98	85	10	H
I	18	86	55	92	47	31	I
J	96	28	50	16	55	69	J
K	74	93	37	63	31	86	K
L	30	42	20	89	14	65	L
M	52	12	16	83	33	75	M

N	67	87	72	49	32	56	N
O	38	46	81	53	17	91	O
P	61	84	50	25	78	33	P
Q	55	12	84	93	50	61	Q
R	16	78	28	37	74	69	R
S	96	18	47	83	25	63	S
T	68	82	19	54	29	43	T
U	21	15	73	90	64	88	U
V	16	93	55	69	37	78	V
W	83	28	75	61	12	92	W
X	74	33	18	50	86	96	X
Y	84	25	31	18	75	52	Y
Z	61	92	96	74	50	83	Z

347

348

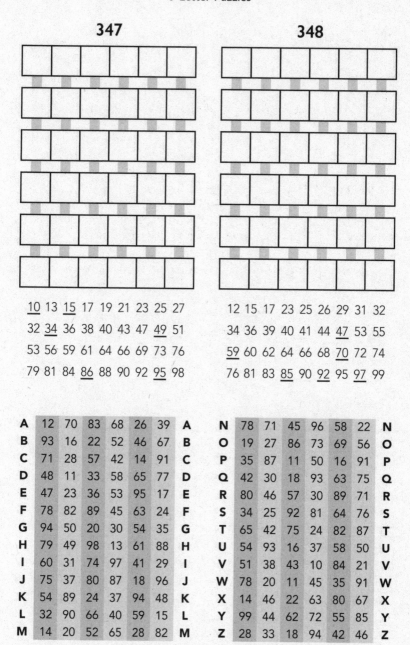

10 13 15 17 19 21 23 25 27
32 34 36 38 40 43 47 49 51
53 56 59 61 64 66 69 73 76
79 81 84 86 88 90 92 95 98

12 15 17 23 25 26 29 31 32
34 36 39 40 41 44 47 53 55
59 60 62 64 66 68 70 72 74
76 81 83 85 90 92 95 97 99

A	12	70	83	68	26	39	**A**
B	93	16	22	52	46	67	**B**
C	71	28	57	42	14	91	**C**
D	48	11	33	58	65	77	**D**
E	47	23	36	53	95	17	**E**
F	78	82	89	45	63	24	**F**
G	94	50	20	30	54	35	**G**
H	79	49	98	13	61	88	**H**
I	60	31	74	97	41	29	**I**
J	75	37	80	87	18	96	**J**
K	54	89	24	37	94	48	**K**
L	32	90	66	40	59	15	**L**
M	14	20	52	65	28	82	**M**

N	78	71	45	96	58	22	**N**
O	19	27	86	73	69	56	**O**
P	35	87	11	50	16	91	**P**
Q	42	30	18	93	63	75	**Q**
R	80	46	57	30	89	71	**R**
S	34	25	92	81	64	76	**S**
T	65	42	75	24	82	87	**T**
U	54	93	16	37	58	50	**U**
V	51	38	43	10	84	21	**V**
W	78	20	11	45	35	91	**W**
X	14	46	22	63	80	67	**X**
Y	99	44	62	72	55	85	**Y**
Z	28	33	18	94	42	46	**Z**

Word Fall

349

(grid of 6 rows × 6 boxes)

11 <u>13</u> 15 18 20 22 24 <u>27</u> 30
32 35 37 39 <u>41</u> 45 48 50 52
<u>54</u> 57 59 61 63 68 70 73 75
78 <u>80</u> 82 85 <u>88</u> 90 92 96 98

350

(grid of 6 rows × 6 boxes)

10 11 <u>14</u> 17 19 21 23 26 28
<u>31</u> 33 35 38 43 45 47 49 51
54 <u>56</u> 58 <u>61</u> 64 66 69 72 74
76 79 <u>83</u> 87 89 92 95 97 <u>99</u>

A	21	74	66	99	33	17	A
B	34	46	77	93	25	40	B
C	78	96	88	63	52	32	C
D	50	22	98	75	18	80	D
E	19	28	79	58	49	83	E
F	56	72	64	43	38	10	F
G	16	65	71	60	84	36	G
H	24	57	85	13	39	48	H
I	11	61	45	92	54	35	I
J	67	44	91	86	81	12	J
K	55	62	67	16	34	44	K
L	51	47	89	23	31	97	L
M	62	84	55	36	40	25	M

N	26	69	14	76	87	95	N
O	41	90	70	30	20	82	O
P	91	46	81	86	12	42	P
Q	71	94	77	60	84	46	Q
R	68	27	59	15	37	73	R
S	55	16	40	93	44	36	S
T	25	86	29	65	91	12	T
U	77	67	71	81	62	53	U
V	42	94	34	55	71	25	V
W	84	46	29	12	65	93	W
X	67	94	34	62	53	42	X
Y	60	77	16	36	81	12	Y
Z	25	93	65	53	29	44	Z